MARY PICKFORD
AND
DOUGLAS FAIRBANKS

Also by Booton Herndon

YOUNG MEN CAN SAVE THE WORLD

FORD: An Unconventional Biography of
the Men and Their Times

THE GREAT LAND

RICKENBACKER (Editor)

MARY PICKFORD
AND
DOUGLAS FAIRBANKS

The Most Popular Couple the World Has Ever Known

by

BOOTON HERNDON

W · W · NORTON & COMPANY · INC ·

New York

Published simultaneously in Canada by George J. McLeod Limited, Toronto.
Printed in the United States of America.
All Rights Reserved

First Edition

Library of Congress Cataloging in Publication Data
Herndon, Booton.
  Mary Pickford and Douglas Fairbanks.

  Bibliography: p.
  Includes index.
  1. Fairbanks, Douglas, 1883–1939. 2. Pickford, Mary, 1893–
3. Moving–picture actors and actresses—United States—Biography. I. Title.
PN2287.F3H4 1977 791.453'028'0922 77–12573

This book was set in Avanta and Bernhard Modern
by Haddon Craftsmen, Inc.
Printing & binding by Haddon Craftsmen, Inc.
Design by Jacques Chazaud

ISBN 0 393 07508 7

2 3 4 5 6 7 8 9 0

For Bonnie—who conceived of the project,
helped research and write it,
and supported it and me to its conclusion.

CONTENTS

LIST OF ILLUSTRATIONS

MARY PICKFORD
AND
DOUGLAS FAIRBANKS

Who would have dreamed that this idealized pair of lovers, "America's Sweetheart" and "The Most Popular Man in the World," tortured themselves with fears that the world would not accept their marriage. *Wisconsin Center for Film and Theater Research*

CHAPTER ONE

Most Popular Couple in the World

Passengers on board the eastbound California Limited the last weekend in May 1920 were twice blessed. From their compartments in the deluxe train, drawn smoothly by a huge coal-burning locomotive over the Continental Divide, they could look out over gorgeous views of the Rockies. Roaring at ninety miles an hour across the plains of Kansas they could visit the well-stocked library in the observation car, consult the latest market news wired to the train at designated stations along the route, or go to the barber or beauty shops on board. They could feast on fresh mountain trout in the dining car. But what made this trip special was the opportunity to see, in person, the two most glamorous stars of motion pictures, Douglas Fairbanks and Mary Pickford, en route to New York and then to Europe on their honeymoon. The papers had been full of their marriage; their real-life story was as romantic as any film.

Those lucky enough to catch a glimpse of the newlyweds could hardly have been disappointed, for both were as attractive in person as they were on the screen. Little Mary was in fact the Girl with the Golden Curls, America's Sweetheart. Her lovely face, with its peaches-and-cream complexion and hazel eyes, was framed with those famous curls. She was even more demure than one would expect, for in the postwar period when ladies of fashion were beginning to reveal a few daring inches of stocking between high-laced shoe and hem, Mary's long-skirted travel costume covered her legs completely. Douglas wished her to dress modestly, she explained to the press, and she was happy to please him.

As for Douglas Fairbanks, his tanned skin, so distinctive at a time when both men and women protected themselves from the sun, was as dark as it appeared in his films, his flashing teeth as dazzling white, his smile as jaunty. He walked with an athletic bounce that was also graceful, and gave off a sense of controlled energy that many described as electric. Dashing Doug was reported to be as irrepressible in real life as he was in films; there were accounts of how, on earlier trips, he had clambered along the sides or tops of the train, peering in the windows of the dining car as he hung upside down from the roof.

Passengers on this train saw no such pranks, however. They saw little of either Doug or Mary, for the two stars remained in their compartment most of the time, visited only by Mary's mother, traveling with her daughter as always, and the secretaries and servants who made up their entourage. After the first glow of their marriage, Douglas and Mary were afraid that their fans, in the third decade of the twentieth century, would not accept the marriage of two divorced persons. Relatives and business associates had advised them against marrying, but they had gone ahead. Now, though they were genuinely in love, they were fearful that the world might not understand, and might stay away from their films.

Both had dreamed of the glory they now had since childhood, and they had worked and suffered to make their dreams come true. For all Mary's feisty film characterizations, for all Doug's strength and agility in performing the most dangerous movie stunts, both were artists of extreme sensitivity. They had suffered many times from imagined rejection; this time they feared it could be real.

In New York they received the press in their eleven-room suite in the Ritz Carlton Hotel. Two warm, likable people, Doug and Mary were popular with the press, and the resulting stories were all favorable. Even before the papers came out, however, word of their arrival had spread throughout New York, and movie fans gathered around the hotel entrance on Madison Avenue, hoping for a look, a touch, perhaps an autograph. They spilled out into the street, and across it—before long the entire block between Forty-sixth and Forty-seventh streets was filled with people. They crowded into the intersections, tying up long lines of horse-drawn vehicles and overheated automobiles and trucks. The two responsible for it all were trapped in their hotel, prisoners of their fans, and they loved it.

But this was, after all, New York, the entertainment center of the world, and they were still worried about how people in less sophisticated parts of the country and abroad would react to their marriage. Since the beginning of World War I, only the United States had been steadily producing films; the 5000 theaters in Great Britain, for example, were almost totally dependent upon the American film industry. Doug and Mary were dependent upon the foreign market for a substantial part of their income.

Aboard the S.S. *Lapland*, bound for Southampton, Doug continued to reassure his bride, and himself. He had brought along a copy of Charles Dickens's *A Child's History of England*, and, to take her mind off her worries, read it aloud to Mary on the way over. She was so excited over the prospect of seeing England for the first time—Doug had been there many times before—that she couldn't sleep the night before they landed.

Mary's excitement over seeing England could not compare with England's excitement over seeing her. It began even before the ship docked. For perhaps the first time in history, two fluttering, sputtering aeroplanes, representing newly organized airline companies, ventured out to meet the ship at sea. Swooping low over the *Lapland*'s deck, the canvas crafts dropped roses and messages of goodwill for the newlyweds. A huge crowd was waiting when the ship swung into the White Star dock, including a delegation with an illuminated scroll signed by 4000 of Mary's admirers. It was never presented, however, for, as reported in a copyrighted story "by special cable to the New York Times," the delegation couldn't get close to her. The people were packed so tight, cheering, waving, pressing forward, that neither Doug nor Mary nor anyone else could make it to the London train, two hundred yards away. Thirty constables were summoned to control the crowd. Doug, as strong in person as he was in his films, hoisted Mary to his shoulders, and the policemen formed a strong circle around them and forced their way through to the train.

The crush at Waterloo Station in London was almost as bad, but they managed to reach their hotel, the Ritz, by teatime. Waiting for them at the hotel were presents from their fans—scones and biscuits, jars of jam, and many tidies, little cloth bags hand-embroidered with an *F* or a *P*, the kinds of things one gives to dear, familiar friends.

No one in England could believe that such loving admirers could get out of hand. On their second day in England, Tuesday, June 22, Doug and Mary were to attend the event of the season, the Theatrical Garden Party on the grounds of Chelsea Hospital. Doug asked their host, George Grossmith, if there would be police protection.

"What rot, dear old chap," Grossmith said, according to an account written by Alexander Woollcott, "Don't worry your silly old bean about that."

As they drove up to the gates in an open car, however, Doug and Mary soon had reason to worry their silly old beans. Accounts of what happened next differ, but whether it was "an amazing scene" (the *New York Times*) or "an extraordinary welcome" (the *Times* of London), the principals had the fright of their lives.

The terror in Mary's eyes, the concern in Doug's, reveal the danger as their frantic admirers press toward them at an English garden party. He has hoisted her on his shoulder to carry her to safety. *Mary Pickford Corporation*

Women put out their hands to Mary, and she reached out to them. But they didn't let go, and she found herself being pulled out of the car. *"Douglas!"* she cried. He quickly grabbed her, but then she was being pulled in two. Fortunately, the car was barely moving, and the chauffeur stopped. Then, according to the *New York Times*, "well-dressed women seemed suddenly to have lost their heads and made such a rush that the police were powerless. The women got the doors open and dragged Mary out, all mad to shake her hand. Mary's cloak was pulled off. . . . She was pressed to the ground."

Four policemen finally pushed the crowd back and once again Doug hoisted Mary to his shoulders. In the crowd's wild rush, however, he was pushed into a tree. Mary became entangled in the branches and was badly scratched. Thrown off balance, Doug careened into a tent in which jellies and preserves were on display. The crowd followed, and within minutes everyone was wading in goo.

It was funny only in retrospect. According to the *Times* of London: ". . . and the crowd was—appalling. One never looks for comfort at this kind of festivity, but one does not expect danger to life and limb." A photograph of Mary perched on Doug's shoulders shows terror in her eyes.

Back at the Ritz, they found both sides of Piccadilly in front of the hotel lined with people. Many had brought campstools with them, determined to stay. His Majesty King George V, Woollcott reported, surreptitiously observed the phenomenon for twenty minutes from a limousine parked in the outskirts of the crowd. At one point, hearing a rumor that Doug and Mary had come down for dinner, hundreds of people burst into the hotel and swarmed through the dining room. "The police had just woke up to the fact that a new portent had invaded London," said the *Times*, "and a strong cordon had a very hard time pretending to keep the crowds in order."

Mary was exhausted and unable to sleep. Doug called for a doctor, who ordered her to leave London immediately. The duke and duchess of Sutherland, old friends of Doug's, came to the rescue, inviting them to their estate, Sutton Court, in Guilford. While constables held back the crowd at the Arlington Street entrance, Doug once more carried Mary to the car. Several women broke through the ranks, the *Times* reported, and leaped on the car, "still clinging like limpets as it drove off."

In the country, away from the crowd, Mary got a good night's sleep. The next morning she awakened early and drew the curtains to let the sunshine in. She found herself, in her nightgown, looking out at a crowd of silent faces looking right back at her. The local people had been waiting quietly all night.

When Doug and Mary left England, the *Times* gave them a farewell editorial:

> Every nice boy, it is said, falls in love with Mary Queen of Scots. . . . Every man with a sixpence to spend on his amusement falls in love with Miss Mary Pickford. . . . The appeal which her acting makes is always to the sense of chivalry which, in however sentimental a form, is characteristic of the English temperament. In this sense she is truly an ambassadress of our race. Our welcome is the recognition of a touch tending to make the whole English-speaking world kin. Centuries were necessary to raise Queen Mary to her pinnacle of devotion; by the alchemy of a machine, centuries have been shortened into days and nights. Thus we would all be Mary's comforters and defenders in her hours of peril. In that enterprise the gentlemen of the world, however humble, stand as of old time, side by side, and shoulder to shoulder.

Mary and her equally famous husband were kin not only to the English-speaking world but to the entire world, for the silent film was a global language. In Holland, they were met with another noisy and nerve-racking reception. Only in Germany, where no American pictures had been shown during the war, were they able to pass unrecognized, but that was worse than being mobbed. Mary later recalled that Doug asked, "Frankly, Mary, how do you feel about it? Do you like being left alone?" She answered, "I definitely do not, Douglas. Let's go some place where we are known. I've had enough obscurity for a lifetime."

At the Swiss border they were told that in the postwar shortage it would take a week to acquire a car. With his famous flashing smile and some of the money it had earned him, Doug bought a car, hired a chauffeur, and he and Mary were on the way to Italy the same day.

In Italy there was more adulation; Doug learned that he was known as "Lampo," or Lightning. France was the finale. In Paris, Doug happened to mention that he and Mary planned to visit Les Halles, the central market, the next morning, and again the press reported a mob scene. As the crowd pushed toward them out of control, they fled across the butchers' tables, slipping on the cotelettes and tournedos.

Finally, their honeymoon over, they sailed for New York where they were met by a delegation including Jack Dempsey and Babe Ruth. The king and queen of motion pictures were home. At last they could believe that they had not sacrificed their careers for their love. Their popularity was not diminished; indeed, it was still growing.

During the first years of their marriage Mary Pickford and Douglas Fairbanks were surely the most popular couple the world has ever known. They were at the peaks of their individual careers during the zenith of the silent cinema; as there was no language barrier, no expensive sound equipment, they were seen and adored by the people of the

They attracted crowds *everywhere*—New York, Moscow, Tokyo, and in this scene, Prague, 1925. *Charles O. Lewis*

As the unquestioned King and Queen of Hollywood, and the entire realm of the silent film, Doug and Mary reigned from Pickfair, on an imposing ridge in Beverly Hills. *Historical Collections, Security Pacific National Bank*

world, in cities, towns, and crossroads. Wherever a portable generator and projector could be set up, in Eskimo village or jungle clearing, Doug and Mary were known and loved. She was the world's most beloved woman, he the most admired man, and it turned out that their marriage, which was no publicity arrangement but the result of a consuming love right out of a D. W. Griffith scenario, enhanced their individual popularity. It is unlikely that any couple will achieve such recognition, receive such adoration, ever again.

As stars of the first magnitude they were loved to the point of danger; not only in England and Europe but later, in Moscow and Tokyo, they were nearly trampled to death by their fans. They had the respect of their peers, and as the recognized king and queen of Hollywood they led by example, bringing dignity to the disheveled, often raunchy social life of the young movie colony. It was Doug and Mary who were first

At the peak of their popularity when this picture was taken in Paris in 1926, they were still genuinely in love, and fully as warm and likable as they appear. *Library of Congress*

visited in Hollywood by European nobility as well as by American socialites and dignitaries. In the early days of the motion picture industry in California it was common to see signs on boarding house lawns in Los Angeles saying "No Jews, dogs, or picture people." Things changed with the ascendancy of Doug and Mary.

They were well rewarded financially. Their yearly salaries of hundreds of thousands of dollars, paid to themselves by themselves, were only a part of their total income. They produced their own films, and, with remarkably few exceptions, their films were profitable. In partnership with D. W. Griffith and Charles Chaplin they founded the giant

United Artists Corporation, which covered the world and which survives today. They selected their own corporate managers, provided leadership that was sometimes daring, and took part in decision-making. They made millions from their films and more millions from investments, particularly in real estate.

They sought the American dream, worked hard, and when they realized the dream they relished it. They enjoyed their adulation, their work, their life, their home, their position, their friends, their money, and all the things—good things, crazy things—that money could buy. Through it all they kept most of their friends. They remained likable people.

Their stardom was no unearned coincidence. They had the physical attributes—Mary's beauty was of that inexplicable type that becomes even more appealing on the screen; Doug's physique and grace on his five-foot-eight, 160-pound frame were the perfect raw material for the magic of the camera, so that his impossible feats appeared to be not only easy, but enormous fun—and they had talent, intelligence, and experience. Perhaps most important of all, as children they had both suffered remarkably similar emotional wounds. Indeed, if it hadn't been for the trauma of their early lives, they could never have reached their amazing pinnacles.

Doug and Mary both lost their fathers when they were very young, Mary's by death, Doug's by desertion. Both were abnormally close to their mothers. Both were intensely narcissistic—they craved affection, attention, recognition. Along with the anxieties that drove them, however, they also had courage, strength, and perseverance. Above all, they had supercolossal, five-star luck, for both happened along at the one moment in history that gave birth to the films. They took advantage of their emotional liabilities, acted out what distressed them for all the world to see, and brought happiness to millions—and to themselves.

Who but Shakespeare could be the playwright for their one appearance together in *The Taming of the Shrew?* Mary said later that Doug played his role far too realistically, in a preview of unhappy days to come.
Wisconsin Center for Film and Theater Research

CHAPTER TWO

Doug:
Denver to Broadway,
1883–1899

Douglas Elton Ulman was five years old when his father left home. It must have been a particularly unpleasant departure, for his mother took extreme measures to expunge his father, even his name, from the family. And it left a permanent mark on Douglas, an unusually sensitive child who had started life unwanted and unhappy. All through his adult life he rarely mentioned either his father or his childhood.

The story of an individual begins with his parents, but in Douglas's case that beginning is obscure. His mother was born Ella Adelaide Marsh in 1847, but where is something of a mystery: her grandchildren assume that she came from Virginia, but one document gives her birthplace as New York. Her image, passed on by her sons and described by her grandchildren, was much more positive. She was beautiful, with a thin waist, chestnut hair, and large, luminous eyes. She considered herself a southern lady. She was selfish, and her sons adored her. They called her Tutu.

Sometime after the Civil War, according to family legend, Ella was living in New Orleans, the wife of John Fairbanks, a wealthy planter, sugar-mill owner, and socialite. How she journeyed to New Orleans during those unsettled days is a mystery, as, indeed, is John Fairbanks himself; neither records of plantation owners nor New Orleans city directories of that period mention him. Ella's first son, also named John, was born in 1873, and, again according to family legend, in that year Fairbanks died. A New York lawyer named Hezekiah Charles Ulman is supposed to have appeared and tried unsuccessfully to protect her estate. Ella and her son next showed up in Georgia, where she married a man named Edward Wilcox and had another son, Norris.

Again H. Charles Ulman appeared, this time ostensibly to help her get a divorce from the hard-drinking Wilcox. In 1880, Ella arrived in Denver, Colorado, with Ulman. She brought her son John with her, but her other son, Norris Wilcox, remained in Georgia with his father's family. Ulman had left a wife and law practice in New York.

Although Ella was later to send him packing, Ulman has attained some prominence in family legends over the years. Among other accomplishments, he is said to have founded the United States Law Association, which the family and friendly biographers have described as the forerunner of the American Bar Association. Investigation shows that Ulman did indeed have law offices in New York from 1872 to 1881, but the U.S. Law Association was only a small publishing operation, with Ulman listed as associate editor. He has also been described as a devotee of the theater, with a striking resemblance to the popular actor Edwin Booth, and even an acquaintanceship with him.

Ulman was forty-nine and Ella thirty-four when they arrived in Denver. Apparently he made no effort to practice law there. He was involved in mining, frequently making trips into the mountains to look at mining properties. John couldn't stand Ulman, got a job as a delivery boy for a local store, and moved in with the owner's family. Ella didn't like being alone, nor did she like Denver, then a dusty—or muddy— pioneer town. Nor did she like giving birth to a third son, Robert, in March 1882, or a fourth, Douglas, on May 23, 1883. She was resentful of Douglas when she carried him; after all, she was thirty-six years old and vain over her trim waist. There is reason to believe that she resnted him even more after he was born, for he was unusually dark-skinned. Many years later Douglas would tease her about being ashamed of him —"Mother would reach down in the baby carriage and pull the blanket over my face when she saw somebody coming," he'd say. She would protest, sometimes angrily.

Whether or not Ella was a resentful mother, something happened during Douglas's first few months of life to disturb his normal pattern of growth. It is an accepted phenomenon in the study of human personality that an infant begins life all wrapped up in itself. With the help of love and support from the mother the infant usually makes an easy transition from his own little world to the big wide one. But either an unhappy grudging mother, or one too selfishly protective, might well not provide both love and support, and the infant may not make the

Sun-worshippers have Douglas Fairbanks to thank, for, more than anyone, he made the suntan first acceptible, then popular—but his mother was ashamed of his dark skin. *Charles O. Lewis*

full transition and remain bound up in himself to a small or large degree. This condition is known as narcissism, and Douglas Fairbanks is a perfect case history of it. Unfortunately, because Narcissus is often identified as a Greek youth who spent his time admiring his own image, narcissists are often thought to be conceited exhibitionists in love with themselves. Those like Fairbanks, however, are not like that at all; they are insecure people who want to be noticed.

Many years later, after studying descriptions of Fairbanks and some of the events of his life, Dr. Seymour Rabinowitz, a professor of psychiatry and a practicing psychoanalyst, called his narcissism "enormous."

"It was so extreme," Dr. Rabinowitz said, "that he must have had a hell of a time relating to other people as individuals. He wouldn't want criticism or discussion from friends, just worshipful adoration."

From babyhood on, as subsequent events made clear, Douglas would be extremely sensitive, easily hurt. He would have a great interest in his own body. He would daydream a lot, with fantasies of wealth, power, popularity. He would expect instant success in everything he tried, and be terribly depressed when he didn't get it. He would constantly cry out for attention, and be crushed if nobody noticed.

He was a glum baby, according to family legend; even after he began talking he was slow to laugh or smile. The neighbors, according to one account, whispered that he was mentally retarded. He was certainly not physically retarded, for he was a most active boy. The picture that comes through is of a miniature Buster Keaton, solemnly climbing things.

At some point Ella seems to have accepted her youngest child, perhaps favoring him. When Ulman was away on his mining trips Douglas would share her only with Robert, who seemed to be a more self-sufficient child. But then Ulman would come riding home, flamboyant, dramatic, theatrical—a formidable rival.

If there is any question about Douglas's craving for attention and the rivalry with his father, the one most important episode of his childhood answers it. He rarely talked about his early life, but this was one event he discussed freely. For one thing, it left him with a scar over his left eye, which became one of the arsenal of devices he used to gain attention.

When Douglas was about four or five years old, he fell off a roof. According to one account he was trying to fly, according to another he had climbed to a precarious position and fell. It really doesn't matter, for undoubtedly little Douglas fell many times off many things, and over the years he screened out all but the one he chose to remember. Before the fall, according to the way he told the story, he never laughed. Then he fell—or jumped or tried to fly—off the roof, knocked himself cold, and regained consciousness in his mother's arms, the center of attention.

"I fell off the roof," he said proudly, and laughed out loud. He had survived a dangerous experience and won a double prize. It was only the beginning of a pattern that was to repeat itself again and again. When Doug needed attention or recognition, he could get it by some daredevil action.

For a couple of years after the fall off the roof Douglas was able to compete with his father. He kept on climbing things, continued to court danger. Perhaps he called attention to himself in other ways for in records of his conversations as an adult run allusions to Ulman's interest in drama, especially Shakespeare. Again according to family legend, Ulman brought home members of troupes playing Denver. It would have been a precocious child indeed who could deliver the soliloquies of the bard at the age of four and five, yet there is some evidence that the boy did indeed attempt some Shakespearean recitation at that age. (Long after his death Mary Pickford remarked, with rueful envy, that he had been exposed to Shakespeare as a child, while she had not.)

Whatever his weapons, Douglas was probably able to keep his rivalry with Ulman within balance. But then the father delivered the crushing blow: he left, taking with him any possibility of a normal resolution of the struggle. Ulman was beginning to drink heavily, and this probably made the departure an ugly one. Douglas never mentioned it, much less discussed it.

One time he did refer to his father by name was when his first wife, Beth, asked why he never drank. She said later that from his tone of voice and the expression on his face she had thought he was going to confess that he had robbed a bank. Instead he told her, for the first time, that his real name was Ulman and that he was part Jewish. When he was twelve, he went on, his father returned to Denver, intercepted his son on the way home from school, and took him into a bar to talk. Ulman had one drink or more, and Douglas, elated at his father's return, invited him home, whiskey breath and all. Ella, furious almost to the point of hysteria, gave her one-time lover a tongue-lashing and sent him away for good. Still in an excited state, she took Douglas to the local office of the Women's Christian Temperance Union and demanded that he sign the temperance pledge. He did sign and he kept the pledge, along with a strong distaste for drinking and drunks, for most of his life.

So, too, did he keep the secret, at least from the public, that his baptismal name was Ulman. He certainly had good reason to think of himself as a Fairbanks, for Ella had wiped Ulman out of her life completely, resuming the name Fairbanks and bestowing it upon Douglas and Robert. She moved to another part of Denver. There had never been any question about their religion; under Hebrew law the religion is passed on through the mother, and because Ella was a Gentile her boys could not be Jews. Douglas had been baptized in the Immaculate Conception Church by Denver's internationally famous archbishop, Joseph Projectus Machebeuf. For the rest of his life Douglas was sensitive and secretive about his Jewish blood. At any rate, at the age of five Douglas lost not only a father but much of his identity.

Douglas's childhood in Denver was about what would be expected of a mischievous boy seeking attention. Many years later a retired schoolteacher recalled a trick Douglas and a friend of his played in the classroom. Each would bring a rock to class. The other boy would throw one rock through the window and Douglas would drop his on the floor with a clatter. Then he'd pick it up and say, "Here it is, teacher."

On another occasion Douglas and Robert released a couple of water-snakes on a crowded streetcar. Douglas even took his mischief into church, once putting vinegar in the wine and soaking the wicks of the altar candles so they wouldn't light.

Douglas was often caught and punished, of course. Punishment in the public schools of Denver in the closing years of the nineteenth century could hardly have been any different from the rest of the country; historians have observed that it was a period of rule by the rod, when students were beaten for trivial things. Sometimes Douglas was beaten so severely he came home with bloodstained underpants.

This was physical punishment. Douglas challenged fear of the unknown as well. All the boys believed that terrible things took place in the backroom of the Chinese laundry; the strange aliens smoked opium

and tortured people. Children crossed the street to avoid walking by
the laundry—"the Chinaman will reach out and grab you." To prove
his bravery to his peers, Douglas announced that he would throw a rock
through the laundry window in broad daylight. He did, and then ran
for his life; in his active and terror-filled imagination the supernatural
Oriental was right behind him, and gaining.

Some thirty years later, in one of the rare interviews in which he
consciously revealed anything about his childhood, Douglas confessed
that he was frightened during his adventures. "I was always afraid," he
said. He seriously didn't understand his compulsion to seek attention,
for he went on to observe that "Robert did not know fear." Robert,
of course, was not compelled to be constantly proving himself and
played less dangerous pranks.

Douglas certainly succeeded in capturing the approval of his school-
mates. One of them, Frank White, recalled being sent to the principal
with Doug to be disciplined. It was a pretty spring day and Doug was
fidgeting. "Let's get out of here," he said. Frank, knowing he was in
enough hot water as it was, sat tight, but Doug climbed out the window
to a ledge and then jumped to the ground. He probably got an awful
licking, but he got a lot of recognition, too.

Another schoolmate, many years later, described the wall around
East High School as being three feet high, eighteen inches wide, and
covering most of the block. He remembered how Doug walked the top
of the wall the entire distance, on his hands. Another time a baseball
was stuck in the crotch of a tree and none of the players could get it.
On a bet Doug leaped, caught a branch, swung his feet up high over
his head, and kicked the ball loose. It stands to reason that, given his
agility and his craving to be noticed, he would attempt many such
stunts—and that he would often collect bruises and guffaws instead of
acclaim. To someone crying out so desperately for attention, it was
worth it, either way.

To his mother, Doug's activities were embarrassing. She enrolled
both Robert and Douglas in Jarvis Hall Military Academy, hoping that
the discipline would straighten them out. Most boys, certainly in the
1890s, liked uniforms, and Doug was surely delighted with the image
he presented in the made-to-measure uniforms of West Point gray—
two complete outfits, including caps, for $32. He was later noted for
his extreme fastidiousness, so most likely he took to the emphasis on

cleanliness and neatness. It's also safe to assume that he liked that bête noir of military school, close-order drill, with its rhythm and movement and the use of the body as a precision instrument. Among the Fairbanks characteristics in later years were an erect, military carriage and a quick-step, bouncy walk.

The two boys stayed at Jarvis Hall for the better part of two years. Ella was taking in roomers, and perhaps boarders, too, but the proceeds would hardly have kept two boys in military school. She was probably helped by her sister Belle, who was married to a man named Weeks. According to family legend, Weeks had made a fortune in whalebone corset stays. Ella's grandchildren remember Belle as an elegant and formidable old lady with two elegant and formidable middle-aged daughters.

As Douglas grew into puberty, he discovered new ways of gaining approval. One was, of course, through the physical appearance and dexterity of his body by dressing well, carrying himself well. But he doesn't seem to have been too interested in the opposite sex. His most memorable case of puppy love, as might be expected, involved one of his teachers, for he had a tendency to seek out mother substitutes to love. He was also influenced by his mother's Victorian, Old South attitudes—there were only two kinds of females: ladies to be placed on pedestals or women of loose morals to be shunned.

Another of Doug's outlets was his growing interest in drama, and Ella nurtured it. John, ten years older than Douglas, was by this time making his own way in the world, and Robert's inclination was toward electricity, which came in handy when the lights went out, but was not as glamorous as the theater. It was Douglas, therefore, whom Ella took to performances of visiting repertory troupes. Surely, at the opera house and on the way home, they would discuss the players and their abilities. Now in her forties, Ella could see little future for herself in Denver. Perhaps she was simply living vicariously through her son, or perhaps she was beginning to think of him as a potential ticket east. In either case, she encouraged his emerging dramatic talents.

Like all public school children, Douglas received a great deal of exposure to drama and dramatic expression. Memorizing and reciting poems and dramatic passages and presenting class plays made up an important part of school life. The Delsarte method of declamation was being taught throughout the country, and Doug loved the sweeping, stylized gestures. To express frustration in the Delsarte method, for example, the actor would hold his clenched hand waist high in front of him, and strike an imaginary table, stamping his foot for emphasis, plus noise.

Even better was the Delsarte method of portraying triumph, a gesture known to everyone who ever attended an opera house performance. As Doug performed it, he stood with feet together, right hand closed over his chest. Then he would step forward and to the right, simultaneously throwing his hand upward and outward, palm up. It became such an identifying characteristic that it's hard to visualize the adult Douglas Fairbanks in any other position. And so, encouraged by his mother, he practiced his Delsarte gestures in front of the mirror and all through the house.

It was worth memorizing poetry or roles in plays to be able to recite or declaim in front of an audience, complete with gestures. Some of his teachers undoubtedly encouraged him, for dramatic activity kept him out of mischief, and he was an engaging youngster anyway.

At the age of ten Doug was taking part in a neighborhood group. A handlettered program for "The Man from the Mts." lists D. Fairbanks as "an old miner." Years later he could still recall some of the lines from those cellar productions—"If you cross this line you're a dead man!"—and a whole stanza from one of his own masterpieces:

> "I love you now. Can you doubt it?"
> But the man arose with a sneer and passed out
>   into the night.
> "God help me, a sinner!" wailed a voice,
> A flutter, a splash, a thousand little bubbles
>   flowed onward to the sea.

Such talent needed cultivation. Denver had an excellent dramatic school, run by Margaret Fealy and her daughter Maude, both of whom had performed on Broadway. Doug became a pupil, and while his exuberance may have exasperated the ladies at times, they surely appreciated his eagerness.

Like other poor boys, Doug worked at odd jobs after school and summers. Although he wasn't lazy, he was hardly a good worker, especially when compared with his brothers. John was driven by poverty and responsibility, and Robert was a stolid plugger, but Doug was inclined to goof off. He was a dreamer, both on the job and hiking over the hills. In dramatic school, however, he proved that he was anything but lazy, as long as his interest was stimulated. He not only memorized his lines and bounced around the stage delivering them, but he was eager to move the furniture around for the different sets and help out in general. When he was fifteen he was good enough to be selected by the Fealys to represent the school with a solo recitation at a variety show at the Broadway Theatre, his name prominent on the formal program. And he was listed—"Master Fairbanks (Douglas)"—in the roster of the Broadway Theatre Stock Company in the fall season of 1897.

Around this time he was working as a bellboy at a Denver hotel. In reminiscing about it later with a friend, the screenwriter Frances Marion, he recalled that what had impressed him most was the handsome leather luggage and steamer trunks with their hotel labels from cities and spas all over the world. Someday, he dreamed, he would travel to those romanatic places, and people would look at the labels on his bags and know that he was somebody. Those labels represented identity. Many teenage boys dream of traveling to far-off places, but Doug had more compelling reasons. A fatherless adolescent, he had an abnormal dependence on and attachment to his mother, but he also had the intelligence to perceive this and the strength to want to break away. But what could he do? How could he get out of Denver?

As is true of so many other episodes in the career of Douglas Fairbanks, the accounts of his departure from Denver vary widely but have one feature in common: all are wrong. Fortunately, the true story of the turning point of his life can be documented.

Probably for financial reasons, the Fairbanks boys left the military academy and returned to public school. The records of East High School, Denver, show that Douglas Elton Fairbanks was enrolled on September 7, 1898; lived at 1629 Franklin Street; his mother's name was Ella; his father's name was not given; and the birthplace of both parents was New York City. He "left" East High on April 3, 1899. Family legend gives the reason for his departure as a lavish and unauthorized use of green paint and ribbons at school on St. Patrick's Day.

On April 17, Frederick Warde, a prominent English actor, began a week's run at the Broadway Theatre in Denver, appearing in *The School for Scandal, Othello, Hamlet, Macbeth,* and *Julius Caesar.*

43221

Warde enjoyed telling young people about the stage and Shakespeare, and gave a talk at East High School. The next day, he wrote later, "a very youthful student called on me and expressed a desire to go on stage. This applicant, though little more than a boy, had an assurance and a persistence in spite of my discouragement, that attracted me."

The boy was, of course, Douglas Fairbanks, then fifteen, and he obviously did not bother to tell Warde that he could hardly have heard him speak at school the day before, having "left" two weeks previously.

Nor did Warde, in his account of this first meeting, make any mention of the dramatic story still being told in Denver today that he had refused to see anyone, and that Douglas had therefore climbed the fire escape and burst through the window to his dressing room. (Three-quarters of a century later, Douglas Jr. was photographed in the window through which his father was purported to have made his entrance. It was, however, the wrong theater.)

It is more likely that Warde welcomed Douglas simply as just another stagestruck youth. Like Doug he had been a fatherless boy, and at the age of fifteen had torn himself away from his mother to go into the theater. Perhaps he saw himself in the youth; at any rate, there was a definite empathy.

"He told me of his life and referred me to his mother for confirmation," Warde continued. "The lady called on me the next day, indorsed all that her son had told me, approved of the boy's ambitions and the result was I engaged him for my company for the following season, to lead the supernumeraries and to play such small parts as his capacity and appearance would permit."

Probably one reason Douglas never told the story this way was because of his mother's role in it; few heroes like to admit that their mothers helped them get their first job.

But the job was for the next season, several months away. Douglas had already taken care of the school situation, and nothing held him in Denver—or, more likely, nothing held his mother in Denver. John was now twenty-six and earning a respectable salary, and Robert was leaving Denver to go into electrical engineering. She could take Douglas to New York! John and Robert agreed to support her. Perhaps her sister Belle promised something from the whalebone fortune. And Douglas had saved twenty-three dollars.

Whenever the move and whatever the circumstances, it was a happy event all around. Giving their adored mother what she wanted was no great sacrifice to Jack and Robert. As for Ella, she was at last leaving Denver for New York, with the dream that her boy was going to be a great theatrical success. Her only wish, she recalled later, was to "live long enough to sit in a theater and hear someone near me point out and whisper, 'There's Mrs. Fairbanks, mother of Douglas, the star.' "

The future star, of course, had it made in every way. Though Jack and Robert had specified that they were going to support only their mother, Doug knew very well his Tutu wouldn't let him starve. He was almost at the point of breaking loose from his emotional dependence on her, but now the trauma would be postponed and eased by going with her to New York. Finally, of course, there would be the biggest thrill of all—embarking on his chosen career, the theater, on Broadway.

CHAPTER THREE

Mary:
Toronto to Biograph,
1893–1909

When Gladys Smith was almost five years old, she was wrenched awake before dawn one morning by a scream so horrible she kept hearing it for the rest of her life. She ran to her mother, only to find her still screaming and beating her head against the wall so hard that the blood was running down her face. That's how the frightened little girl learned her father had died. It's always painful for a child to lose a parent; Gladys had an unforgettable scene in her memory to remind her of it.

If her father had lived, the world would probably never have heard of Mary Pickford, née Gladys Smith. She was just another pretty child of a lower-middle-class Toronto family. Her father, John Charles Smith, was the son of English Protestant immigrants; her mother, Charlotte Hennessey, the daughter of Irish Catholic immigrants. They had a happy marriage, a comfortable house, an adequate income, and three children in four years—Gladys Marie, Lottie (named for Charlotte), and John, Jr. Gladys, with her father's golden hair, was the prettiest, but she was a sickly child. Born April 8, 1893, she was little more than a year old when Lottie arrived. Her mother had her hands full and couldn't give Gladys all the attention she cried for. Her aunt and grandmother helped, but what she remembered, she wrote years later, was when Papa picked her up and held her.

It's natural for a little girl three or four years old to be in love with her father and to compete with her mother. At the age of five or six she usually makes a healthy adjustment. She helps with the housework, tries on her mother's hats and high-heeled shoes, smears on lipstick, and passes through the father-worshipping stage without scars.

But Gladys did not have the opportunity to resolve the phase herself.

Her father was injured in an accident at work, lingered on for a while, and then, on that awful night, he died. Gladys wasn't old enough to understand death, but she understood rejection—her father had left her. She cried and cried, but the tears eventually went away. The emotional injury never went away, but affected her major thoughts and actions for the rest of her life. Time and again she would seek out a man to take her father's place, then goad him into repeating the pattern of rejection. She was emotionally bound by her clutching attachment to her mother. She would constantly crave attention and affection from her fellow man, and be utterly miserable if she did not receive it. Her self-esteem would require an enormous amount of reinforcement. An average child might be happy with a word, a hug, a smile, but Gladys would need the applause of an audience, or money, or presents.

In one of her most vivid memories, recounted almost six decades later, she ran to meet her father as he came home from work—and he went right by her to pick up baby Lottie instead. This may have happened once or twice, but it could hardly have been typical for she also remembered her father as a warm and kindly man. It was, rather, what Gladys chose to remember—being rejected by her father.

She also remembered that, shortly after her father's death, she asked her mother, "Mama, have you next month's rent, and money for coal?" Again, whether or not the episode actually happened, the fact that she remembered it and chose to recount it was significant. Although only five when her father left her, she shared in her mother's concerns.

A wealthy, childless couple who knew the Smiths well offered to adopt Gladys, and her mother, wanting to do the best she could for her daughter, considered giving her up. She told the little girl of the pony she'd have, and ice cream, and chicken every day. When Gladys realized what this was all about, she cried out, "Mama, don't you want me anymore?" Both of them burst into tears and threw their arms around each other, and there was no adoption. But for a long time Gladys had nightmares in which Mama died or went away, and the fears persisted when she was awake. She resolved that she would let nothing come between her and her mother, and her sister and brother. So when Charlotte took in boarders and did dressmaking to support the family, Gladys helped with the housework and cooking, and looked after the children.

A nice young couple rented the bedroom John and Charlotte had shared. The husband was the stage manager for the Cummings Stock Company and, seeing the family's financial condition, offered Gladys and Lottie the opportunity to make some money by appearing in a forthcoming play that would have openings for children.

At first Charlotte refused permission; she believed that women in the theater were scandalous and smoked cigarettes. But the young man was very nice, and they could certainly use money. She agreed to meet the cast and found them to be perfectly respectable people, and brought in her two girls. The play was *The Silver King,* to open September 19, 1898. Lottie, who was barely four, was given a walk-on part. Gladys, now five and a half, was given two roles. In the first act she played a spiteful little girl who stamps her foot, tosses her head, and says one nasty line: "Don't speak to her, girls. Her father killed a man." In the second act she was a little boy who sits on the floor playing with toys.

On opening night she played her unpleasant little role routinely, but in the second act, while the action of the play went on around her, she built a pile of blocks and then knocked them down with a clatter. It brought a laugh from the audience, but at just the wrong time, for it was during the denouement of the play. An insensitive stage manager could probably have wiped out the child's theatrical career then and there by fussing at her. Instead, he praised her for thinking up the little bit of business, then suggested a more opportune time when the play could use some laughter. Thus her first theatrical father, in those six evenings and two matinees, made it possible for her to receive both her first applause and her first money, two great reinforcements for an insecure little girl. Five dollars bought a lot of coal in Toronto in 1898. During the run of the play, instead of playing with the other children when she was offstage, Gladys crouched in the drafty wings, a shawl around her shoulders, watching the girl who played the child lead.

Her second appearance was a mere walk-on, but she was on the same bill with a real touring professional, Elsie Janis, a teenager receiving a fortune, seventy-five dollars a week. Her mother traveled with her, and if Charlotte still had any aversion to the theater, it disappeared after talking with Mrs. Janis.

Two years after Gladys's debut in *The Silver King,* her mother learned that it was going to be put on again by another group. She dressed Gladys up and took her to see the casting director, Anne

Blancke. Charlotte suggested that Gladys take the same role she had played before, but Gladys had her own idea. She did not want to be that spiteful little girl again—she wanted the warmth and applause given to the child lead. Charlotte tried to shush her, but Gladys pleaded, and Miss Blancke agreed to give her a chance. Minutes later, under the street light waiting for the trolley, Gladys began studying for the role. Because of her nightmares and waking fears Gladys had been kept out of school and had not yet learned to read, but Charlotte read the lines to her and she repeated them. They continued studying on the streetcar; when they reached home Gladys knew the first act.

By the time she was eight years old Gladys was so well known in Toronto that the program for *East Lynne* announced: "The souvenirs for tonight will be of Gladys Smith, the little tot whose work has been so much admired." She had learned to love the theater, its atmosphere and excitement, but most of all she enjoyed being admired, the reflection of her image from the audience. During the sad scenes when she was dying on stage, she would peek into the darkened theater and count the patches of white where handkerchiefs dabbed at tearful eyes. She had also developed poise and stage presence. Once in *Uncle Tom's Cabin* the actor playing Uncle Tom forgot his lines at the dramatic moment when he was holding the frail child in his arms. Gladys put her hand on his woolly wig, brought his head down to hers, and whispered his lines to him. It was so natural that the audience accepted it completely.

In the spring of 1901, Hal Reid, a New York playwright, brought his latest work, *At the Little Red Schoolhouse,* to Toronto for its first performance anywhere. Reid himself had a role in it, as did both Gladys and her sister Lottie. Later, in three separate autobiographies published over a period of forty years, she was to say that Reid and the play changed the course of her life. As she recounted the episode, Reid was so pleased with her and the rest of the family that he promised all four Smiths they would have roles when the play opened in New York that fall. On the strength of his promise, the story continues, Charlotte sold her furniture and prepared to leave Toronto. But the call did not come; Reid had sold the play without providing for the Smith family, or even letting them know. Charlotte and the children, having burned their bridges, had to turn to relatives to survive.

In the meantime, according to this account, the play went on the

Though too young to read in 1900, Mary was so elated at the opportunity to play Cissy Denver that she learned the first act on the way home on the streetcar as her mother read her lines. *Mary Pickford Corporation*

road with Lillian Gish—then Lillian Niles—in Gladys's role, but in Buffalo she had to drop out of the play for a time. Somebody remembered Gladys, and she was asked to come to Buffalo. Charlotte insisted that if the entire family didn't go, no one would. The management finally agreed, and the Smiths joined the troupe for twenty dollars a week to begin their life in show business.

But this account is not accurate. Contemporary issues of the chronicle of show business, the *New York Dramatic Mirror,* show that *At the Little Red Schoolhouse* made its debut in Toronto the first week of April, 1901; revised and retitled *In Convict Stripes* it opened in Detroit not in the fall of that year but in September 1902. Lillian Niles was indeed in the cast (so was Walter Huston). It did play in Buffalo, in the last week of January, but the first time Gladys Smith was listed in the cast was in the New York City engagement, March 16–21, 1903.

Why was her memory a full year off? One conjecture is that Reid had indeed made some unfulfilled promise, and her resulting sense of rejection was so strong that in time she came to associate him with the miserable experience she really did suffer.

What actually happened, according to the *Dramatic Mirror,* was that the entire family somehow managed to join the touring company of *The Fatal Wedding.* "Baby Gladys Smith" had the leading child role as the Little Mother, Lottie was her understudy, Johnny had a small role, and even Charlotte made an appearance as an Irish maid named Bridget. Charlotte had lied to get the part, saying that she was experienced, and was frightened to death. At the first performance Gladys and Lottie got down on their knees in the dressing room and prayed during their mother's scene in the first act: "Oh, Lord, please don't let Mama forget her lines."

Mama remembered them, but there were times when she wished she hadn't, and that the whole family had been fired. For the tour, in the season of 1901–02, turned out to be nineteen weeks of one-night stands in small towns throughout Pennsylvania (Pottsville *and* Pottstown), Ohio, and New York State.

After a couple of weeks the days all ran together in a daze of exhaustion—arrive in town, usually in the afternoon, and walk to the hotel; wash and iron clothes and sometimes mend them; wash Gladys's hair and put it up in rags; prepare something to eat. Charlotte became a genius at stretching food. One of her tricks was to drain a can of vegetables, mix the liquid with flour, then heat it all together—it was a lot more filling that way. At supper Gladys helped feed the children and then they walked to the theater, or what passed for the theater. There, no matter how dreary the surroundings, her adrenalin would flow and she would project her energy and talent out past the footlights. Then, drained of that energy, she'd get dressed, walk back to the hotel with the family, help Mama put the children to bed, and fall in herself for a few hours of sleep until it was time to go to the station to catch the train out. Sometimes they had to leave as early as two or three in the morning, and she'd drag her body out of bed after only a few hours sleep, help Mama rouse and dress the two younger children, boneless lumps of exhaustion, and head for the railroad station.

As the winter went on, the walk to the station was frequently through a foot or more of snow. Gladys and Mama played games to keep the children moving—Mama couldn't carry them as she had the suitcase. They'd pretend to be a band, going oompah, oompah—anything to keep Lottie and Johnny marching on to the station, knuckles in their eyes, noses running, whimpering with the cold and lack of sleep.

At the station they waited on the hard benches for the train, with Charlotte and Gladys taking turns staying awake to make sure they wouldn't miss it. When the train came in they again roused the protesting children, herded them on board, and plopped down on the hard, red plush seats of the day coach. She would always hate that color. Using coats and suitcases for pillows, they curled up as comfortably as they could, and as the milk train rattled on through the night, jolting to a stop at every hamlet, all four caught another shift of sleep. As the train clattered on into morning they ate cold sandwiches made the night before. Charlotte and Gladys went over the clothing, noting what needed to be mended, washed, or pressed. Charlotte had a couple of primers and helped Gladys and Lottie practice reading and writing. Lottie and Johnny had some formal schooling later, but Gladys never had any other than at these odd moments on trains or in hotels and rooming houses. She learned what and when she could.

The roles Charlotte and Gladys played in real life went through a transition, then became established. When Gladys had first appeared on stage she was just another little girl who had chanced upon a way to add a few dollars to the family income. Now that she was largely responsible for their entire livelihood, she and Charlotte became even

BABY GLADYS SMITH

The Little Mother   In The Fatal Wedding Co
FRANK WENDT, Photo Artist,   Boonton, N. J.

Left to the imagination in this picture of 1901 is the dreary, miserable life of the repertory troupe, through which eight-year-old Mary supported her family. *Mary Pickford Corporation*

more dependent upon each other. Gladys was the breadwinner and Charlotte, though mother and adult, tended to play a supportive role. In her mother's eyes Gladys was no longer a child. One day Gladys came in and found Charlotte roughhousing with Lottie and Johnny. All three were rolling around on the floor and laughing. When Charlotte saw Gladys her expression changed. "That's enough, now," she said to the children, patting her hair back in place.

Many years later when both were grown, Johnny was talking with his older sister about those days. "Poor kid," he said, apparently realizing it for the first time, "you never had a childhood, did you?" It was true that, chronologically speaking, Gladys had had a childhood, but it was a childhood without play and that kind of childhood lasts a long, long time.

Once committed to the concept that they were a theatrical family, the Smiths had no choice but to return to New York every year to find work. The center of the entertainment world might have been thrilling to some, but the little group from Toronto had neither the time nor the money to enjoy it. They stayed in the cheapest theatrical rooming houses. They could not afford to see the shows on Broadway. Though they had come to New York to find work, there was little hope that they would find roles in New York plays. But there were many worlds in show business at that time; traveling repertory troupes—everybody called them rep troupes—were very popular and it was with them that many actors and actresses pursued their careers.

Out in the hinterland at the turn of the century there were enough audiences to support rep troupes by the score. Many cities and towns boasted three-tiered opera houses. Because the prices for admission to the rep shows were ten cents for the gallery, twenty cents for the balcony, and thirty cents for the main floor, opera houses were known to troupers as the ten-twent-thirts.

But before trooping out to the ten-twent-thirts, show people had first to troop up and down Broadway to the booking offices. The casting season was in the summer, when the sidewalks were hot, the booking offices roasting. Trudging along Broadway with its steaming piles of horse dung, or sitting for hours in waiting rooms jammed with job seekers, Lottie and Johnny fussed and cried, while Charlotte and Gladys hushed them and tried to look cool and poised.

This was how actors, both adults and children, spent their summers; it was the hardest part of their work. It seems cruelly ironic that theater people, surely the most narcissistic of all groups and fearfully sensitive to rejection, functioned in a system that subjected them to repeated rejection of the most demeaning kind.

But Charlotte and Gladys and the children kept going back. Sometimes they were able to find plays that had something for all of them; miserable as the tours might be, the family could stay together. But some job-hunting summers, no matter how many muggy offices they visited, they could find no troupes with places for all four, and they had to split up. On the first separation the troupe Charlotte and Johnny were with left first, and Gladys and Lottie saw them off. They all waved bravely as the train pulled out. But once it was gone Gladys and Lottie threw their arms around each other and wept on the platform while Mama and Johnny threw their arms around each other and wept on the train.

Then Gladys and Lottie left with their troupe. Charlotte had arranged for her two daughters to be cared for by a couple in the company, but the couple didn't like children, and showed it. They'd send the two girls to the theater alone. The alleyway to the stage entrance was dark. Gladys and Lottie either heard rats scurrying around or thought they did. Night after night they'd stop at the alleyway, hold hands, and take a deep breath. "Let's go!" Gladys would cry, and they'd race to the stage door.

Late one night, she recalled later, the troupe arrived in Baltimore and got on a streetcar to go to the hotel. The caretakers ignored their two little charges. Gladys tossed her curls. "We'll take care of ourselves," she told Lottie.

They saw a tavern with an inn on its upper floors. Gladys and Lottie got off the streetcar and went into the tavern, where Gladys primly introduced herself and her sister as actresses and asked for a room for the night. After the proprietor got over his shock, he called his wife. She gave the little girls a room, something to eat, and tucked them in.

They cuddled together in the double bed and cried themselves to sleep. Gladys was eleven years old; Lottie was ten. It was Christmas Eve.

By the time Gladys was twelve she knew how to travel better than most adults, certainly better than most women of 1905. She knew how to get around in a town she had never seen before, how to get a room at a reasonable price, how to eat cheaply, when to walk rather than spend a nickel for a streetcar.

Her spare time was spent talking theater with other people in the business. During the annual job hunt one summer the Smiths fell in with another husbandless, fatherless family, Mary Gish and her two daughters, Lillian and Dorothy. Gladys and Lillian, with more than ten years' theatrical experience between them, became friends, discussing the theater, practicing their roles, and sharing theatrical secrets.

Both knew they should see real professionals perform, and talked about it wistfully, for neither could afford the price of admission to the theater. Gladys had last appeared in *The Child Wife,* and she had cards printed that read:

Gladys Smith
THE CHILD WIFE COMPANY

She and Lillian dressed up and went to a theater playing a show both were dying to see. Gladys presented her card and asked to see the manager. He looked at the card, and then at the two poised little girls.

"Do you recognize professionals?" Gladys asked, in her most professional voice.

The manager smiled. "Of course," he said, and ushered them in. Gladys enjoyed that show and others to which her card opened the doors, but she never forgot that her prime mission was to observe and to learn. No producer or agent looking for talent ever studied the actors more intently than she did.

Since her father's death Gladys had learned the importance of money; she knew that it did not rain down from the skies but came from hard work, good performances, and Mama's haggling. When she and Lottie first went out on tour without Charlotte, they changed their weekly salary into one-dollar bills, which Gladys kept in a chamois bag tied around her neck. The two girls counted it together every night. When they had $68—sixty-eight big dollar bills crammed into one small bag—they bought a money order and sent it to Mama. Working so hard for money, trying to make it stretch to feed and clothe her family, hammered home its absolute necessity. All things flowed from money.

In the summer of 1906 weeks of search turned up only one role for the entire family—a role for Gladys playing a boy in a melodrama. Charlotte and the two younger children would have to go back to Toronto and live with relatives on what Gladys could send them. It would mean a grubby, pinch-penny existence for all of them, but most of all for the thirteen-year-old breadwinner out on the road.

After the arrangements were made, the manager of the troupe said that in order to play the boy Gladys would have to cut her hair. That was too much. "I won't do it," she said. She realized the immensity of her proclamation. If she didn't work there would be no income at all. But her hair represented the last defense of her self-esteem. The tears streamed down her cheeks but her lips were set. She meant what she said.

The manager backed down. "How about a wig?" he asked. Gladys nodded. The wig she wore was bright red, and, to fit over her thick hair, seemed as big as a pumpkin. She looked ridiculous, and the part matched her appearance. She was Patsy Poor, brave little exploited mine boy. She even had a death scene. "Dear God," pumpkin-headed Patsy said, dying, "don't open the gates wide, it's only Patsy."

The other players were also contemptuous of the vehicle in which they were appearing, and Gladys was mired in an atmosphere of dejection and fear. Stories were told of stock companies going bankrupt in tank towns, leaving the players to get home as best they could. To Gladys, sole support of her family, counting the house at each performance took on a new meaning. She began having nightmares that would stay with her the rest of her life. In one she would come out on stage to see only vacant seats—that meant the company would close down. In another she'd forget her lines and stand there in panic—that meant she'd be fired. She'd wake up crying, unheard and uncomforted. The dread stayed with her, and before every performance her hands were sweaty, her heart pounding, and she wanted to throw up. Once on stage, of course, the fright disappeared; she was a professional.

She was by this time a capable actress; she had been directed in a score of roles by many professionals. She had studied other players, and thought about her own work. The sensation that came over her when the audience applauded, laughed, or cried was the most important thing in life, and over the years in the ten-twent-thirt proving ground, she had learned every trick in the book to make them do it. She could laugh on cue, with a natural freshness. She could cry just as easily, or turn on a bright smile, a puzzled frown, a look of horror, of surprise, of sadness. She could dominate an audience, even the rough crowd in the ten-cent gallery. Once, when the catcalls were so loud that the thirty-cent customers couldn't hear, she lost her temper, put her hands on her hips, and, head tilted, lips in a pout, glared back. The noise died down, and then they applauded the feisty little creature. After that she had used that combination—arms akimbo, head on the side, angry expression under angelic curls—on many occasions.

As Patsy Poor, however, deprived of her curls and her cute little girl expressions, she felt far removed from the audience. She was playing a character with whom she could not empathize; she couldn't imagine being a red-headed boy who worked in a mine.

"I have never known a heavier sense of fatigue and depression than I felt night after night as we went through with this awful play," she wrote later in the most poignantly frank of her autobiographies, one in which she referred to "the utter wretchedness of this sort of life." Never before had she played to such bored and apathetic faces. And she was desperately lonely for Mama and the children.

One night, for no reason she could pinpoint later other than that she just couldn't stand it anymore, she resolved to leave the troupe. She would not grow up to be like these dull, frightened players. She would make one last effort to find happiness in the theater, and, if this effort failed, she would quit. She had heard that a girl could earn five dollars a week pulling out basting threads. That would be her security blanket: a routine job, five dollars a week, and Mama. She was then thirteen years old.

And so she quit the tour, telling the manager her fantasy: she was going to New York and work for David Belasco, Broadway's most successful and colorful impresario. With the memory of the manager's incredulous expression, and some twenty dollar bills stuffed in her waistband, she went to New York. As her family was still in Toronto, she moved in with a family she had stayed with before, sleeping in a Morris chair in the living room, and cleaning house and doing the shopping in exchange.

Boldness is relative. Gladys sent off to the *Ladies Home Journal* for a kit that told her how to sell subscriptions door to door; she studied it but could not get up the nerve to knock on even one door. But she had the nerve to go to the office of the great Belasco again and again, and to send him letters and photographs. She wrote actresses who had appeared in his productions, asking for introductions to Belasco. The only response she received was from Belasco's office boy, who kept telling her, with what must have been malicious humor, to come back "next Monday." She kept coming back next Monday all summer.

An actress who had achieved stardom in Belasco productions was Blanche Bates. When Miss Bates opened at a Brooklyn theater where Gladys knew the doorkeeper, Gladys went to the theater and did indeed get as far as the star's dressing room. She would later tell the story in different ways, but in every version Miss Bates was too tired to see anybody. For some reason her colored maid sympathized with Gladys, and as reconstructed in horrible dialect in a 1916 account, said, "Miss Blanche, I'se done been with you foh fifteen years and I ain't never axed no favor from you. . . ." But she did ax it, and Miss Bates shouted to Gladys through the partially opened door to go to Belasco and "tell him that Miss Bates sent you and because she is interested in you he must give you a fine position." Miss Bates, when asked about it for publication several years later, not only described "that slip of a child with golden curls and blue eyes . . . lighting up the dingy dressing room of that Brooklyn theater like a flash of sunshine," but took full credit for knowing that Belasco needed a child actress and persuading him to give Gladys a chance. As for Belasco, his version was simply that this girl had been pestering him and one day he agreed to see her.

Whether Gladys did or did not see Miss Bates personally, it seems probable that she did make such an insistent fuss in Belasco's office— "But Blanche Bates sent me!"—that his curiosity was aroused. It happened that he was just about to go into rehearsal with *The Warrens of Virginia* and had not yet chosen the child who would play an important role in it. He told Gladys to come to the theater after the evening performance.

The audience had left, the members of the cast were in their dressing rooms, the stage deserted, and Gladys was scared to death as she approached David Belasco that night. He was a truly theatrical figure, wearing, as always, a black suit and a priest's collar. His thick snow-white hair surrounded his head like a corona, and his dark eyes reflected the dim lights.

He studied her for a moment. "Well, young lady," he said. "So you want to be an actress."

"Oh, no, sir," Gladys said. "I've *been* an actress for eight years!" Her fear was over; she was onstage. "I want to be a real actress now. I've been doing dreadful parts in dreadful plays. I've wasted eight years, and I mustn't lose any more time."

For a tryout, Belasco suggested she read some poems he had with him.

"Oh, no, sir," she said. "Please! I don't know those poems. If I try to read them to you, I can't do myself justice. I'm going to do a scene from one of the plays I've been in. You won't like it. I know it's awful —it's what I want to get away from. But it's the only kind of thing I really know."

Belasco shrugged. "Have it your own way," he said. He called up to the electrician and asked for lights, then stepped over the rail into the stage box and sat down to enjoy the show.

Gladys ran around the stage busily, getting two chairs and placing them just so. "This chair is a poor woman and this one is a policeman who's going to take her to prison. And I'm a little boy who's pleading with him to give her a chance."

Never had Patsy Poor pleaded with such passionate appeal. Gladys was not pleading with a policeman for some woman's freedom: she was pleading directly to David Belasco for her own future. And Belasco, with his genius, saw genius in the scruffy little girl shouting those corny lines. She finished, body tense, hands clutched, face set, eyes glowing. There was a long silence.

"Put out the lights," Belasco told the electrician, and came back onstage. He said nothing, but took her head in both his hands and, in the dim house lights, looked at the drained face framed by the golden curls.

"I think we will make a real actress of you, little girl," he said. "What's your name?"

Gladys had been giving herself more glamorous names. "Gladys Milbourne," she said, and quickly added, "but I'm Gladys Smith in Toronto." He shook his head and she rushed on. "My saint's name is Marie. That's French for Mary."

"Mary's good. But Mary Smith . . . what are some other family names?"

Mary remembered Hennessey, of course, and Grandmother Pickford, names on her mother's side.

"Pickford, that's the one. From now on you're Mary Pickford."

Overcome with the new name and without Charlotte there to haggle, Mary Pickford said she would accept whatever salary Belasco would give her. He offered her $25 a week to play the part of Betty in his new play *The Warrens of Virginia*. She sent a triumphant letter home telling everything—job, Belasco, new name, everybody come.

Mary Pickford played Betty, on Broadway and on the road, for sixteen months. David Belasco had guessed right. He himself often

This was the role, Betty, in *The Warrens of Virginia,* for which Mary besieged Belasco. Belasco himself bought her the doll. *Mary Pickford Corporation,*

marveled at the way the little Canadian girl handled the part of the southern girl. Mary had begun working on a southern accent the very night she got the role. She was the first to arrive for rehearsals, the last to leave. She was always working on a new delivery, a different expression or movement.

"Oh, Mr. David," she'd say, "I thought of something for my part. Tell me what *you* think of it."

She'd go through it while Belasco watched. "I think you're right," he'd say, "but remember, always keep it natural."

Once when he was telling her a story he noticed that her expressions were changing, her body moving, as he talked. He often told her stories after that, just to watch her illustrate them. So eminently successful a theatrical producer as Belasco surely possessed highly developed perceptive powers, and, whether or not he had become a father figure to her, he gave her his attention and appreciation and received the maximum return from her in her performances.

The Warrens of Virginia was warmly emotional, good theater. Audiences liked it *and* the child known as Mary Pickford. She felt their response, that wonderful reflection of her own image, and now that response was coming from expensively dressed audiences in one of Broadway's finest theaters. She knew she was pleasing the great Belasco. She was selling happiness, and receiving money: Belasco gave her a five-dollar raise. Thirty dollars a week was a good salary for anyone in 1908. Mary kept five and gave the rest to Mama. With what Charlotte and the other children were able to pick up, the family could well afford to be together again.

The play closed in the spring of 1909. Belasco had nothing else with a part in it for Mary. She understood. She threw her arms around him, promising that if he ever wanted her back, she'd come. Then she left, out of a job at the close of the season, the worst possible time. About the only thing she could hope for was summer stock, the open-air theater with the flies and the bugs and the low salaries.

Charlotte had another idea. A showgirl she knew had earned five dollars in one day at a motion picture studio.

"Why don't you try pictures?" she asked.

"Oh, Mama, not that," Mary said. One afternoon in Chicago, on tour with *The Warrens,* she had gone to a motion picture show, and it had been a bad experience. She would never have gone to one of the dingy nickelodeons—vacant stores with a sheet hung on the wall for a screen—but the attraction called *Hale's Tours and Scenes of the World* was supposed to be different. It also cost twice as much—ten cents. The ticket taker was dressed like a train conductor and stood at the end of a simulated railroad car. Mary went in and sat down. Suddenly bells clanged, and the car started rocking back and forth, and flickering scenes of landscapes appeared on the screen. Other people in the audience gasped in amazement at the pictures actually moving before their eyes, but all Mary felt was nausea—she'd paid a dime to get seasick in the middle of Chicago.

That was enough moviegoing for Mary. She disapproved of Lottie and Johnny wasting their pennies (children got in two-for-a-nickel) at the grubby nickelodeons in New York, and protested when Charlotte let them go. As for working in pictures, she felt it completely beneath the dignity of a Belasco actress. She went to a couple of motion picture companies to keep Charlotte happy, but was relieved when nothing came of it.

But the savings Mary had put away ran out, and Charlotte urged her to try again. She could, Charlotte suggested, wear her new silk stockings.

The bribe was irresistible to a sixteen-year-old girl, even if she was a Belasco actress. Mary put on her silk stockings, the blue serge suit she had bought for Easter, and a white straw hat. She would go, she decided, to a company called Biograph, on Fourteenth Street, but she had no intention of wasting all that finery on picture people. She walked down Broadway, took a crosstown car on Fourteenth, and asked for a transfer. After being turned down at Biograph she would use it to go back up Broadway to the theater district where her costume would be appreciated, without spending another nickel.

But Mary never used the transfer, for she was not turned down at Biograph. She was hired to play in motion pictures.

CHAPTER FOUR

Doug:
Broadway to Triangle,
1899–1915

When Douglas Fairbanks arrived in New York in the spring of 1899, shortly after his sixteenth birthday, he found a city that had everything. The whole country was prosperous, and much of its wealth was pouring into New York. Its population was more than three million and it was the center of many elements in American life, but it was Broadway that fascinated the stagestruck boy.

From Thirteenth Street all the way uptown to Forty-fifth, there were theaters, theaters, theaters—the first-class houses alone numbered nearly forty. They offered standard fare, the kind of theater a prosperous nation wanted—melodramas, comedies, and sentimental romances. Theatergoers came to laugh or cry, to be soothed or flattered. Plays offering the right formula were rewarded with long runs: *The Count of Monte Cristo* had been playing on Broadway since the year Doug was born, and it was going to continue for another couple of seasons. And where there were theaters there were also vaudeville houses, restaurants and hotels and saloons, billiard halls and barbershops, penny arcades and peep shows. The nights were as bright as the days; in just another year Broadway would be dubbed the Great White Way. Up and down its broad thoroughfare moved cable cars, hansom cabs, private carriages, and even an occasional horseless carriage sputtering along. It was made to order for the young Douglas Fairbanks. Years later his mother remembered him coming home one evening and declaring: "Someday everyone in New York's going to know who I am."

In 1921, at the height of his success, Fairbanks looked back on that first visit to New York. As reported in a Sunday supplement (the *Boston Post*) the quotation is probably not exact, but it has a ring of sincerity.

He [Fairbanks] was struck with the glory of the theatre. "At home," he explains, "I saw good crowds go to the opera house. I saw the great stars get their share of applause. And, of course, I had read of the great triumphs of famous actors. But it wasn't until I reached here" (he was talking in New York and he waved his hand toward the great gaps in the sky made by brick-and-stone giants) "that I realized what a vital force is the theatre, how many hundreds of thousands go to its stage to be amused, or interested, to cry or to weep, how it can play upon their hearts and move their minds. It was then I discovered what an accomplishment it was to be a great actor.

"I devoured the theatrical comments in the press. I walked about town studying the bill posters and window notices. My ambition was set aflame. I would be an actor."

The story went on to recount how Doug ran across the name of his father's friend, Frederick Warde, sought him out, and, at the age of seventeen "I was appointed to play François in *Richelieu.*"

According to his entry in *Who's Who in the Theatre,* Fairbanks "made his first appearance on the stage at the Academy of Music, Richmond, Virginia, 10 Sept., 1900, as Florio in *The Duke's Jester.*" True, the *Richmond Dispatch* of September 9, 1900, carried an advertisement for *The Duke's Jester* at the Academy the following night, although it did not mention Fairbanks. A year earlier, however, when Douglas was sixteen, the *New York Dramatic Mirror* of September 9, 1899, listed D. Fairbanks as the last name on the F. Warde Company, scheduled to open in Philadelphia on September 11. And Warde himself, in his autobiography, set the season Fairbanks joined the company as that of 1899–1900.

"The youth," Warde continued, "was of rather less than average height but of athletic build, with frank attractive features. . . . Douglas remained with me two years and fully justified his ambition to become an actor. His work was earnest and sincere, his personality agreeable, and his energy and ambition unlimited."

This is about as much as is known for sure about Douglas's association with Warde. It has been said that he drove the serious British actor nearly out of his mind with his high spirits, but the record shows that Warde signed him on again for a second season. Warde obviously liked young people, and it's quite probable that on the long train rides between towns, and during the hours between shows, Warde spent some time with young Fairbanks. Warde himself was fascinated by

America, and Doug could not have had a better guide and foster father than this Englishman who had been touring the country for twenty-five years. Warde was not only an actor, but a student of the theater and a man of letters. In later years Fairbanks proved himself to be most literate for a first-year high school dropout; Warde could well have been a factor in his continuing education.

Doug's role as leader of the supernumeraries undoubtedly provided him with invaluable training in personal relations. Supes, or spear-carriers, come in all ages, and not only have to be shown what to do onstage, but kept quiet and out of sight when off. A sixteen-year-old boy would achieve the best results by getting people to work with him, rather than trying to boss them around. Wherever he learned it, this proved to be a priceless attribute in later years.

A well-known figure in the repertory theater, Warde traveled comfortably. On trains, in hotels, at theaters, Doug would be close to successful men with labels on their suitcases, and propinquity to success was a goading reminder to Doug Fairbanks that he wanted it for himself.

Why, then, did Doug leave the Warde troupe? The standard answer has always been that he left to attend Harvard University. Indeed, not only every biographer of Douglas Fairbanks but also his obituary in all the major papers including the *New York Times* states that he was a student at Harvard. Alastair Cooke, in his monograph on Fairbanks for the Museum of Modern Art, even set his attendance as January to May, 1901.

It is not possible to analyze every episode reported to have occurred in the life of Douglas Fairbanks to determine whether it actually happened, but an exploration of at least one is essential to a better understanding of his unusual personality. The Harvard affair is a good example.

In the opening years of the twentieth century periodicals rarely ran feature stories about theatrical people, and direct sources on Fairbanks are available only back to around 1910. In "A Dressing Room Chat with Douglas Fairbanks" published in the *Theatre Magazine* in 1912, "B.L." wrote: "At the Colorado School of Mines and later at Harvard University he was popular for his fun-loving spirit and his irresistible sense of humor." In 1916, in *The American Magazine,* he was quoted as saying he "went to the Colorado College of Mines for a time, then to Harvard." The first major piece on him in the *New York Times* Sunday drama section, February 4, 1917, states that he decided he needed a liberal arts education, enrolled at Harvard as a special student, and studied Latin, French, and English literature. A seven-part series in the *Boston Sunday Post* in 1921 says he received his high school diploma at sixteen and then attended the Colorado School of Mines. Then, said the *Post*, "he made a trip to Cambridge, Mass. He wanted to enter Harvard, he told the dean. But Denver High School was not sufficient for entrance. So Doug took a special course in Latin, French and English to help him in his acting." Doug is quoted at length on his "long tramps along the Charles" and on the practical application of the psychology of William James to his career in the theater.

And so it goes, through the official studio biographies right up to the present. David Niven, a Fairbanks admirer who said Doug had "a hold on the filmgoers of the world, young and old, that has never to this day been equalled," described him in *Bring on the Empty Horses* as "an ex-Harvard graduate." The program of the American Film Institute's retrospective of Douglas Fairbanks at the Kennedy Center in Washington, D.C., in 1974, listed "a few months at Harvard" as one of his "youthful dalliances."

Douglas Fairbanks, Jr., in his remarks introducing the retrospective, said, "Father always said that he left Harvard, but Harvard says that he got kicked out." A handsome man of great charm, Doug Jr. smiled, lowered his voice, and added conspiratorily, "I'm inclined to believe Harvard."

It really doesn't matter, of course, but the truth is that Fairbanks neither left nor got kicked out of Harvard. He was never *in* Harvard. Even in 1901 the nation's leading educational institution was not accepting students with less than one year of high school.

As for the possibility of his having special student status, this was checked in seven separate listings by Harvard University archivists, but no mention was found of Douglas Fairbanks.

And so it can be positively stated that he never attended Harvard —but that doesn't mean he was never there. "He may have audited a class," Letitia Fairbanks, daughter of Robert and the family historian, suggested. "Uncle Doug was good at that. He could just visit a place and make you think he'd lived there all his life."

In 1973 Lorillard Tailer, who knew Fairbanks for some thirty years and traveled around Europe with him one summer, recalled that they first met in 1915 or 1916. "Grizzy Lorillard introduced us," Tailer recalled. "Doug and Grizzy were at Harvard together."

Griswold Lorillard was, like Tailer, a grandson of the incredibly wealthy financier, industrialist, and socialite, Pierre Lorillard. When a student at Harvard, class of 1908, he lived at 9 Bow Street, Cambridge, known as the Gold Coast.

But, Tailer was told, Fairbanks did not attend Harvard. "Of course he did," Tailer answered. "Grizzy used to bring him up to Tuxedo Park [home of the Lorillards] all the time. The other Lorillards were stuffed shirts, but not Grizzy. If he liked you he liked you, and that was it. He liked Doug and so did I. Anyway, that's where they met, at Harvard."

So there the matter rests. Whether in 1901 at the age of seventeen, or later, during long runs of plays in Boston, Doug must have had some exposure to Harvard. He may, as has also been suggested, have made his first acquaintance with a gymnasium there and begun to take gymnastics seriously. He may also, as he later recounted, have met there two young men with whom he worked his way to Europe on a cattle boat; he identified them as Charles "Little" Owen and John "Jack" Beardsley—although there's no record of them at Harvard, either. Nor, incidentally, is there any record of Doug's attendance at the Colorado School of Mines.

Fairbanks's tendency toward exaggeration, prevarication, or down-right mendacity has always been accepted as a part of the man by his friends and relatives. Douglas Jr., gently remonstrating with a biographer who had presented one of his father's stories as truth, gave an illustration: Doug Sr. told his first wife a thrilling and detailed story about a bullfight in Seville; she didn't find out for years that he had never seen a bullfight, never been to Spain.

Why would a man tell the world he went to Harvard, saw a bullfight, and all the other things Douglas Fairbanks claimed to have done, if he had never done them? He was trying to impress people, of course, including himself. The psychiatric explanation is that he was counter-ing inner fears and depression by building up his own self-esteem; he would not permit objective reality to interfere.

In the case of the entertainer, however, particularly the comedian (and as we shall see, Fairbanks was a comedian), the individual is willing, sometimes even eager, to settle for far less than self-esteem. He doesn't build himself up by impressing people; he simply gains their attention by amusing them. What many comedians do for a living is make fools of themselves in public. For all the laughter they evoke, for all their seeming appreciation of it, they are often unhappy people. Would a happy person deliberately bruise both his body and his ego with a pratfall in exchange for a laugh? Or, as a stand-up comedian, ridicule himself, his wife, his parents, his children, his ethnic group? Throughout the life of Douglas Fairbanks his ego can often be heard calling "Admire me, idolize me." It can also be heard to plea, "Like me, look at me, notice me, laugh at me, but don't ignore me!" For to be ignored was to be rejected.

He was often eager to poke fun at himself. He frequently mentioned, for example, a review he said he got in Duluth that reported that "Warde's supporting company was bad but worst of all was Douglas Fairbanks." (Researchers in Duluth can find no mention of Warde, his company, or Fairbanks.) It would not only bring a laugh, but elicit a feeling of rapport, as all actors have at some time or another given a bad performance or received a caustic review. The Duluth review, invented or real, made Fairbanks one of the fellows.

And so in the Fairbanks story, which has to be based at least in part on his accounts of his experiences, there are episodes both ridiculous and sublime, perhaps true, perhaps with some foundation of truth, perhaps made up completely. For in gaining the positives of adulation or recognition, he was blotting out the negatives of his childhood and a father who was not married to his mother, and who was a drunk and a Jew in a moralistic, anti-Semitic society, a father who didn't even care enough about him to stay.

Over the next few years then, Douglas Fairbanks's life was filled with adventures, real or imaginary. He probably did go to England on a cattle boat, and then on to Paris, for his Aunt Belle seems to have been living in Paris at that time (he would not have mentioned Aunt Belle for that would have taken the hardship out of the adventure). He may have made more than one such trip; he often referred to the one with his fellow non-Harvards, Little Owen and Jack Beardsley, and an actor named Hale Hamilton once mentioned a cattle-boat trip he had made with Fairbanks at a later time. On his first trip to Paris, Fairbanks later said, he worked as a laborer and learned to speak the Parisian argot. But in later years when someone made a suggestion he would ask, *"Vous avez raison?"* He meant, "Do you have a reason?" apparently unaware that the idiom actually means "Are you right?"

After leaving Warde, Douglas had several jobs, but it's uncertain whether they were serious attempts to begin new careers or just ways to earn money when no parts were available; probably a little of both. He worked in a law office for a time, perhaps intending to follow his father in that profession. He also worked in a brokerage house, and there are several stories about that venture. One is that he was given to jumping over chairs, often with customers in them, while running messages. Another is that on a day when a stock was fluctuating between 113 and 114, he wrote different combinations of the numbers on the board—131, 141. If he did, he probably received all the attention he needed that day.

However he was earning money, he was always doodling, in big block capitals, the word SUCCESS. That was his goal. A likable young man, he probably went into each new job with enthusiasm and a positive attitude, along with dreams of immediate success. But when SUCCESS was slow in coming, his enthusiasm was quick to wane.

If through some miracle he had encountered success in some prosaic field like business or law, would his enthusiasm have remained high? Of course not. Whether he knew it or not, an indispensable ingredient of success for Douglas Fairbanks was an audience.

He was lucky, for he had good looks, talent, lots of nerve, and plenty of contacts. And with his mother providing a place to eat and sleep and constant encouragement, he had staying power; he could remain in New York, making the rounds. When he was still eighteen he landed his first role on Broadway, in a play starring two well-known leads, Herbert Kelcey and Effie Shannon. It closed after a modest run but Doug was remembered; he obtained another Broadway role after a summer of idleness, and then went on tour with a good show for most of a year.

For the next couple of years Douglas's life was certainly no example of how to get ahead in the theater. Demanding more and more attention, he was fired from one show for interpolating crazy lines and wild bits of business, and quit another when he didn't get a raise. He made a second trip to London on a speculative business venture that collapsed, but while there, perhaps through friends in the theater, perhaps through Harvard connections, however tenuous, he met the American impresario Lee Shubert. So it was that Douglas Fairbanks was hired in London as a chorus boy in *Fantana,* a Japanese operetta opening in New York. It was a big success and so was Doug. Among the first-nighters on January 16, 1905, was Grace George, the Broadway star and wife of the producer, William Brady. Miss George noticed the young man hoofing away and felt that he exuded more virility and personality than the more smooth-stepping chorus boys. She came back to see him again, and then she told her husband about him.

Brady, who'd made a fortune promoting prizefights before becoming a Broadway producer, also liked Doug's athletic energy and physique. The next day, out of the blue, Doug received a wire offering him a five-year contract at a starting salary of forty dollars a week. He thought it was a practical joke and wired Brady back to ask if he had really sent it. He had.

Two months later, at the age of twenty-two, Doug Fairbanks saw his name in lights on a Broadway theater. He hired a hansom cab and he and his mother drove around the block again and again, admiring the sight. The world could have stopped that night for both of them. Doug took several bows, and as for Ella, she heard someone whisper those wonderful words, pointing to her, "There's Douglas Fairbanks's mother!"

The play itself, *A Case of Frenzied Finance,* was a dog, but Doug's performance satisfied Brady that he had made a good investment. He kept his new discovery busy, both on Broadway and on the road.

A contract was a wonderful thing in those days, especially when, for *Clothes* in 1906, Brady raised his salary to fifty dollars a week, a guaranteed income. An actor could make the rounds of the theatrical agents for months, get a part and rehearse in it for weeks, then see the play bomb and not receive a penny. At that time, and for many years to come, the average actor had no guarantee at all. Perhaps even more important to Fairbanks than financial security was the constant ego boost he got from Brady. The producer was fascinated with Doug's energy, and he came to rehearsals just to see what Doug would do next. Doug didn't disappoint him; during rehearsals for one show he walked up and down a flight of stairs on his hands. Brady was ecstatic.

But still Doug doodled SUCCESS. Association with Grizzy Lorillard and his set made it clear just what a pittance fifty dollars a week was, no matter how regularly it came in. He was now interested in golf, tennis, even polo, and though he was welcome at Tuxedo Park, he was only on the fringe of society.

Doug didn't know it, but after a performance of a play called *The Pit* two members of that stratum of society to which he would have liked to belong had discussed him fervently. They were Daniel J. Sully, who didn't like the character Fairbanks played and criticized both role and actor, and his daughter Beth, who defended the actor with unusual vehemence. Not long after, she arranged a meeting with the young actor. She was already enamored of Broadway, and to her this hand-some, active leading man was the epitome of what the theater was all about. She fell head over heels in love with Douglas Fairbanks.

For all his popularity and the resulting availability of girls from Delmonico's to the Epworth League, Doug's sex life was unusually limited. It was probably difficult for him to love anyone in a natural sense; he was not only too wrapped up in himself but also still wrapped up in his mother. Moreover, he had never forgotten that there were only two kinds of women: those who were on a pedestal and those who weren't.

Beth Sully was definitely on a pedestal. She was dark-haired, a little plump, and just aggressive enough to be flattering—she was very much like Doug's mother. And she was also Society. The Sully summer home was a mansion at Watch Hill, Rhode Island. At one time, it was said, Dan Sully had cornered every bale of cotton in the world. He had lost much of that fortune, but he was still considered wealthy.

Doug would certainly not have married a girl solely for her wealth and social position, but he would hardly have married even a pretty girl who looked like his mother if she had not had those extra attributes. One thing we know for sure from what happened later: he was genu-inely fond of her. Even though Doug's mother and Beth's father were not pleased, Doug and Beth became engaged.

Sully could not prevent his headstrong daughter from marrying the man of her choice, but he insisted that his future son-in-law leave the stage for the greater promise, and security, of business. Doug agreed; here was certainly the road to instant success. As for Beth, who had not sought a businessman but an actor, it is not known whether she protested the arrangement or wisely suspected that she would soon have the actor, and the excitement of the theater, back again.

They were married in June 1907. The wedding and reception at

For an actor as unpredictable and prone to skylarking as Doug Fairbanks, progress to stardom on Broadway was remarkably smooth. His performances were as engaging and as confident as he appears in this 1912 publicity photo. *Library of Congress*

Watch Hill were described in detail in the society pages; the groom's departure from the theater had already been noted in the theatrical pages. After a honeymoon in England, the couple made their residence in New York where Doug worked for the Buchan Soap Company, owned by Dan Sully, in the Flatiron Building. His job was selling soap, 12–23 brand soap.

Doug went about his new career with enthusiasm. He sought endorsements from his fellow actors and one day at the Lambs Club he persuaded the famous Wilton Mackaye to shave with his product. As

Mackaye was lathering up Doug told him a story. Mackaye burst out laughing and got a mouthful of 12–23.

"I'll tell you what you can say, Doug," Mackaye spluttered, "you can say this is the best damned soap I ever tasted."

Doug and Beth were happy together. They took a comfortable corner suite at the modern Algonquin Hotel, on Forty-fourth Street east of Sixth Avenue, a block and a half from Broadway, where the recently erected Times Building had brought respectability to what had been the seedy uptown fringe of the theater district. Doug, like many successful members of the theatrical profession, had stayed there before, and Beth loved the hotel, the neighborhood, and her husband. Her mother had often advised her, "Never withhold yourself from the man you marry," and Beth was quite willing to obey, especially with the handsome, dynamic former actor now on his way to equal rewards in the world of business. Doug had the best of everything—the love of a good woman who also happened to be a wealthy society lady with a very strong resemblance to his mother, friends from both the theater and society, and a future loaded with success.

Within two months he was back on Broadway playing the lead in *All for a Girl* for William Brady. One account says the soap company was in trouble, another that Brady lured his favorite actor back with a good part. Whatever the reason, Beth was delighted and the Sully family became resigned to having an actor in the family. As for Doug, he was so happy to be back in the theater that, during one matinee, he started smiling and couldn't stop, his teeth flashing across the footlights throughout the play. Brady was fascinated with this new portrayal by his ever-surprising star, and advertised "The Fairbanks Smile" in all the papers the next day. The play itself departed swiftly, but the new, smiling Douglas Fairbanks remained: he had accidentally created a new character.

He enhanced it in the vehicles Brady created for him in the next couple of years. In *The Cub* he played a big-city newspaper reporter on a dangerous assignment in the Kentucky mountains. In one scene the stage direction called for him to run up a flight of stairs to a balcony and there take the heroine in his arms. Fooling around at rehearsal one day, Doug got a running start, jumped, caught the floor of the balcony, and pulled himself up. The action was incorporated in the play, with the additional business of the heroine bending over and kissing him as he held himself up. Brady had planned to put *The Cub* on the road after a limited run in New York, but Doug's athletics were so popular that he held the play in town, playing musical chairs with available theaters.

In *A Gentleman of Leisure,* by the young English writer P. G. Wodehouse, Fairbanks played another exciting scene, a fight with a burglar. The action was accompanied by the sound of frightful bumps and banging, grunts and groans, and the final exultant cry of victory —but all this time the stage remained completely dark. When the lights came up on the disheveled set there was a touseled Fairbanks, teeth flashing, sitting triumphantly on top of the vanquished villain.

When his contract with Brady expired, he signed with Cohan and Harris Productions, the highly successful partnership of George M. Cohan and Sam H. Harris. His first play under their management was *Officer 666;* the lead for the Broadway cast was already filled when Fairbanks signed but he played it for a long and lucrative engagement on the road. In Chicago an actor named Lewis Waller told Fairbanks of a play he had seen in London, and from Waller's description Fairbanks knew it would be the perfect vehicle for his particular talent and personality. His enthusiasm and conviction were so strong that, still without seeing the play, he persuaded Cohan and Harris to bring it to New York, complete with its author, James Bernard Fagan, as director. The play was a satire on the British idea of the hyperactive American, and when Fagan saw Douglas Fairbanks he could hardly believe him. There was his character in the flesh, Hawthorne of *Hawthorne of the U.S.A.*

The twenty-nine-year-old actor took full advantage of Fagan's reaction to him and practically directed himself; he'd put his arm around Fagan's shoulder, enveloping him with warmth and vitality, and propose some exaggerated bit of acrobatics that Fagan nearly always accepted. In the first act Doug made his entrance, and an immediate impact on the audience, by leaping over a wall. In the second act he decked one villain with a roundhouse swing, hit another with a chair, leaped over a table as the first villain arose to knock him down again, and then dove headfirst through a window to make his exit. That scene brought shouts of excitement from the audience.

None of these antics was difficult for Doug. Though the roundhouse swing actually missed the villain's jaw by inches, the illusion was so strong that the audience accepted it completely. The chair was constructed to break on contact, the leap over the table was easy, and after the dive through the open window he landed on a pile of mattresses. The most difficult thing in the play for Doug was an entrance he made while singing. Fagan, apparently believing that Americans sing as they go forth to save the princess, had his hero trip out on the stage singing:

> If you ask me why I love you
> I will ask you if you know
> Why the tiny stars above you
> Fade with the dawning's glow.

Doug could carry a tune, but he had trouble finding the key. The stage manager would give him the starting note, and then push him out.

Hawthorne of the U.S.A. was a great success wherever it played. The *Chicago News* review was typical: "Douglas Fairbanks, his charm and boyish spontaneity in full blast, has never been more delightful."

From the time of his first starring role on Broadway in *All for a Girl*, when he was twenty-five, Fairbanks introduced at least one play a season. He averaged twenty weeks a year in New York at a salary as high as $800 a week, and did well in the Boston and Chicago runs. Audiences loved his breezy, athletic charm, and critics gave him good reviews—sometimes *too* good. In Boston, for example, a reviewer described *Hawthorne* as though it were a circus; another reported on it as a prizefight. Reporters sought Doug out; he was friendly, personable, and good copy.

One story on him carried the subhead "A Few Glimpses at an Actor Who Is Really Likable," and the reporter, David H. Wallace in *New York Magazine,* after mentioning Doug's "agreeable nature," "genuine laugh," and "buoyant vitality" wrote, "He had a fast walk, with shoulders bent slightly forward, a healthy swing and a snappy step, that survives the days of college track teams."

Asked about his famous personality, Fairbanks replied, "Of course they keep telling me I have personality. But that's nothing unusual. Everyone has personality, but they don't all show it. I believe in letting go."

Under the title "Douglas E. (Electricity) Fairbanks," an unidentified reporter wrote:

Standing—or rather sitting—about five foot eight, with very dark complexion and hair, he made a very striking appearance. Dressed in a very classy, tight-fitting, double-breasted suit, and with a nifty hat perched on his head, he was all there, to use the vernacular. Smile? Oh, yes! I should say the smile was especially prominent. . . . Seated beside him in the hotel lobby, I soon found that he knew everybody in the hotel. He had a word for them all, to the girl at the desk—"Chuck me a box of coffin-nails," he called, and caught them in his hat. A publicity man from "Chi" wanted some photographs, a friend wanted to borrow some money, a Mr. Brown wanted him on the phone, a reporter wanted an interview, a friend had a dinner party waiting, and dozens of friends stopped to pass the time of day and purloin a cigaret. At last he began to talk:

"I attended a military academy in Denver, my home town; then went to the Colorado College of Mines for a time, and later to Harvard. The most trying moment of my life was while a student at Cambridge. Two friends and myself worked our way to Europe on a cattle boat. We landed in England, and then crossed into France and walked to Paris. We had great sport with the Frenchmen and the Martinique negroes. . . . They couldn't understand us, and we called them all kinds of American pet names, and they would shrug their shoulders and walk away while we stood and laughed. I tried it on a six-foot-two shade one day, and he understood English. I had no more than said it, when—bing!—I landed under a table, with blood running from a gash in my cheek where he had hit me. I looked up just in time to see friend Beardsley square off and send a right, clear from Omaha. . . . [He] went down as if he had been hit by a forty-two centimeter shell, and we beat it. Blood was running from his eyes and he was in bad shape. The three of us hid in the morgue overnight, and got out of Paris the next day. We don't know to this day whether we killed that fellow or not."

His fellow actors may have chuckled at such nonsense—they knew Doug for an easygoing fellow who liked boxing but hated fights—but they didn't resent him or his publicity. Everybody liked him. When the Lambs Club gave a tribute to the dean of actors, Thomas Wise, who had been the star of a show with which Doug had toured for two years, the fine old thespian, responding to the ovation, threw his arm over Doug's shoulder and said, "I'm happy to be on the stage with such a fine kid."

Doug was also developing his own way of life. Long tours could have been boring to a man who didn't drink, didn't like long meals, and couldn't sit still to read. Doug thought of many other ways to entertain himself. He could always head for the nearest gym or athletic club for a strenuous workout, or, even better, some kind of game. Few other actors were interested in that kind of activity.

Doug had friends, and friends of friends, from punchy fighters to real Harvard men. Whatever their interest, he liked to discuss it with them, and if they had no special interest he'd invent one, suggesting a two-minute discourse on astrology, or the labor movement, or anything that came to mind.

He was an excellent raconteur and had a wealth of experiences to draw on. Some were imaginary, like the bullfight in Seville, but some had at least a foundation in reality, like his hike across Cuba, from Havana to Batabanó, to win a bet. A similar story with Yucatán as locale, however, pushes credibility too far.

During the inevitable periods when there was no one with him Doug worked out a dozen ways to make the time go by. He practiced sleight-of-hand tricks: he could produce a card or a coin from someone's ear or make knots in handkerchiefs disappear. Dressing was also a game for him. He'd stand as far as he could from the clothes rack and stretch to pick off a suit, and put on his shoes and socks while standing up. He tried to develop an elasticity of movement when he walked, and carried his head high—"Did you ever see a man crying with his head up?" He always bounded up stairs two or three at a time.

One day at the Algonquin, with nothing to do and nobody to do it with, he happened to run across Margaret Case, the daughter of the owner of the hotel. The little girl often went up to the roof of the hotel to watch Doug take his laps around the penthouse or to skip rope with him.

"Let's go up to the roof," Doug suggested, Margaret reported years later. Walking around on the roof, they noticed a small door the size of a dumbwaiter in the cornice on the front of the hotel. Doug pulled on the handle, the door squeaked open, and they looked inside. The cornice was hollow.

"I wonder what's inside," Doug said. Margaret, being smaller, crawled in first and Doug followed, scraping his back and elbows. They found themselves in a long cylinder, only three or four feet high, that extended the width of the hotel over Forty-fourth Street. There was no way for Doug to squeeze past Margaret so she led the way through the dark tunnel to the end, and they couldn't turn around, so they had to crawl backwards to the entrance.

They had dislodged so much debris that the door was stuck shut. They hammered and shouted, but no one could hear them. After an interminable time, the hotel carpenter happened to come up for a smoke, heard them, and dug them out. Just another afternoon in the life of Douglas Fairbanks.

To his friends, and there were scores of them, and the theatergoing public Doug appeared to have the world in his pocket. Forgiven by Dan Sully for not sticking with soap, he and Beth were welcome at Watch Hill during the summer season. They spent a season in London, renting an impressive town house on the Thames. Doug returned from such junkets in debt, but he accepted the obligation almost gratefully. Having to pay back the money he'd borrowed gave him an additional incentive to find a fitting play and knock himself out performing in it.

Doug had the perfect national hero to admire—Theodore Roosevelt, who became president when Doug was eighteen. He was surely impressed by Roosevelt's emphasis on exercise—the "tennis cabinet," jujitsu lessons, and long, brisk rides in Rock Creek Park before breakfast. It was Roosevelt who, when a coal strike threatened to cut off the heat in schools and homes, used his presidential office to end the strike fairly. Action! Power! Roosevelt even waded into the rising new sport of college football when it was nearly outlawed as being too vicious and dangerous, and forced the reforms that both saved it and sent its popularity zooming.

Fairbanks might well have become interested in national affairs anyway, but having an activist in the White House during those formative years surely helped. He developed a simplistic kind of patriotism, a belief in the land of opportunity for those who strove to achieve, and an interest in what was going on in the country and the world. Like Roosevelt, Doug carried himself erectly and walked briskly. He shook hands exactly like Roosevelt, pulling you in close to him, nose to nose. He learned it directly, for he visited his idol in the White House. He came away in ecstasy, because TR knew who he was!

Of the few people who knew who Douglas Fairbanks really was, one was H. Charles Ulman, now in his seventies, who emerged from Brooklyn to share in his son's good fortune. Whether Doug had made regular contributions to support his father or simply gave him a handout now and then is not known. But he did not make the relationship public and, more importantly, neither did Ulman. On the few occasions he mentioned his father, Doug referred to him as John Fairbanks, so he must have had some uneasy moments worrying whether Ulman, or Ulman's wife, would reveal his true identity. His fears were justified after Ulman died in February, 1915. The brief obit in the *New York Times* did not mention Fairbanks, but Ulman's widow let Douglas know that she intended to apply, publicly, for a government pension (Ulman had served as an officer in the Civil War). The action could reveal not only Fairbanks's parentage, but also the fact that his father had been married to someone other than Doug's mother when Doug was born. Through intermediaries, Doug provided Ulman's widow with a private pension and there was no publicity.

It is easy to accept Doug's feelings as a son, not so easy to understand his actions as a father. Douglas Jr. was born December 9, 1909. Place of birth was not the Algonquin, but the Apthorp Apartments. Both Doug and Beth felt it would not look good if their baby was born in a hotel, and the Apthorp was very fashionable. Dan Sully paid the rent, and after the event the family moved back to the Algonquin. By this time there were four in all, for the baby had an Irish nurse, Dee-Dee. It was Dee-Dee who gave the child a name, for his parents seemed to be unable to—there could be only one Doug or Douglas. They referred to him as the boy, and in Dee-Dee's brogue it came out "bye." From then on Douglas Fairbanks, Jr., was called Bye by both family and friends.

Fairbanks must have resented the attention paid to his son. He was not cruel to the boy—Doug would never be cruel—but he ignored him. As Bye grew into a chubby child and Doug was forced on rare occasions to take him out, he was obviously uncomfortable at being seen with him. This reserve and restraint, so unusual to Doug, rubbed off on the boy. Doug Jr. later recalled that once his mother kissed him in public —and he burst into tears of embarrassment.

One area in which narcissistic people can break through their preoccupation with themselves is in their relationship with their children, but Fairbanks's self-absorption was so extreme that he couldn't bring his own son into his life.

Beth must have been a most understanding woman who gave her son love in double quantities, for he grew up to be a kind and gentle man, grateful to his father for eventually becoming his friend, and forgiving of his actions without really understanding them. Reminiscing one

This portrait of the poised performer and proud father with his five-year-old son belies the inner tensions of Douglas Fairbanks, himself lonely and insecure and often a forgetful parent. *George Eastman House*

evening, Douglas Jr. quoted a line from the play in which he was appearing about how a bull sires offspring and then forgets them. "That's the way many males are about children," he said. "The father doesn't have the same intense biological urge for nurturing children that the mother has."

Fairbanks's emotional turmoil as his son grew older was accompanied by a prosaic, chronological fact: time was passing and the popular

Broadway juvenile was getting older, too. Even *Hawthorne* could not run forever, and even its star could have weeks of idleness between plays. There were moments of doubt. Had he gone as far as he could go in the theater? Would his success last?

About this time he was presented with an opportunity to which he reacted, for the first time in his life, with a cautious, play-it-safe attitude.

It began when he met the Aitken brothers, Harry and Roy, in the Algonquin lobby. Depressed and restless when alone, Doug continually sought companionship and, as there were always people in the Algonquin (it was the in thing to come to the hotel after the theater for the specialty of the house—hot chocolate), Doug spent a good deal of time there, drinking hot chocolate, talking with friends, and meeting new people.

Harry and Roy Aitken, teetotalers like Doug, also enjoyed the Algonquin's hot chocolate, Roy Aitken recalled some sixty years later, and it wasn't long before they all became fast friends. Just a few years older than Doug, the Aitkens had started out in their hometown, Waukesha, Wisconsin, showing flickers on a sheet in an empty store for a nickel admission, and had come a long way since then. They had a seven-room apartment on Fifty-seventh Street, a butler, and a housekeeper. Their suits were made by a tailor in Savile Row. And their automobiles—Roy alone had a Rolls Royce, a Renault, and a Leon Bollée! He had brought the Leon Bollée, a yellow roadster with green leather upholstery, over from London just before the war. When he drove over to the Algonquin for hot chocolate in the Leon Bollée, everybody stopped to watch.

Doug liked the Aitkens and they liked him, but they were hurt by his prejudice against their means of livelihood, motion pictures. Doug had seen few films, and he hadn't been impressed. When the Aitkens offered to drive him to motion picture theaters in the Leon Bollée, he went, but although he liked the ride, he still didn't like the flickers. He didn't like the grubby theaters, the short, jerky films, the players waving their hands, the lack of dialogue, the odd titles that described what was going on. Even when the Aitkens took him to a regular Broadway theater to see *Cabiria*, a film made in Italy that was more than two hours long—eight times longer than the usual one-reel picture—he didn't like it. He pointed out that it didn't do anything that couldn't be done in the theater, and in the theater the actors could talk. The

Aitkens had to agree, but they told him that a film they were financing would change his mind. It was being made in California by a man generally considered to be the best director of all, D. W. Griffith—David Wark Griffith. Doug had never heard of him.

The Aitkens' Mutual Film Company released a series of short films featuring the Mutual Girl, a beautiful young woman named Norma Phillips. Harry Aitken had met her on a ship coming back from London, and this was his way of getting to know her better. Each week she interviewed a prominent guest—questions and answers ran on the screen as printed titles—and then the guest would do something for the camera. Douglas Fairbanks was the guest in the film released December 7, 1914. It was apparently not preserved, but mention has been made of a "screen test" in which he jumped over a park bench, among other things, and it could well have been the film with the Mutual Girl. Few people got a chance to go before a motion picture camera in those days and Doug must have enjoyed it, and appreciated the agile grace of the man—himself—on the screen.

He did not consider going into pictures at the time. With one or two exceptions, picture people were lucky to get one-tenth of what he was making, and were looked down on. Nor would the Aitkens, who were paying their best-known players—Lillian Gish, Mae Marsh, Miriam Cooper—only thirty and forty dollars a week, have insulted him with an offer. At that point it was simply a matter of friendship and curiosity.

But this changed, as did history, when the Aitkens presented the film they had financed. Costing $110,000, it was by far the most expensive motion picture ever made up to that time. It was also the greatest, for it was *The Birth of a Nation*. No other representative of any art form —music, literature, painting, drama—has made such an impact. Nor has any other art form reached maturity so swiftly. Presented in a legitimate theater at a two-dollar top, *The Birth of a Nation* brought motion pictures respectability.

It also brought instant wealth to the industry. Just one of the millionaires it made was Louis B. Mayer, later head of Metro-Goldwyn-Mayer; he obtained the rights to show the film in New England and made more than a million with it in that area alone. No one knows how much money *The Birth of a Nation* has brought in over the years, for people like Mayer did not give and the Aitkens did not demand honest accountings, but it is believed to have made more than any other film until *The Godfather* was released in 1972.

With this bonanza Harry Aitken, the dominant brother, went to Wall Street and got investment bankers to come into his newest venture, the Triangle Film Corporation. He could also afford to make generous offers to Broadway actors to lure them to his California studios. One of those actors was his friend Doug Fairbanks.

Doug had been at the opening of *The Birth of a Nation*—it is easy to picture him leaping to his feet and cheering with the rest of the dinner-jacketed, evening-gowned audience—and had gone back several times to see how it was done. He met D. W. Griffith, whom the Aitkens had brought to New York for the opening and often took to the Algonquin. Griffith, who had gone into pictures only because he was starving in the theater, admired Douglas Fairbanks, and Fairbanks, like all of New York, was impressed with the man acknowledged to be the best director in pictures. He told friends that he might go into pictures if he could work with Griffith. Griffith told the Aitkens that they should get Fairbanks into films.

The details of Aitken's first offer are not known, but we do know Fairbanks's reasons for declining. The dashing star of *Hawthorne*, the bon vivant of both the theatrical and the polo set, the pre-jet-set traveler who would take off for London on a whim—Douglas Fairbanks was afraid that being in pictures would cheapen his stage image, perhaps even destroy it. After appearing in films he might not be able to get a part in the theater, and if he did, his salary might be reduced, perhaps severely.

This was a side of Douglas Fairbanks that few were aware of. The public, his friends, the journalists, saw the Doug of *Hawthorne of the U.S.A.* constantly putting on a performance. It probably never occurred to any of them that he could be insecure, fearful, depressed. After all, few ever saw him alone. Indeed, he had so many friends in so many circles who saw him only when he bounced into their lives that they probably never realized how seldom he was alone, how desperately he sought *not* to be alone. As he turned thirty-two, the fear of jeopardizing his stage career and giving up his life in New York by taking a flyer in the flickers was too strong.

But the Aitkens and Griffith persisted. Doug had to admit that California sounded wonderful; he'd always wanted to see the country west of the Rockies. The show in which he was playing closed and he was at liberty, but still he resisted the Aitken pressure.

If Fairbanks had been deliberately holding out for better terms he could not have been more successful, for Harry Aitken, as driven in his ways as Fairbanks was in his, couldn't stand being refused. He raised the salary offer to $2000 a week for a trial period of ten weeks—$20,000 to an unemployed actor for a summer in California—and agreed to the stipulation that Fairbanks would be personally directed by D. W. Griffith. He could take Beth and Bye—and Beth, who had a strong influence over her child-husband's decisions, wanted to go. There was only one perquisite Doug requested that he did not get: Roy Aitken wouldn't sell him the Leon Bollée. "With the war on in Europe," Roy explained apologetically, "I couldn't get another one."

Doug signed the contract. On June 26, 1915, he began his career in motion pictures.

CHAPTER FIVE

Mary: "Little Mary," 1909–1915

The brownstone building at 11 East Fourteenth Street occupied by the Biograph studio had once been a grand mansion. The large foyer, its parquet floor now badly worn, opened into the ballroom. The people waiting on the hard benches could see the lucky ones who were working today milling around inside. Mary Pickford, sixteen years and eleven days old this nineteenth day of April 1909, had no intention of spending the day on a bench hoping someone would call her. After a few minutes she got up, smoothed her new navy-blue suit, straightened her white sailor hat, and started to leave.

A tall hawk-nosed man strode out of the ballroom, stopped her, and without introducing himself demanded, "Have you had any stage experience?"

Mary tilted her head to the side and looked up at him as haughtily as she could. "Ten years," she said. "The last two for Belasco."

The tall man was a frustrated actor who believed David Belasco to be the greatest living influence in the American theater. He was thirty-four years old and had never even met Belasco, but he was not going to let this young girl know that he was impressed.

"Well," he said, "you're too little and too fat, but I may give you a chance. My name's Griffith. What's yours?"

Mary told him, but she was furious. She was just under five feet tall and weighed 115 pounds; a little plump, perhaps, but not fat. His arrogant, patronizing attitude offended her. She did not know that he was David Wark Griffith, the sole director of the Biograph Company, with authority to hire her for five dollars a day. Nor did she know that Linda Arvidson, a motion picture actress secretly married to Griffith, had called his attention to her and that he had studied her for several moments before approaching her. Over her protests he pulled her back into a dirty little dressing room and, with no chaperone present, made her take off her hat and began putting makeup on her face. He was, he said, going to give her a screen test. Even though she was angry and a little frightened, she noticed that the makeup was not the pinkish shade used in the theater, but stark white. He outlined her eyes with a heavy black pencil. Her reflection in the mirror looked more like a clown than a girl.

He took her out to the ballroom, grabbed a mandolin from somebody, and handed it to her. She had no idea how to hold it, and he showed her. He told her to strum the mandolin and look natural. Several actors and actresses gathered around to watch, laughing and talking among themselves. Then the harsh blue lights went on and a man started cranking a big black box pointing right at her. Mary was confused and flustered, and one of the actors, impatient, said, "Get on with the dame." That did it. To Mary the term "dame" was an insult. She stamped her foot and demanded an apology. Griffith stopped the camera with an angry shout. She had ruined the shot. Wasting film was a cardinal sin, and he bawled her out in front of the entire company.

For all her ten years on the stage, Mary was a sensitive sixteen year-old girl with very little experience in life away from the formal atmosphere of the theater. She had associated almost exclusively with older people, and if they had not been solicitous, at least they had been courteous. In the informal, raucous milieu of the studio she was confused and hurt. She would have stormed out of Biograph right then if it had not been for the money. She wanted her five dollars.

Work went on until eight o'clock that night. Griffith himself handed her blue card to the cashier, who in turn handed her a five-dollar bill, and asked her to come back the next day. Mary was still hurt and angry. The average girl would probably have taken the money and left, never to return, but not Mary. Her self-esteem was badly bruised and she desperately needed a reinforcement. Griffith had not praised her, no audience had applauded her, and there was only one way to get the gratification her ego was craving.

"I'm a Belasco actress, Mr. Griffith," she said. "Five dollars isn't enough. I'll have to have ten."

Ten dollars was twice what the other players, including Griffith's wife, were getting. This girl had appeared in only one scene and had messed that up the first time (it was never used). Why should he even consider her brazen request? For whatever reason, perhaps because he wanted to show this Belasco actress and even himself that he had power too, he acceded.

"All right," he said, laughing. "Ten from tomorrow on. But don't let anybody else know or there'll be a riot."

Mary was so excited that she ran several blocks through a heavy April shower, ruining her suit and hat, to show Mama her five dollars and tell about the promise of ten more the next day. That night she couldn't sleep, and got up before dawn to practice expressions of joy, sorrow, anger, and love for Mr. Griffith. (In her final autobiography Miss Pickford wrote that she was excited only about the money, and turned and tossed in dread of going back to the studio the next day. In her earlier reminiscences, however, the descriptions of her eagerness to go to the studio are more convincing.)

The next morning Griffith told her how pretty she looked, and commented that it must take two maids to comb out those golden curls.

"Oh, no," Mary said, "I do it all myself," She prattled on, and neither then nor later did she realize the significance of the question and her answer. She had passed a major test: Griffith had a predilection for poor girls, self-sufficient girls.

In addition to paying Mary an extra five dollars for the day's work, Griffith sent Linda Arvidson to Best's to buy a costume suitable for a ten-year-old child, the role Mary would play that day. She returned with a light-blue linen dress, light-blue stockings, and patent-leather shoes. Miss Arvidson recalled later that she spent about twenty dollars; Mary gave the figure ten-fifty. Whatever the amount, it was a lavish expenditure for Biograph. But it was justified, because the radiance of the child wearing the pretty dress for the first time comes through dramatically on the film even today.

More important, Mary's first appearance in film, so fortunately preserved, demonstrates the dramatic power of the motion picture camera. Viewing this one short segment is essential to any serious study of the cinema.

The film is *Her First Biscuits.* It was originally a half-reel, or split-reel, film; that is, it took up only half a standard 1000-foot reel. Often

This silly scene in a ridiculous 1909 flicker is of unparalleled importance
to scholars and fans alike. Available to viewers in the Library of Congress,
Her First Biscuits demonstrates the magic of the camera in enhancing the
characteristics of certain rare individuals, and as her very first appearance,
it demonstrates the magic of Mary Pickford. *Library of Congress*

the studio did not have a story good enough to fill at least three-quarters of a reel (twelve to fourteen minutes) and so a comedy or light romance, anything that could be shown in half the time, would be filmed. Then, of course, a similar story would have to be found to fill up the other half. *Her First Biscuits* is 514 feet, and it runs a little more than seven minutes.

In the film a bride bakes biscuits for the first time. Her husband is too smart to eat them—the premise that a bride's first biscuits were inedible was a standing joke in America at the time—and he takes them to work. He runs a casting office, where a strange assortment of people —actors and actresses, a fat man, a midget—come in one by one and sneak a biscuit, eat it, then fall down in a faint. The husband drags each one into a back room. Then they all recover and move around gesticulating until the husband opens the door and lets them out.

That's all there is to the film, except that, for no apparent reason, this child suddenly appears in the crowd in the back room. Perhaps Linda Arvidson had not returned from Best's in time for Mary to be in the first part of the film, or perhaps she was in it and was cut out for some reason. It makes no difference; what matters is the shot in which Mary appears. The cliché is the best way to say it—she lights up the screen. She does nothing but stand there, look at the camera, smile, and make a few simple gestures, yet she pulls your eyes away from the others in the scene. Her photogenic quality is so strong it's eerie. The effect continues after the film is over; some viewers say they remember her in a blue dress, although, of course, the film is scratchy black and white. Others remember her as being larger than anyone else, although she was less than five feet tall.

It has been said that the camera is honest, it does not lie, but that is often not true: inexplicably, the camera portrays some people as looking better than they really do, others worse. In some rare individuals it highlights and transmits a striking quality. It takes nothing away from Mary Pickford to say that she could not have been as beautiful as that glowing child on the screen. Rather, whatever it is that makes one person in a million so photogenic that the rest of us look at her with fascination, reflecting emotions from love to hate—whatever that is, Mary Pickford had it. You can see it there on the screen, just the way the camera recorded it on April 20, 1909.

Mary had other, more definable properties; she was just right for pictures. The harsh lights needed to expose the crude film then in use added years to a woman's face by illuminating and emphasizing every line and flaw. A young woman's role was ideally played, therefore, by a teenage girl with a smooth complexion. But in the early 1900s few teenage girls had sufficient poise to perform before the camera; Mary, with all her ten years on the stage, had been most uncomfortable her first time. Her appearance in *Her First Biscuits,* pointless as it was, proved that, in addition to the magical quality of being photogenic, she had the rare combination of acting experience and a youthful complexion.

Mary and motion pictures combined in another coincidence: each was precisely ready for the other. Both were adolescents. The camera that made it possible to take motion pictures had been perfected three years before she was born; the projector that made it possible to show those pictures on a screen, two years after. In the early 1890s motion pictures were short filmstrips shown in individual viewers in penny arcades. A traveling salesman waiting for a train could drop a coin in a box, squint through a peephole, and see a few seconds of clouds moving, a woman dancing, or even, in the raciest strip of all, *The Kiss,* a rather homely man and woman kissing.

With a projector, this same strip of pictures could be shown on a large screen—a bedsheet would do—to many people at once, for a nickel apiece. In small cities and towns, where the rep troupes came through only a few times a season, and in working-class neighborhoods in the big cities, where the average man made a dollar a day and couldn't afford to take his family to the theater, motion pictures began attracting audiences. The new pastime was even bigger in immigrant neighborhoods; a greenhorn right off the boat could understand pictures.

And so the new industry developed not upward into a higher form of art, but outward to the people who could afford a nickel. (For a few years a franchised operation called Hale's Tours attracted middle-class customers to central locations, but the public lost interest in travel scenes.) When film manufacturers began turning out pictures that told stories the industry went into the second stage of expansion. Movies were no longer mere curiosities—they were entertainment. Small merchants discovered this great new opportunity: they could take the customer's money and send him away happy *without wrapping up a thing*—it was a license to steal!

In 1905, when an imaginative proprietor of a business consisting of a projector, a sheet, and some chairs set up in a vacant store combined the American word for five cents with the Greek word for theater and came up with *nickelodeon,* there were probably about five hundred such operations in the country. By the time the image of Mary Pickford was first projected, there were more than five thousand nickelodeons in North America alone. Programs lasted from a half-hour to an hour, requiring anywhere from two one-reel films to several shorter ones, and they changed every day.

A half-dozen major companies and several smaller ones, located in New York, Philadelphia, and Chicago, were attempting to meet this swelling demand. In ten months as a director, D. W. Griffith had turned out more than a hundred pictures for Biograph, one of the larger companies—*Her First Biscuits* was number 113. Thus Mary Pickford, extremely industrious, driven by insecurity and a craving for adoration, and seeking a surrogate father, fell into the hands of a director who was also work-oriented and who enjoyed being a father figure to the female members of the company: he called them "my children."

Griffith, too, had come to motion pictures through hunger. A stage-struck product of a Kentucky dirt farm, he had traveled the country with grubby rep troupes, often being stranded when they'd gone broke, had written a play that flopped, and, with his wife, was penniless as usual when he received five dollars for his first day's work in pictures. He went back for more, and one of the Biograph owners noticed his energy and enthusiasm. The company needed a director. The two cameramen on the payroll were offered the job, but they were insulted; they considered the director a flunky who simply moved people and things in position for them to photograph. None of the other regulars wanted the job either, and that left Griffith. He agreed to try one film, provided he could keep working for five dollars a day if it didn't turn out, and made it and eleven more in the next month. Biograph gave him a contract for a year at fifty dollars a week plus a bonus of five mills for every foot of film (*Her First Biscuits* put an extra two-fifty in his pocket). In addition he could give his wife work at five dollars a day; they kept their marriage secret so as not to endanger her earnings. Griffith had security he had never known before.

At that time the reward was ostensibly financial and nothing more, for he worked in complete anonymity. Biograph, like other companies, did not identify director, players, or anyone connected with its films.

Who cared? Certainly not the immigrants and rubes who packed the vacant stores called nickelodeons. The first film manufacturers, which was what they called themselves, considered their products to be nothing more than merchandise. It cost around fifty cents per foot to make a film; copies were run off for next to nothing and sold at the standard price of ten cents a foot, no more, no less, regardless of who made it, directed it, or played in it. All any company wanted from any director was quantity. But Griffith, working in a medium for which he had at first felt contempt, gave Biograph quality, too. He produced at least two films a week, and they were innovative, bright with imagination and creativity.

There must have been some motivation in addition to money. Frustrated actor, poet, playwright, at some point Griffith made the discovery that just as a playwright or actor could employ words or actions to gratify his ego, so the director could call upon many entities—story, characters, scenery, photography, presentation—to project himself through film. It may seem paradoxical to assign so narcissistic a motive to so faceless and nameless an individual as a 1909 movie director, but what other explanation is there? Griffith later demonstrated the priority he placed on self-esteem and vanity over money. Officially credited or not, he began to identify with his product.

Mary Pickford came along just when he was beginning to know what to do with her. She was just one of the many devices at his disposal, but his use of her would benefit them both. The better he made her look, the better he looked. Both were willing, more than anyone else in the company if not in the entire industry, to apply their talents, thoughts, and efforts over long hours. The films they first made strictly for money became extensions of themselves.

In their relationship Griffith was an alternating current, keeping Mary off balance. The first day he had sought her out, then called her little and fat. The second day he had complimented her on her hair, then, just before quitting time, told her she was going to play a love scene the next day and asked if she had any experience in that kind of role.

Mary had never been kissed romantically, onstage or off. She had never even had a date, or gone to a dance. But of course she said she had played many love scenes.

Just then a carpenter walked by carrying a papier-mâché pillar.

Griffith told him to set the pillar down and told Mary to make love to it. Flushed and embarrassed, she said she couldn't make love to a pillar. Griffith looked around, saw Owen Moore, a slender actor with sexy eyes and slicked-down hair, and called him over.

"Miss Pickford doesn't like to make love to a pillar," Griffith said. "Let's see if she can do any better with you."

Owen moved in smoothly, obviously enjoying this kind of work. Mary hesitantly raised her arms. She fought back her fears—*ten dollars*. But she resolved that there would be no kissing, no matter what Griffith said.

She tried to remember the love scenes she had seen. She looked up at Owen with what she hoped was a loving expression as he put his arms around her and pulled her to him. She could feel her heart pounding. She turned her face away at the last moment, but apparently Griffith was satisfied. He cast Moore in the role of her sweetheart; they would repeat the scene for the camera the next day. Mary went home excited and frightened.

When it came time to shoot the love scene, Griffith sent everyone out of the studio. Only Mary and Owen, Griffith and the cameraman, Billy Bitzer, remained. In the strange greenish light of the mercury lamps, Mary tried to look poised and natural.

"Camera!" Griffith ordered. Bitzer, peering into the black box, began turning the crank. Griffith spoke to Mary softly. "Pickford, you're no longer a child. You're a woman in love. See that man? He is the man you love. He has been away a long, long time. Now he has returned. Go to him. Put your arms around him. Hold him. Kiss him with all the warmth you have in you. Ah, that's right. Cut."

Little Mary and the handsome, experienced actor stood locked together for a moment, then released each other. Breathless, Mary put her hand to her face, brushed back her curls. This scene, and her entire performance in *The Violin Maker of Cremona*, a sappy film taking up a whole reel, are moving and convincing. She is sweet, pretty, appealing, and mature. It is difficult to believe that this was her first romantic role, for she handles it delightfully. Perhaps Griffith put her through the demeaning experience of the evening before to prepare her for the actual scene.

Within weeks Mary played a child, a sweetheart, a mother of teenage children, a Mexican girl, and other roles. That was the way Griffith ran the company, like a repertory theater. He rehearsed each scene two or three times and photographed it only when he was completely satisfied. To players who had worked for other companies his method was unusual, for other directors wasted no time on rehearsals, but Mary accepted it.

She needed little rehearsal, anyway. Belasco was noted for his emphasis on the economy of gesture and Mary had absorbed his methods. His accent on naturalness, the elimination of exaggerated, corny gestures, fit this new medium perfectly. Even in a Belasco production it was sometimes necessary to overplay an emotion for the benefit of those far from the stage, but the eye of the camera, especially in Biograph's crowded ballroom studio, was never more than twenty feet away. As the players had no lines to speak, they had to use gestures to tell the story, but even so the pantomime could be done naturally, without chewing up the scenery, as they called it.

As always, Mary watched the other actors and actresses both rehearsing and filming, studying how they got their emotions across without words. It should have been the other way around; in many scenes in those early films Mary is an oasis of natural appeal in the midst of exaggerated gestures. She practiced before the mirror, emphasizing facial expressions—the frown, the smile, the wrinkled nose, the pout. As she became more at ease in the new medium, she realized how much she could learn from Griffith. Later she said that she had learned more about acting under his direction than in all her years in the theater, and he recalled that she had never stopped listening and learning. He also commented on a phenomenon that Belasco had noted, too—that often, just when he would think of a gesture for her, she would perform it as though she had read his thought.

Griffith had positive ideas about practically everything that went into the portrayal of a character. A southern Victorian, he believed that his heroines should be pure, sweet, kind, and neat. In a film in which Mary played a poor girl who, naturally, found love and riches at the end of the reel, she put on a woeful assortment of clothing, including a worn coat with a scraggly fur collar and a ridiculous hat with a little bird on it. When she came into the room she took off her hat and coat and threw them on the bed, then went into the action that had been rehearsed.

"Stop the camera!" Griffith shouted. Everyone looked at him in alarm. "Pickford," he said, "you must never come in like that, throwing your hat on the bed and putting your coat down without shaking it. No heroine is untidy."

Mary said, "Yes, sir," picked up her coat and hat and went out. At first she was angry, but then she thought, well, he may be right. She entered, took off her coat, shook it and brushed the collar with her hand, then took off her hat and fussed with the silly little bird. She hung the coat carefully on a chair and placed the hat down just so.

"Very good," Griffith said.

She rebelled against some of Griffith's notions. He loved to portray his heroines as flighty girls, skipping around like bunnies, pointing their fingers at bluebirds, tilting their heads, resting their cheeks against the back of their hands. Mary protested vehemently and refused to perform the more odious actions.

Both volatile, they had their fights, too. Once, wearing a heavy velvet dress much too large for her and pinned up in the back, Mary felt so hot and ridiculous that she couldn't produce the emotion Griffith wanted. They rehearsed it ten, twelve times. Impatient, he shook her. She bit him. She cried and declared that she was through with him and pictures forever. He shouted good riddance. But as she was leaving he ran after her and apologized, and she came back. The tears flowed— and, of course, the camera recorded every one.

Their relationship extended beyond rehearsals and filming. Much younger and more serious than the other members of the company, Mary rarely joined in the gossip sessions during slack periods. As a poignant indication of just how young she was, she remembered, many decades later, playing with the mercury spilled from a broken lamp. Griffith was always working, and she would often join him when he was cutting, or editing, the film. He was pleased that she was interested, and loved having an audience. He explained cutting to her. It was a completely new process in entertainment. In the theater, the curtain came down after a scene and the audience waited while the stagehands changed the scenery and the actors changed their clothes. Griffith, however, could accomplish all that in a moment with a snip of the scissors and a touch of glue, so that the action flowed, uninterrupted, from scene to scene. Other filmmakers were beginning to study his pictures, for he was ahead of everybody else in the world in this new art.

A film could be cut in several ways, he explained to Mary. He could show something happening in one place, then cut the film and glue in another strip to show a simultaneous happening somewhere else. The climax of many pictures of this era was a chase scene—the villains chasing the hero, the hero racing to save the heroine. Griffith would shoot the pursuers and the pursued separately, then cut the film so that the audience would see first one, then the other. People in vacant-store theaters would often leap to their feet and shout with tension as Griffith switched back and forth from hero to villain.

The cutting operation, looking and snipping and pasting, was more fun than many activities available to teenage girls, and Mary came back often to watch Griffith and, occasionally, help him. She studied the performances of the cast, including her own, and made mental notes on how to improve her work.

She examined the way she photographed and began to experiment with makeup with Billy Bitzer, the cameraman. He was delighted to talk about photography with this golden-haired girl, and explained how the strong lights bounced off her white skin, taking the detail and expression out. In the theater she had used pink makeup to deepen the color, but pink has red in it, which comes out black on film. Bitzer concocted creams and powders using tan instead of pink and photographed Mary wearing them. Then the two studied the results of their experiments, Mary chattering away, Billy grunting back in his German accent.

Each inspired the other to try new techniques and procedures. One day after shooting an outdoor scene in the countryside, Bitzer saw Mary and Owen Moore standing and talking in a striking composition. He wanted to photograph it, but the sun was behind them. No cameraman ever shot into the sun because the faces would be in shadow. But with Mary's encouragement, Bitzer took a few feet of film anyway, right into the sun. Developed, it presented a lovely picture, and the sun shining through Mary's hair brought out new highlights. But the striking thing about it was the clear image of her face and Owen's. It happened that they had been standing on a patch of white gravel, which reflected light on their faces.

Bitzer showed the take to Griffith, who also admired it. Bitzer experimented further with Mary and Owen as subjects, seating them at a table covered with white oilcloth, the sun behind them. Again, with the reflected light, they photographed beautifully. He used the technique in several films after that, and other cameramen went out of their minds trying to figure out how he had done it. Shooting into the sun with reflected light eventually became an accepted practice; Mary's encouragement had helped Bitzer stumble on it.

She was also interested in the first step in filmmaking, the story. Griffith contributed many stories himself, and others were bought from whoever took the time to write them down. Although Mary had had no formal education, the prospect of extra money was motivation enough. She laboriously wrote out a simple plot, and when Griffith gave her fifteen dollars for it, she wrote more. Plots were easy to find; Mary rewrote *Thaïs* in one page and got twenty-five dollars for it. Only a page was necessary, for all that Griffith needed was a story line. He did the rest, breaking it down into scenes in his head.

Sometime later Mary was directly involved in a milestone in filmmaking. When she first came into films, scenes were photographed as though they were onstage. The camera, a big black box, was fixed in one position with a definite field of vision; the area was the same whether occupied by one person or ten.

Directing a film called *Friends,* in which Mary played the interesting role of a girl living alone over a western saloon, Griffith suddenly said "Let's have some fun," and suggested that Bitzer move the camera in closer to her. Bitzer pushed the heavy thing forward until everything but the upper part of Mary's body was cut out of the picture.

Mary could hardly wait to see the results. Griffith called her when the film came back from the laboratory and they went to the screening room—formerly the master bedroom in the old mansion. He started the projector and suddenly there she was, filling the screen. But even in the shock and wonder of seeing her first close-up, Mary's first thought was that she had on too much eye shadow.

The close-up had been done before, but it was its use in *Friends* that made a revolutionary impact on both industry and audiences. Biograph executives complained that they were paying Mary enough; they wanted to see all of her. Criticisms on esthetic grounds ranged from vague expressions of displeasure over something new to the warning that the sight of a disembodied head on the screen would frighten pregnant ladies. But audiences were generally ready for this obvious development, and Mary herself, who is lovely in the shot, helped the

From the time Mary's father died, through her working childhood, on to her emergence as America's Sweetheart, and into her reign as queen of the cinema, Mary's relationship to her mother was one of mutual love and intense dependence. *Mary Pickford Corporation*

close-up gain acceptance. The close-up is one of the great separations between stage and screen; it enables the actor and director to present the most dramatic and intimate expressions of emotion, the audience to receive them without distraction. The slightest movement of an eyebrow in a cinema close-up can say more than the gamut of Delsarte gestures on a stage.

If the camera could be moved closer to the action, it could also be moved up, back, and to the sides. The long shot, dramatically depicting an entire troop of cavalry galloping across the plain, was received with almost as much astonishment as the close-up. But the most important result of this experimentation was the concept of the moving camera. By moving the camera, or by using additional cameras and different lenses, the director could now photograph the entire scene as well as individual characters from different distances and angles. Selecting views from each camera—called shots—and gluing them in sequence, he could present a scene in a continuous flow of many different shots, bringing the audience into intimate relationship with each character. There is a wonderful vitality in these early films of 1909 to 1914, reflecting enthusiasm and delight as Griffith and Bitzer and the players, like Mary, who were interested in film techniques worked with the new toy.

Mary's interest in filmmaking had developed gradually; at the beginning it was strictly a job. In her first week at Biograph Griffith had offered to pay her a guaranteed salary of forty dollars a week, instead of a chancy ten dollars a day, and she accepted. After eight o'clock at night all players received extra pay, and Mary frequently stayed on. Selling an occasional story brought in more money. Lottie and Johnny began playing roles and Mama came to the studio, too. Donald Crisp, who worked for Biograph in 1910, said that Charlotte cleaned up the place, including the one toilet serving the entire building. Whether or not this is true, the family was together, and eating well.

Mary still needed constant appreciation, especially after Griffith decided that, with her hazel eyes, which photographed dark, and her high cheekbones, and with a black horsehair wig and a dark stain on her face, she was well suited for Indian roles. She wore a leather dress —clammy in the morning, hot during the day—and with the wig and the stain she was miserable. She complained that she didn't even look like herself. Griffith, with a strange obtuseness, rarely gave her the praise she needed. She had to have compensation, so she asked for a raise.

"Well, if you're a good sport I'll see what I can do," Griffith said.

Not long after, Mary was playing a scene in which she and her sweetheart paddle a canoe to safety and which was being filmed on the swift, cold Passaic River in New Jersey. The canoe turned over and Mary had some frigid and frightened moments before she was rescued. Griffith threw a blanket around her, called off the shooting for the day, and took her back to civilization. Shivering, wrapped in the blanket, her wet hair falling down around her face, Mary turned her eyes up to him.

"Wasn't I a good sport, Mr. Griffith?" she asked. She got the raise.

Discomfort and danger were just a part of the day's work. Mary hiked over the hills in her leather dress, leggings, and horsehair wig. Over the protests of the company's owners, who pointed out that the countryside in Harlem was just as rustic and much closer, Griffith took the players all the way to Fort Lee, New Jersey, crossing the Hudson River on the 125th Street ferry, to film the outdoor scenes. When winter came he persuaded the Biograph management to set up an operation in Los Angeles. He had played with a rep troupe in California—it had gone broke and he'd picked hops for enough money to get home—and he remembered the constant sunshine and the many different kinds of terrain. A couple of other New York–based companies had spent the winter there, with successful results.

Mary was the only member of her family asked to make the trip, but at the last minute Griffith let Johnny come along. Mary wasn't very excited about going to California that January of 1910; she was unhappy at being so far from Mama, and the five-day train ride only emphasized the distance. There was nothing glamorous about Los Angeles, then a drab, hick town populated largely by retired midwestern farmers.

She and Johnny and two girls in the company rented two rooms with connecting bath for $5.50 per person per week near the Biograph lot on the corner of Grand Avenue and Washington Street. It was called a lot because that's what it was, a vacant lot, and so began the custom that resulted in multimillion-dollar studios being called lots. Griffith had a crew of carpenters build a small stage six inches off the ground for interiors. Walls were canvas flats with windows and doors painted on; they moved when the wind blew. There was no roof, for the only light came from the sun.

Mary was in Biograph's first California picture, filmed at the San Gabriel mission. Some of the titles and subtitles of the films she made in California indicate the type of role she played: *The Thread of Destiny: A Tale of the Old Southwest; The Twisted Trail: A Story of Fate in the Mountain Wilds; A Rich Revenge: A Comedy of the California Oil Fields; Ramona: A Story of the White Man's Injustice to the Indian; A Romance of the Western Hills.* She was in her leather dress, horsehair wig, and leggings from sunup to sundown, broiling on the barren mountains and deserts near Los Angeles.

When she wasn't tramping over the hills she was riding over the hills. A rodeo rider, six foot three in romantic-looking cowboy clothes, got a crush on her, helped her overcome her fear of the "owl-eyed beasts that know a tenderfoot before he comes within a hundred yards of the corral," and taught her to ride. Unfortunately for the cowboy, Mary's interest in him ended abruptly when he showed up in Los Angeles in a too-tight store-bought suit and whitewall haircut.

Nor did her new ability to ride always work to her advantage. While making *The Two Brothers,* her horse fell and rolled over. She managed to scramble away through the dust just in time to escape being crushed. In the final chase scene, her horse broke loose again. All that in one reel!

The days ran together and when Sunday came all she wanted to do was sleep. Later she could recall only two pleasant experiences from that first time in California. One day, riding the trolley car through Hollywood, a nice little town where the flowers spilled down from the front yards into the road, she saw an expanse of poppies and got off the car to pick a bunch to take to her room. And one night she was returning home with Griffith after work—he had the only automobile —through another outlying town, Pasadena. She looked up to see palm trees silhouetted against the sky. Poppies and palms: they were Mary's most memorable moments.

Johnny—now called Jack Pickford—had enough fun for the two of them. He doubled for the girls, riding horseback and taking falls. A skinny youngster starving for attention, he was willing to do anything if coaxed or praised. Sometimes after work the men would dare him to take a drink and laugh at him when he'd reel around giggling. Jack was not slow; he'd take a couple of drinks and put on a drunk act. One night a couple of actors going to a whorehouse offered to take him along. He was too embarrassed; he was hairless where it mattered. Somebody pulled a mustache out of a makeup kit and provided him with a handsome thatch of pubic hair. The girls at the house thought that was a riot and gave him special attention. By the time he left Los Angeles, Jack, at fourteen, was well educated in whiskey and women.

With living expenses paid, extra pay for stories and overtime, and little opportunity to spend it, Mary saved quite a bit of money in three months in California. Jack threw his in and the total came to $1200. They'd never seen so much money before. They put it all in fifty-dollar bills and when they got home they arranged the bills on the kitchen table, then called Charlotte. She smiled. "Oh, stage money," she said.

"No, Mama, it's real," Mary and Jack shouted. Jack threw a handful of bills in the air. Then Mama and Mary, Lottie and Jack, giggling and laughing and shrieking, all began throwing the money around the room. It was the happiest reunion they had ever had.

Unhappy Bride

Mary had been looking forward to another reunion, this one with Owen Moore. From the first time the handsome actor had held her in his arms, she had felt an attraction for him. That first summer Griffith had made several films in the Orange Mountains west of New York, putting up the company in a small summer hotel. The setting was lovely—a lake, an old canal, stone farmhouses, green pastures. After dinner Mary would find herself alone with Owen, strolling by the canal, floating in a little boat on the pond as the evening star came out, sitting on the verandah as the frogs sang in the pond and the fireflies made holes of light in the midsummer night.

When they returned to New York, Mary brought Owen home to dinner. After all, he lived in a small furnished room and ate in cheap restaurants. Although he was blessed with romantic good looks, the ability to wear clothes well, and an air of sophistication, underneath Owen was just another Irish farm boy. His family had immigrated to America when he was eleven, settling on a farm in Ohio. Like his older brothers, Owen had started out with small stock companies, first in the summer, then whenever he could get a job. And finally he had drifted to New York and Biograph.

Perhaps Charlotte would have disapproved of any young man, but in Owen's case she had good reasons. He was seven years older than Mary, a $5-a-day actor with limited talent and a liking for the bottle. Charlotte surely knew, for everyone else did, that Owen frequently came to work with a hangover. Just as Mary was a typical Griffith leading lady, strong and self-reliant in that she worked hard and supported her family, Owen Moore was a typical Griffith leading man, handsome, personable, and weak—the master wanted no competition.

Charlotte told Mary not to bring him home again. Mary later speculated that if her mother had made Owen welcome and not disapproved of him, if she had been able to see more of him, and openly, their relationship would never have become more than a teenage infatuation.

And she was probably right. She was only sixteen when she first met Owen, seventeen when she had to decide whether to obey her mother or see him covertly. She was caught in an intense symbiosis with her mother; she cried herself to sleep many a night in the awful fear that her mother would die and leave her. "Even in my happiest moments," she recalled, "it would stab through me like a knife." Economic necessity was another factor in their relationship, for Mary and her mother needed each other for survival. They also shared an excessive amount of physical contact. Adolescent girls frequently pull away from their mothers' petting and stroking, but Charlotte's constant fussing over her, doing her hair, was a part of her professional life. She felt trapped, smothered. But she wasn't defeated. She proved it in the only way she had to assert herself: she met Owen Moore clandestinely.

One of Mary's biographers has implied that these meetings resulted in a premarital pregnancy. The contention is based on a report that she was a little plump during the shooting of *A Call to Arms* and insisted on draping herself in a cape—on a hot day in June—between takes. The baby was lost, this story goes on, when Mary fell off a horse; indeed, this accident has been given as the reason Mary never had children.

Mary herself never discussed such a delicate matter, but the story is improbable. Even if she were carried away by emotion on her reunion with Owen, only a little more than two months elapsed between her return to New York in the second week of April and the shooting of *A Call to Arms* in the last week of June, rather a short time to be showing signs of pregnancy. There is a less scandalous medical explanation for her inability to have children, which will be discussed later.

It is far more probable that Mary, like the good Catholic girl of high morals that she was, placed the price of marriage on her virginity. Yet when Owen asked her to marry him, she refused, saying that Mama would never permit it. And then he stumbled on the ultimate argument.

"If you don't marry me," he said, "I'll leave and you'll never see me again!"

He had presented the unbearable alternative. The one thing worse than being apart from her mother would be another rejection by a man she loved. There seem to be no other considerations involved in the decision. Where and how they would live after they were married? She apparently never thought about it. Couldn't she have talked to someone, anyone, about this decision that would surely change her life? Apparently not, for she didn't. Couldn't she have called on her own inner resources in evaluating so potentially destructive an involvement? Absolutely not. Mary, after all, did not have a healthy self-esteem. She had no inner security. She lived in fear of losing everything, in need of constant reinforcement from without.

Only because losing him would be worse, Mary agreed to marry Owen. The wedding of any mail-order bride would have been more romantic. After work one dreary day in January 1911, Mary borrowed a long dress and high-heeled shoes from the wardrobe department, and went with Owen across the Hudson River to Jersey City. While waiting for the justice of the peace, Mary realized the enormity of what she was doing. She didn't love Owen. She didn't want to leave Mama. She'd run out of the building, go back to New York! But then she realized she couldn't run in her long dress and high-heeled shoes, and she didn't have any money for the fare home. So she married Owen Moore. After the ceremony she went straight home, crawled into the double bed she shared with Lottie, and cried. . . .

The life of Mary Pickford, including her unconsummated marriage with her secret husband, is so inextricably meshed with the cinema that even as she and Owen were leading their strange, secret life as newlyweds, sleeping in their respective beds blocks apart, the events of her professional life were of greater importance. For it was during this period that she began to have an influence on the shaping of the film industry.

Mary's first contribution to the cinema was, simply, to be recognized. People who went to nickelodeons saw her, remembered her, and wanted to see her again. By coincidence, they called her "Little Mary," simply because the titles in a couple of her pictures referred to the character as "Little Mary," complete with quotation marks. Benjamin B. Hampton, a highly respected corporate executive who made a comprehensive survey of the industry some years later, wrote, " 'Little

Mary's' films began to stir audiences definitely in 1909, and it is probable that she was the first player ever to register deeply and generally
in the minds of screen patrons."

But it was only by such names as "Little Mary" and "The Girl with
the Curls" that she was known, for Biograph did not identify her or
anyone else. Audiences not only did not know Mary's name, they had
no way of knowing when her films would be shown. Nickelodeon
operators received the films for the day every morning. Even if they had
known who would appear in the one-reel or split-reel features, they
would not have had time to advertise the fact—if they had advertised
at all. Programs were not repeated two days in a row. But when "Little
Mary" was appearing word would be passed around the neighborhood
and people would come specifically to see her. A few exhibitors
throughout the country recognized the potential of identifying "Little
Mary," advertised her films, and perhaps even showed them for two or
three days at the same nickelodeon. But Jeremiah J. Kennedy, wearing
three hats as president of Biograph, of the Motion Picture Patents
Company, the trust of which Biograph was a member, and of General
Film Company, which distributed the films of the trust, saw no reason
to change the method of operation. The trust, composed of the ten
major film companies, was based on the patents held by Thomas A.
Edison on the motion picture camera; by controlling nearly all the
cameras then in use, the trust controlled the market. For a fee of two
dollars a week—the collections were brought to the office in laundry
bags—it licensed nickelodeon operators to rent films for ten cents a
foot. A 1000-foot film cost $750 to $1000 to make, and hundreds of
copies would rent many times over at $100 a day. In October 1910,
there were 9480 picture theaters licensed in the United States alone.
Motion pictures were a gold mine. The companies kept their earnings
to themselves, but it has been estimated that Edison, as holder of the
patents, received $10,000 a week. Executives of the trust rarely, if ever,
went to nickelodeons and probably had no idea that movie audiences
knew one character from another.

But some of the nickelodeon operators, who were closer to their
audiences and who liked the flickers themselves, began to realize that
they could attract more customers if they could tell them who was
going to appear, particularly if it was somebody like Little Mary. One
of the more enterprising exhibitors was a former clothing store manager

named Carl Laemmle. Typical of the new breed of entrepreneur, he was far removed from the old-line Anglo-Saxon bankers and business-men prominent in the motion picture trust. A German immigrant, he was so enthusiastic about taking people's money without having to wrap up something for them in return, that he presented the best programs he could arrange in a pleasant and comfortable setting. He looked at pictures himself and listened to his customers talking as they left the theater; he knew what they wanted. People were willing to pay a dime to attend his nickelodeon. But the two-dollar levy infuriated Laemmle and he set out to fight the big boys on their own terms. He organized the Independent Motion Picture Company, procured a bootleg camera, and went into business. He knew that people would pay to see Little Mary, and he asked her to come with IMP. Mary, of course, brought Charlotte into the discussions, and Charlotte maneuv-ered Laemmle up to $175 a week for Mary, plus work for Lottie and Jack. That much money for a seventeen-year-old girl provided a large dose of reinforcement for Mary's ego, and, in addition, the enthsiastic Laemmle made her feel wanted. Biograph did not attempt to match the financial offer, and Griffith did not attempt to match the expres-sions of praise and appreciation she craved. In her discussions with Charlotte, Mary convinced herself that Griffith's disciplined direction was stifling her development, and thus found an artistic reason to give for her departure. And, finally, Laemmle also hired Owen Moore. Mary and Owen had been working together at IMP less than a month when they were married.

Mary was now caught up in a real-life combination of intrigues more complex than any one-reel picture. The trust hired private detectives to check on IMP's use of its cameras, and there was always the danger that they might break a few heads along with the camera. Other companies were sending parties south to Florida and west to California; Laemmle, reasoning that only outside the United States would his company be safe, sent a party to Cuba. He chartered a small vessel, tried to keep its destination secret, and gave orders to the captain to make sure he was not being followed.

On board were Mary and Charlotte, Lottie and Jack, Owen Moore, director Thomas H. Ince, and the rest of the players and technicians. Few had made an ocean voyage before, and it was all very exciting. On the second day out of New York, Owen finally managed to get Mary alone. They were in the bunk together when Charlotte burst in and caught them. As Ince reported later, "The old lady blew her top." She demanded that the captain turn the ship around and go back to New York; when he refused she ordered Ince to make him. But the ship sailed on to Cuba.

In her final autobiography, Mary said only that it was on that vessel that she told her family she was married, after which her mother cried for three days and nights, Lottie would not speak to her, and Jack stood by the rail holding his little dog, the tears streaming down his face. She left out the circumstances surrounding the revelation, which make the extreme reactions more credible.

She probably saw no more of Owen on the voyage, and in Havana he went on a three-day drunk. The quarters the advance man had secured proved to be uninhabitable. The food tasted funny; the property man was keeping the cold cream in the refrigerator and the Cuban cook used it for lard. Ince, who had bluffed his way into the job, had never directed before. At least two accounts of the Havana experience include a melodramatic adventure in which Owen struck Ince's assistant for insulting Mary and would have been put in a Cuban jail had not Charlotte, by an elaborate ruse, arranged for him and Mary to be smuggled aboard a New York–bound ship.

Though this episode seems a little hard to accept, there's no doubt that the Cuban experience was unpleasant. In later accounts Mary spoke of being the only "white girl" in the community and of being stared at by the "natives." Her hair kept coming uncurled in the humid heat and had to be rewound, and either because of inferior equipment and film, inexperienced technicians, or both, it photographed dark. With all the delays, bickering, and inexperience, the players had to work eighteen-hour days.

As the company was built entirely around Mary, she worked harder than anyone else. An IMP announcement of *The Fisher Maid* described it as "9996 feet of thrilling drama with 'Little Mary' in nearly every foot." "Little Mary" did not refer to Mary as a child, incidentally, but to Little Mary, the star. Golden curls and all, she played a neglected wife in eleven of her thirty-three IMP films, and once she was a coquette. In one film she played the part of a navy wife who suspects her husband, stationed in Havana, of being unfaithful. She goes to Havana, disguises herself as a Cuban girl, and arranges a meeting with him; he *is* unfaithful, but, as the infidelity is with her, it's okay.

In later years Mary, with her tendency to feel that when she was unhappy everything else was also all wrong, described her IMP films as being poor, and historians have gone along with this subjective judgment. The films do not exist today, but contemporary reviews are available, and they are generally favorable. Here are some comments from the *Motion Picture World:* about *First Misunderstanding—* "Clearly told and . . . sufficiently attractive to hold the interest of the audience from beginning to end"; *Maid or Man—*"It is another of the Little Mary series and you must not miss a single blessed one of these"; *Artful Kate—*"Sometimes the pictures seem to almost talk in their strength and the excellence of the acting. . . . The company deserves congratulations upon producing such a good film"; *The Fair Dentist—* "Easily the funniest thing this reviewer has seen for over a week. . . . The reviewer wasn't the first to laugh, but he fears he laughed the loudest. . . . The dentist really is pretty. We'd hate to have any exhibitor miss this film."

The *World* did pan a few of the IMP productions. *In the Sultan's Garden,* for example, was described as "artistically one of the weakest that the IMP company has released in some time."

Regardless of the quality of the films, Mary obviously was miserable making them. She lost eighteen pounds and was diagnosed as tubercular. Charlotte took her back to New York where the malady proved to be only fatigue. Somehow Owen and Mary got Charlotte's consent to live together while she rested. Owen took her to a modest suite in the Hotel Flanders, and, for a few days, they seem to have been happy. According to people who knew him, Owen was a likable human being, and without Mama hanging around he could have been perfectly capable of giving Mary, so sweet and helpless, the attention, consideration, and love she wanted, and she could have reciprocated. But as she recovered she became eager to start working again and had to discuss the situation repeatedly with Charlotte. Owen, frozen out, went on a week's drunk.

Laemmle hastened Mary's return to work by promising to replace Ince with William Clifford. His first film was *In the Sultan's Garden,* in which the wicked sultan's henchmen tie Mary in a sack and throw her into the Bosporus.

It was easy to film Mary being put in the sack and then cut, replace

Mary returned to Belasco for her last Broadway role in *A Good Little Devil* with Ernest Truex. For the first time in entertainment history, people came to the legitimate theater to see a motion picture player! *Academy of Motion Picture Arts and Sciences*

her with a dummy, and shoot the sack being thrown into the sea. But popping out of the water had to be the real thing. Mary agreed to do it—it was part of the job. Clifford arranged the scene on the Hudson River, with every safety precaution: an anchored barge to shoot from, a police cutter standing by, and two lifeguards treading water just out of camera range.

With her mother watching anxiously from the barge, Mary went in and under, and surfaced for the camera. It was a good take, but the man running the cutter was so busy watching the action that he lost control. Mary saw the boat bearing down on her, but, unable to swim in her harem clothes, she was helpless.

Something grabbed her legs and pulled her down. She heard bumps and a strange roar above, then felt herself being pushed up. When she broke water, flailing and gasping, the first thing she saw were her mother's panic-filled eyes, almost on a level with her own.

What had happened was that one of the lifeguards had dived, grabbed her, and pulled her down deep enough to avoid the propeller. The cutter had crashed into the barge and knocked Charlotte flat, and she was sprawled out, screaming and peering into the water when Mary came up.

Working for IMP in New York was not a happy time either. Her pictures pulled in the audiences, but Mary was ashamed of them. Her home life, what little time her work schedule left for it, was as bad as her opinion of her films. Owen, who had an ego of his own, began to resent being less important than his teenage bride.

Mary understood, and she got a chance to do something about it. While she was grinding out films for Carl Laemmle and he was vacationing in Germany at Carlsbad spa, another former exhibitor, Harry E. Aitken, asked her to work for his new company, Majestic. Charlotte got him up to $275 a week—a figure that people said would break the industry—and Mary quietly specified that Owen be hired as her director, figuring it would be good for his ego.

The deal went through in the fall of 1911, but it didn't solve the problem. As Mary's director, Owen took out on her during the day, in front of the cast, his frustrations of the night. Mary took his sarcasm, never telling him that she was responsible for his having the job. Caught between her mother and Owen, she couldn't please either of them. He would get drunk, she would run to mother—or was it the other way around? After five pictures with Aitken she returned to Biograph. She was so glad to be back that she buried her face in Griffith's chest and cried.

By this time Mary had established a predictable pattern. Even considering that persons in the entertainment world move around, she changed employers more frequently than most. She would be drawn to a father-lover—Reid, Belasco, Griffith, Moore, Laemmle, Aitken— only to subconsciously anticipate and effect rejection; in her mind it

Though today we think of Mary as playing only "Little Mary," in fact she played many adult roles, as in this IMP production of 1911, *The Fair Dentist. George Eastman House*

was always the other who was disloyal first. Examined with this criterion in mind, the twists and turns in her career that at first appear to be diverse actually have one thread in common.

After a year, and some two dozen films with Griffith, she provoked a fight and fled to Belasco. She gave a delightful performance in the difficult role of a blind girl in *Good Little Devil*, but when the show reopened in the fall of 1913, after a summer recess, Mary wasn't in it. She had a new father figure, and was making a film for him in California. He was Adolph Zukor, and in some respects he would influence the motion picture industry, with Mary's help, almost as much as Griffith.

Zukor, a tiny, quiet man—he was no taller than Mary and was sometimes referred to behind his back as Creepy—was another of the immigrant exhibitors who brought innovations to the industry. One night on a streetcar an idea had come to him and he jotted it down. The next day he was finally able to decipher it—Famous Players in Famous Plays. The phrase represented not only a positive program, but a philosophy: Zukor believed that the public had the capacity to appreciate the finest actors and actresses in established vehicles. This simple concept would cause a revolution in filmmaking, financing, and exhibition, for Zukor intended to present famous plays in their entirety—four or even five reels, if necessary. At that time films of more than a reel were extremely unusual; of the 141 films Mary Pickford made through 1912, for instance, only one was longer, a two-reeler. There were many reasons for not making longer films. A four-reel film required much more work and money than four one-reel films, and, of course, would have to take in much more at the box office to pay back the investment. It would quadruple the gamble, for almost everyone but Zukor believed that the public was not ready for hour-long films.

Zukor was aware of the risks, but he was willing to take them and pay for them. He recognized Mary Pickford as the number one attraction in pictures, and after some lengthy haggling with Charlotte he agreed to her demands: $500 a week. Mary was just twenty years old.

For a time it seemed that she had at last found a father. Zukor accepted her as a member of his family, and she later wrote that her years with him were the happiest in her film career, even though she got off to a most unfortunate start. In *Caprice,* her third film for Zukor, the script called for her to carry another girl to safety in a burning schoolhouse. The girl was heavy, and Mary strained herself, suffering serious internal injuries. Later Mary also referred to having suffered a ruptured appendix during this period. Whatever the cause, she collapsed and was taken to the hospital in a serious condition. It was this condition that rendered her incapable of having children.

Owen hurried to her side when he heard that she was in the hospital; unfortunately, he was drunk. There was a nasty scene, Mary cried, and her doctor, doubtlessly encouraged by Charlotte, issued orders that Owen was not to see her again. Mary remained in a serious condition for several days, and was left both physically and emotionally drained. Zukor, in the finest tradition of the father surrogate, took Mary and Charlotte to California to recuperate; Owen, sulking, was left behind. Zukor also took his director, Edwin S. Porter, and rented a farmhouse near Hollywood for headquarters, just in case.

Sure enough, Mary's idea of recuperating was to make a film. She borrowed an idea from a story she had read in some magazine. "The author will see the film and write us and we'll pay him," she told Zukor—and he did and they did. It was a decidedly adult story for Little Mary, and deliberately so. Now almost twenty-one, reborn in a sense after her serious illness, she was determined to put Little Mary behind her and be her age. In the story, a man and a woman are shipwrecked on a desert island—that kept the cast down. They fall in love and declare themselves married, and she has a baby. Then the man's wife finds him, and Mary, baby in her arms, jumps off a cliff into the sea. The whole thing, called *Hearts Adrift*, was shot on the beach. Though it was December—and it can be chilly even in California—and Mary ran around in a grass skirt, she was soon tan and healthy.

She was also, she thought, through forever with grubby and little girl roles. What she wanted was glamorous, romantic leads. When Porter told her about a book called *Tess of the Storm Country* and asked her to read it she refused; Tess was one of the characters she was determined to escape. But just *look* at it, Porter pleaded. Mary did, and couldn't resist the role: a poor, uneducated girl, dirty and dressed in rags, who, after several twists and turns of plot, proves her inherent goodness and marries the wealthy, handsome young hero.

Charlotte found ragged dresses for Mary and helped make her up so that she looked unkempt yet appealing. Porter, who was also the cameraman and had no assistants, contributed little in the line of direction, and Mary worked out her own characterization. A Japanese fishing village in Santa Monica was perfect for the exterior shots of the squatters' cabins, and interiors were shot in the yard behind the farmhouse, with natural light. Zukor did not even have a laboratory in California; exposed film was sent all the way back to New York for processing, so there was no way of knowing whether the takes were good.

Nor did they know the importance of the daily shipments to Zukor. In his dream of presenting quality, feature-length films to the public, he had overextended himself. He borrowed on his life insurance, his wife's jewels. *Tess* cost close to $10,000. Everything Adolph Zukor had, including his pride, rested on this dirty-faced girl.

Overall, *Tess* is unimaginative and static; Porter did not use advanced techniques, not even close-ups. But in the scenes in which Mary appears, and she is in most of them, she is so alive, so convincing, so appealing that nothing else matters. The ragged little girl grabs your heart.

It is not just her photogenic quality, although that jumps out of the screen; it is her technique as well. In one scene the hero enters Mary's cabin to find her holding a baby and jumps to the conclusion that the child is hers. A word from Mary and he will understand and take her in his arms, but she must keep the child's identity a secret, and is silent. He berates her and storms out.

On the screen Mary reduces all the emotions of this scene into one little gesture. She turns up her hand, holds it for a split second, then lets it fall. This one gesture reveals all her helplessness and sorrow. Only great talent, augmented by experience, could convey so much with such simplicity.

Tess of the Storm Country, released March 30, 1914, was a hook that dragged people into theaters across the country and around the world. It proved that Zukor was right; motion picture audiences had the taste and judgment to pay to see their favorites in feature pictures. It not only paid Zukor's debts but gave him the bankroll to continue. It is known as the film that built Paramount Pictures Corporation, for Zukor went on to control Paramount.

When Mary returned east, Zukor took her to tea on Broadway. She told him that another company had offered her more money, and she would have to leave.

"Sweetheart, honey," Zukor said softly, "would you like to have your salary doubled?"

Mary, now making $1000 a week and still not twenty-one, squeezed his hand and kissed him. They sat quietly as dusk fell on Broadway. The lights on the theater marquee came on and then, suddenly, across the street, she saw it: her name in lights. It was the most thrilling sight of her career. The realization that Zukor—"that dear, sweet man"—had

planned for her to see it for the first time in just that way made it all
the more wonderful.

For all his thoughtfulness as her stand-in father, five-foot, fortyish
Adolph Zukor lacked romantic appeal. Mary turned again and again
to her handsome, moody husband, but each rapprochement ended in
a battle. Years later, Mary gave a running account of their difficulties
—the many times he abused or embarrassed her when he was drunk,
the many times he left her. Owen never spoke publicly about his life
with Mary, or privately either, according to one of his friends, Allan
Dwan, the director. "Owen was a gentleman," Dwan said.

It is thus possible that it was Owen who was the aggrieved marriage
partner. Hardly a sophisticate, he was faced with several problems that
would have challenged a marriage counselor. Though he was fairly well
known in films, still his wife was making far more money than he was.
She and her mother were often a united front against him. And there
was Mary's strange pattern of being receptive, then almost seeking
rejection. Whatever the cause, however, there seems to be no doubt
that Owen did drink heavily and brought on several ugly scenes. Mary
reported one occasion when they were staying at the Biltmore and
came back late from an after-theater party with Charlotte.

"Where's *she* staying?" Owen demanded, in front of everybody in
the hotel lobby.

"With us," Mary replied.

"The hell she is," Owen said. After an angry exchange, he left.

There was another story about a similar evening when the three
checked into a hotel, taking a large suite. "You take that room, Owen,"
Charlotte said, motioning to the smaller bedroom. "Mary and I will
sleep in here."

They were often separated by the necessity of making films on
separate coasts; on the other hand, they were sometimes able to work
together as well as live together. They made two consecutive films in
late 1914, for example. The following year, when Allan Dwan was
directing Mary in *A Girl of Yesterday* (it was not a successful working relationship; each was too strong), Mary and Owen went to
Dwan's wedding at the chapel at San Juan Capistrano. Both Catholics, they remembered in the picturesque setting that they had not
been married in the church, and asked the priest to perform the
ceremony. But, even with the repeat performance, the marriage still

was not successful. Owen, Mary said, finally told her bluntly that he preferred the bottle. Mary became resigned to having a marriage without happiness.

That was the situation in the fall of 1915, when she and Owen were invited to Elsie Janis's house at Tarrytown one Sunday, where, among the guests, was the dashing Broadway star Douglas Fairbanks.

CHAPTER SIX

Doug:
The Making of a Star,
1915

"When you're dealing with million-dollar stars whose characters were created by hundred-dollar-a-week press agents," Richard Schickel, the film critic and historian, once advised, "it's easier to go along with the legend than the facts."

The legend of how Douglas Fairbanks first found success in motion pictures has many variations, all connected by one haunting thread: he had failed to make an impression as a screen actor when he first went to California in 1915, and the film that represented his last chance had been placed on the shelf, when, through a lucky circumstance, it was shown in a New York theater. The audience loved it, and Fairbanks was off to a running start in pictures.

The way his niece Letitia Fairbanks tells the story, Fairbanks was considered a failure by both D. W. Griffith and Harry Aitken, head of Triangle, after he had made only one film, *The Lamb*. Only because a new theater, the Knickerbocker, requested a Griffith film for its big opening and the Triangle executives had nothing else did they reluctantly provide it. Big hit.

That is the simplest form of the legend. The most dramatic is the one put forward by Anita Loos, the tiny screenwriter who was also with Griffith in 1915. In her version of the Fairbanks film beginnings, Griffith and the Triangle executives had given up on him when John Emerson, an actor-director imported from the stage, discovered a scenario written by Anita and proposed that he direct Fairbanks in it. Griffith opposed the project for two reasons: Fairbanks couldn't act and the script wouldn't play. Emerson persevered and got permission to shoot it. Griffith didn't like it and ordered it shelved. The reason, according to Loos, was that too much of the picture was in the subtitles, the printed words on the screen; before then, she explained, the titles were very short, like "Next Morning."

Somehow, of course, the film managed to get to New York by mistake and to the Roxy Theater, managed by the famous S. R. "Roxy" Rothapfel. Roxy protested, as he had advertised another film, but put it on while a messenger hurried over to the Exchange with the scheduled picture. By the time it arrived, however, the theater was rocking with laughter and the audience insisted on seeing the rest of the Fairbanks film with the Loos subtitles. The picture was a hit and Fairbanks became a star. As for the subtitles, Miss Loos reported that their success in this film began a trend toward both humor and sophistication in motion pictures, and paraphrased the *New York Times*'s review the next day as extolling the new maturity of the films as evidenced by the subtitles.

Dramatic as these legends and their variations may sound, they are largely untrue, and they do not give a fair portrayal of Douglas Fairbanks. He had far more to do with his own career than to be accidentally pushed into popularity. In his case, the facts are better than the legend, and further, they are right there before our eyes in moving figures ten feet tall. It is true that in the case of many of the pioneers of the cinema, and certainly of Douglas Fairbanks, many of the usual biographical materials either do not exist or are unreliable. He rarely sat still long enough to write a letter, for example. Written reminiscences of those who knew him and worked with him often turn out to be blatant efforts to display their own exaggerated contributions. Press releases of the time ranged from all-fact to all-imagination, as did feature stories and interviews.

Nor did Fairbanks seem to care. One of his nieces, Mary Margaret Fairbanks Chappelet, recalls that he gave up any hope of being accurately reported early in his career. It could be pointed out that much of the inaccuracy was based on his own fantasies, dutifully recorded by reporters who probably considered themselves as conscientious as any, but this would only prove his point. Whether made up by himself or his press agents, the stories were printed.

But there is one reliable source for the development of Fairbanks's career in this visual art, and that is the visual art itself. Fairbanks on the screen—his face, acting, and actions—gives a good picture of Fairbanks off the screen.

Like a new kid in the neighborhood who gets all dressed up to go to his first party and then finds out he is not welcome, Douglas Fairbanks reported to the Griffith lot at 4500 Sunset Boulevard in Hollywood the last week of July 1915 to find himself resented and ignored by most of the players. Between the time the Aitken brothers and Griffith had so persistently pursued him in New York and his arrival in California, many changes had taken place. *The Birth of a Nation* was reaping so much money that the Aitkens and their partners were going around New York hiring players from the stage at enormous salaries, and, what was worse, bragging about it. To the people of the Griffith company whose work in *The Birth* had made it all possible but who were still making less than $100 a week, reports of salaries of one and two thousand a week did not sit so well. Nor did the reason given for such figures—that Broadway stars required such salaries as a form of hardship pay. It had not been so long since the Griffith players considered themselves only temporary refugees from the stage, but since *The Birth of a Nation* they were beginning to take pride in their association with Griffith if not with pictures.

Their resentment fell undiluted on Fairbanks, for he was the first of the stage stars to arrive. To make it worse, there was nothing for him to do. Harry Aitken had telegraphed Griffith that he was coming and to get a scenario ready, but Griffith had delegated the project to someone else, a middle-aged secretary named Mary O'Connor. He had no time for either Fairbanks or a script, for he was just getting involved in a project that would absorb him completely for another year. Though *The Birth of a Nation* was making a fortune, it was also receiving some criticism; it did, after all, present a vicious vilification of Negroes, a glorious hagiography of the Ku Klux Klan. But Griffith considered any criticism of it a most outrageous form of censorship. He became obsessed with the twofold desire to make an even greater picture and to make it on the theme of intolerance through the ages. When Fairbanks arrived, Griffith was beginning to devote all his time and energy to the film that became the flawed masterpiece *Intolerance*. All Fairbanks could do was report to the lot and wait.

"I remember seeing him just hanging around, watching Griffith direct and getting in the way," Miriam Cooper, one of Griffith's stars, said sixty years later. "He looked so silly. None of us had anything to do with him."

Being ignored was the worst thing that could happen to Fairbanks and he persisted in attempting to break down the barriers. He was fascinated by every aspect of picture-making and, in his eager way, he asked questions of everyone. There is solid evidence that he took his grin and his questions to at least one other lot. Another member of the Triangle family, the comedy director Mack Sennett, had his Keystone studios at Edendale, another small town a couple of miles east, and Fairbanks probably drove over to pay a visit. Sennett, a former boiler-maker, was unusually crude and coarse even for a comedian, but he was a good friend to those who knew him. As will be shown later, he wound up being helpful to Doug.

On the Griffith lot there were always cowboys hanging around. One of them, Jim Kidd, a lean, hard, old-timer in his sixties with bona fide —or so everybody believed—notches in his six-shooter, patrolled the lot on horseback. Fairbanks was interested in the Wild West, and in search of someone to bounce his libido off of, he naturally struck up a conversation with Kidd. Kidd just as naturally arranged the standard practical joke for an easterner, a bucking bronco. What Kidd and the other cowboys didn't know was that Fairbanks was strong, had ridden swift polo ponies that could turn on a dime, and, most important of all, would rather break a leg trying than back down from a challenge. As we have seen, with Fairbanks, the loss of self-esteem meant depression, and that was worse than fear. So he hung on, gave the bronco a good ride, and when he was finally thrown, he got up with the Fairbanks smile plastered on his face. From that moment he was in with Kidd and the cowboys. Learning to ride western style and roll cigarettes with one hand augmented their admiration.

But this was of small value when it came time to work with the film crew. The story prepared for him was based loosely on one of his Broadway hits, *The New Henrietta*. Griffith may well have seen him in it; he played the role of a wealthy, foppish young man called Bertie, the Lamb of Wall Street. The working titles gave the plot away: *Blood Will Tell* was the first, then *A Man and the Test*. When the chips were down, Bertie would come through.

In spite of the proviso that Griffith himself would direct Fairbanks's films, it was assigned to William Christy Cabanné, one of Griffith's best-known assistants. Cabanné was a hard-working but unimaginative director who followed the master's pattern as closely as he could. On a five-reel picture such as this, Griffith would not use a complete scenario but rather a story line from which he would shoot each day's film out of his head or from some scribbled words on a scrap of paper. The cameraman assigned to the job was William E. Fildew, who was not too well known; the trade papers never spelled his name the same way twice. Fairbanks's leading lady would be Seena Owen, a pretty girl who was the daughter of a studio seamstress. With this group, after nine days of idleness, Douglas Fairbanks was thrown into shooting his first picture.

Among the cowboys on the Griffith lot, Doug found a companionship—earned the hard way, on and off a bucking bronco—which gave him the confidence and presence he shows in the last reels of *The Lamb*.
Wisconsin Center for Film and Theater Research

One episode in the film reveals something of what went on behind the scenes in the first few days of shooting. It takes place on the beach, when Bertie fails to go to the rescue of a damsel in distress. After his rival saves the girl from the surf, Bertie berates himself. It's an awful scene. Followed by the subtitle, "I am a coward! A coward!" he goes through the broad Delsartean gestures of the stage, clutching his forehead with one hand, flailing about with the other. He even falls down. Such broad gestures may have been necessary on the stage in order to get the point across to the last row in the peanut gallery, but in a shot in which Fairbanks nearly filled the screen the exaggeration was not only unnecessary but ludicrous. Doug had not learned that the camera isolates the character for the audience, but Cabanné, the director, knew it and still let him flail away.

Another interesting feature of that scene is Fairbanks's makeup. His face looks like a witch doctor's, caked with white clay. According to some accounts, this was the result of some malevolent fun the makeup department had with the Broadway actor. He, of course, unwittingly presented them with a difficult problem. His dark skin, burned browner by two weeks in the California sun, had to be coated heavily with makeup; suntan had not yet come into vogue, and both heroes and heroines had to have fair white skins.

In addition, Fairbanks was also worked harder than he had ever been before. He was a birdlike man, restless, nervous, with a fast pulse rate. He was capable of intensive bursts of activity rather than steady, prolonged effort. In the theater, rehearsals had been of comparatively short duration, and in performances he would usually pop on and off stage; even with intermissions the total time was rarely as much as three hours. The motion picture day by contrast began at eight in the morning and went on until five or six o'clock at night, six days a week. Fairbanks was not in front of the camera all day long, of course, but he had to be ready to be in front of the camera all day long. The filmmaking process was often boring and wearisome to actors, for scenes were not shot from beginning to end, but in short takes separated by interminable periods of preparation on the part of the crew.

These aspects of film work caused a high rate of attrition among stage actors transplanted to pictures. Along with Doug, Sir Herbert Beerbohm Tree, the great Shakespearean, was signed by Harry Aitken with great fanfare for a large amount of money. He collapsed so completely under the strain of playing Macbeth in short takes and in silence that a $30-a-week bit player had to finish up for him.

Another Aitken Broadway import, Raymond Hitchcock, was so baffled by the camera that Mack Sennett had to insert himself in Hitchcock's first film, *My Valet,* to lead him around.

Of all the established stage personalities signed by Triangle during that period only Fairbanks achieved any permanent success. His first film shows not only how he adapted to both on-screen and off-screen demands of his new career, but also some of the positive and pleasant features of films and filmmaking.

In developing Bertie's character, at the very beginning of the film Fairbanks walks with his legs wide apart in a funny, teetering motion; in cutaway coat he looks like a penguin. That walk could have come only from his visit with Mack Sennett. Sennett had taught it to Charlie Chaplin the year before—Chaplin had added a rear-end wiggle to create his own effect. Fairbanks can be seen experimenting with it, gradually discarding it as both Bertie the character and Fairbanks the man become more sure of themselves.

In one of these scenes Bertie and his girl are visiting an army unit; Fairbanks is obviously having a great time manning a machine gun, holding on with both hands to the double handles, swinging the gun about as it vibrates like a triphammer. There's a light in his eyes and charisma in his appeal. The shot, which takes less than a minute, was the result of a spur-of-the-moment junket to San Diego, where the army's very first armored cars were passing through on a test run. The army was pleased to show them off, the scene was worked into the film, and the whole day was fun.

The most fun of all, based entirely on Fairbanks's obvious delight with the whole episode, was in the boxing scenes. In the theater, although Fairbanks had stopped the show with the fight in *Hawthorne, U.S.A.,* the action was really not satisfactory. It is not possible to knock a man unconscious six nights and two matinees a week. The blows had to be faked, therefore, and even with the most perfect timing and the best sound effects, the illusion of a solid hit could not be presented to everyone in the theater. From some angles the blow would appear to connect, but from others it would obviously miss.

Watching Fairbanks, as Bertie, box with his trainer, played by a battered-nosed ex-pug named Tom Kennedy, is like watching a kid with a new toy. The camera is monoptic; it has no depth perception. Any film actor with fair timing can appear to deliver a mighty blow on his opponent without actually touching him; Fairbanks, with his superb timing, could make it look all the more real. In this scene, his first of many movie fights, he is clearly enjoying the discovery of just how much he can get away with.

The film had everything in it but the kitchen sink—Indians, cow-

Restricted on the stage, Doug found in films a thousand and one ways to use that marvelous, gymnastic physique as well as his love for deception. Just how high, really, is that bench, and where is Doug in relation to it? Only he and the camera know. The Academy of Motion Picture Arts and Sciences

boys, Mexican revolutionaries, the United States cavalry with pennants flying, an automobile race, a snake, and even a 1915 pusher-type airplane that actually flies. As the film rolls on in Cabanné's parody of Griffith, and Bertie the Lamb changes from the soft socialite to the brave hero, Douglas Fairbanks can be seen changing, too.

It is surely not coincidence that the most noticeable metamorphosis occurs when the action moves from the eastern drawing room to the western desert. It was actually shot on Griffith's property in the desolate San Fernando Valley across the Santa Monica mountains from Hollywood. In these scenes Fairbanks is surrounded by his friends the cowboys, and he is secure. He runs, fights, fires the machine gun, pulls himself up on the top of an adobe hut, dives on the back of a villain, and takes complete command. The hesitant neophyte feeling his way with a silly walk and ghastly makeup has become a confident professional, enjoying every second of it.

Any notion that the Aitkens considered dropping Fairbanks at the expiration of his contract is as ridiculous as the notion that consideration was given to shortening, shelving, or delaying the film. Negotiations on a long-term contract began after its first screening. As for the film, it had been selected for the grand opening of the entire Triangle program before it was either completed or titled. When it was finished toward the end of August, three weeks after it was begun, Harry Aitken saw it, approved the final title, *The Lamb,* and reconfirmed its selection for the first Triangle program to be shown.

This event had far more meaning to the history of the cinema than the mere opening of a theater. It was the introduction to the public of an entirely new concept within the young film industry. This new concept, the company on which it was founded, and Douglas Fairbanks, who would carry much of the load, all made their debut together. They were the same cinematic age, for though Harry Aitken had been working on it for months previously, the Triangle Film Company, Incorporated, had been officially organized just one week before its first star arrived in Hollywood. Although it would effect substantial changes in the motion picture industry, Triangle's operating principle was completely ignored by the moviegoing public, which already numbered a daily audience of eighteen million people in the United States alone, and even by the general and trade press. The name Triangle, in the public mind, referred to the company's three producing studios: the Kay-Bee Film Company, under the direction of William Ince at the lot he modestly called Inceville, located four miles up the beach road from Santa Monica; the Keystone Company, headed by the comedy director Mack Sennett, on Alessandro Street in Edendale; and the Fine Arts Film Company, headed by D. W. Griffith himself, in Hollywood. Triangle was at first known as S.I.G. from the initials of its three key producers, until Aitken realized that the acronym had an unhealthy sound.

But these were only some of the companies making up Triangle; it was the first conglomerate in the film industry. It was also the beginning of high finance in pictures. Harry Aitken had taken his prospectus to Wall Street. Triangle's first offering was oversubscribed at $5 a share. And this interest was based not on the three producing companies of Triangle, but on its attempt to combine, for the first time, the three operations of the entire industry—production, distribution, and exhibition—under one corporate roof.

Making pictures—production—was by far the most glamorous operation in the industry, but by no means the most profitable. The producer's income came from the distributing companies or exchanges, located in major cities and serving distinct geographical areas over the United States, Canada, and the world. The distributors' income, in turn, came from the exhibitors—the theaters—in those areas. The normal procedure was for the exhibitor to keep 30 percent of his receipts and turn over 70 percent to the distributor, who in turn kept 30 percent and turned over 70 percent to the producer. That was the way it worked in theory; in actuality there was no way either producer or distributor could collect his full percentage because there was no way of getting an honest accounting. It was common practice for the theater owner to keep two sets of books, one for his own use and one for the distributor, and the distributor to emulate that example with a phony set for the producer. But Triangle, by leasing or otherwise controlling the theaters in which its programs were shown, and by having its own distribution centers and studios, was able to audit its finances across the board, from box office receipts taken in to dividends paid out. It seemed as foolproof—or as crookproof—a system as could be devised for the chicanery-ridden industry.

To get this ambitious set of undertakings off to a fitting start, Aitken leased one of New York's finest legitimate theaters, the Knickerbocker, at Broadway and Thirty-eighth Street. Any fear of the owners that their theater might be cheapened was dispelled by Aitken's public announcement, which was written into the lease, that the admission would be a two-dollar top.

At a time when most picture theaters charged five or ten cents admission, this was big news in the entertainment world. True, *The Birth of a Nation* had opened with a two-dollar top, but that was a spectacle: Triangle would offer only its own program of three films. The complete price range, for evenings and Saturday matinees, was 50¢, 75¢, $1, and $2, and for other matinees, 25¢, 50¢, 75¢, $1.

For Triangle's grand opening at the Knickerbocker, and for the subsequent openings of Triangle theaters across the country, Aitken chose Ince's *The Iron Strain,* a five-reel film with Dustin Farnum; Sennett's two-reel comedy *My Valet,* starring Raymond Hitchcock; and from Griffith, Douglas Fairbanks in *The Lamb.*

Even Harry Aitken could not have wished for a more successful premiere that Thursday night, September 23, 1915. Among the formally attired celebrities were Mr. and Mrs. William Randolph Hearst, Ignace Paderewski, and Otto Kahn, director of the Metropolitan Opera. It had not been long since some detractors of the cinema had declared that no one could watch the flickers for more than a few minutes, but this sophisticated audience sat happily through twelve reels, some three hours of film watching, broken by two intermissions.

The *Motion Picture World* covered the event as a news story under the heading "Triangle's Auspicious Opening." It reported that "unquestionably the honors of the evening went to the Griffith production, *The Lamb,* in which Douglas Fairbanks had the leading part. . . . The audience fairly rose with excitement . . . a new star . . . a comedian who wins through interesting personality and delightful characterization. . . . He holds the eye so strongly, and without apparent effort, that he is the whole play from beginning to end."

The *Motion Picture News* reported that "young Douglas Fairbanks, an excellent actor on the stage, transplanted to the screen . . . becomes a delight to the eye."

But the greatest accolade was that of The *New York Times,* which covered the premiere as a news story:

MOVIES TAKE OVER
THE KNICKERBOCKER

Three Feature Photoplays Are
Shown There at the Two-
Dollar Scale

GRIFFITH FILM THE BEST

While Douglas Fairbanks Runs
Away With All the Acting Honors
at His Screen Debut

... anyone who goes with a movie mind will find at least one picture that is an exceedingly good sample of the best work now being done for the screen and will meet a new movie actor who is certain to build an enormous following in that considerable multitude which is possessed of a passion for the cinema. The picture is "The Lamb." The supervising director was David W. Griffith, the genius of the motion picture world who established the record with "The Birth of a Nation." The actor is one Douglas Fairbanks. . . .

The Lamb is cleverly and ingeniously done all the way through. Parts of it strike the high and peculiar Griffith tempo. . . .

For Mr. Fairbanks last evening was in the nature of a triumph. For some years a favorite comedian of the legitimate stage, he then made his first appearance in motion pictures. For some mysterious reason he succeeds where others fail. His engaging personality easily and undeniably "registers" —as the film folk say. He is amusing, grapphic [*sic*], individual, effortless. He even has a humorous walk of his own, and no one in last evening's audience at The Knick will be overcome with surprise if he attains a motion picture popularity such as the distinguished Mr. Chaplin has experienced. It is not surprising that, after seeing this film in the studios, the directors hurried out and legally bound Mr. Fairbanks hand and foot for the next three years.

On seeing *The Lamb* today the first notion is that if it was that good, the other movies of the day must have been atrocious. On second thought, however, this opinion becomes chronologically chauvinistic. *The Lamb* had a lot going for it at the time. Today we are accustomed to a smoother execution of Griffith innovations; Cabanné's rapid cutting between the Indians closing in and the cavalry galloping to the rescue was a blatant and mechanical imitation. To the 1915 audience, not burdened with such sophistry, the technique was new, and, as the *World* reported, they "fairly rose with excitement."

Bertie the Lamb also had a peculiar appeal to audiences of that era; it was a time when Americans were fans of the wealthy—crowds would flock to Grand Central Station to see the multimillionaires returning from the Harvard-Yale football game in their private railway cars. At that point in the American dream, people identified with Bertie; that's who they—or their children—would be someday. The character as Fairbanks played him was appealing at the beginning and a true-blue red-blooded American at the end. The flaws at the opening of the film —overacting, weird makeup—were either overlooked or forgiven by reviewers; they were not mentioned.

All this was apart from Douglas Fairbanks himself, which is like attempting to separate the stars from the sky. As noted in the case of Mary Pickford, the motion picture camera makes some people stand out on the screen. Fairbanks was one of those few so blessed. Even without his derring-do, he had something audiences liked. That was luck, but watching him in the film today, we can see him earnestly working, building on his gift.

Fairbanks was not able to enjoy his movie premiere in New York; he had to work in California. Indeed, that was one of the most hectic weeks in his life.

First, he finished shooting his second picture. Called *Double Trouble,* it is double awful; Fairbanks plays two roles in it, both badly. A straight dramatic vehicle with little opportunity for action, it is interesting only as a biographical source. Critics have commented on Fairbanks's avoidance of love scenes, and *Double Trouble* shows why: he attempted love scenes in both roles, hero and heavy, and was stiff and unconvincing in both. He apparently could not overcome that strange inhibiting combination of narcissism and Victorian prudery. He also overacted atrociously, perhaps through sheer sophomoric exuberance. The important thing is that in *Double Trouble* he saw what he could not do, and he didn't do it again. At a time when the most acclaimed stars of the stage were failing personally before the cameras, Douglas Fairbanks obviously had the intelligence to profit from his cinematic mistakes.

Double Trouble would soon be forgotten; a decision made that week in September would affect his entire life. His ten-week option was running out, and the Aitkens wanted him to sign a long-term contract. At a time when a Dodge touring car cost $795, a bicycle $18.50, an electric iron $2.48, sirloin 16 cents a pound and hamburger 12½, strawberries 11 cents a quart, and books $1.35, when the income tax was 1 percent over $4000, the amount of money Harry Aitken was proffering was a fortune. But money was never Douglas Fairbanks's only goal. There were other things involved, and he and Beth, who was sometimes more of a mother and a manager than a wife, must have discussed them.

Neither wanted to remain in California the year around. They liked New York, Broadway, good restaurants, society and theatrical people, nightlife. In contrast, Hollywood closed down tight at sundown, and Los Angeles, an inconvenient distance by either streetcar or by automobile over a narrow country road, wasn't much livelier. The area reflected the characteristics of its residents, retired farmers and small businessmen from the Midwest. There weren't any good restaurants, much less theaters and after-theater gathering places. Fairbanks at least had full days at the studio, but Beth was stuck in hicktown. She found the cowboys and Indians whom Fairbanks enjoyed offensive to her eyes and her nostrils. When Douglas Jr. came home from the lot with stories of being picked up by Eagle Eye, the studio Indian, she rushed him to the bathtub.

Another problem was D. W. Griffith. He seemed to disapprove of Fairbanks. Cabanné had apparently reported that Fairbanks was making suggestions on the set—"Hey, let's do it this way!" he'd say, and his enthusiasm was hard to resist. Griffith, pompous in his new acclaim, resented such independence, particularly from a newcomer. The truth of the matter, of course, was that Griffith resented any strong masculine figure who might endanger his role as father and hero to the girls of the company.

One day when the Aitken brothers were in Hollywood Fairbanks proposed taking a short film of them. They agreed, and Fairbanks went through the elaborate motions of directing them as Billy Bitzer, Griffith's number one cameraman, cranked away. When it was over Fairbanks broke up laughing; he had told Bitzer not to load the camera. The Aitkens took the joke, but Griffith was shocked at this familiarity with authority.

Fairbanks liked the money and he was beginning to like pictures, but

Hollywood was boring and Griffith was becoming difficult. And Beth wanted to go back to New York.

It was at this point, according to Anita Loos, that John Emerson discovered her scripts and persuaded Griffith to let him use one for Fairbanks. It is more likely that Emerson, who had an in with Aitken and a knack for using other people's talents, worked out a scheme to enable him to ride back to New York on Fairbanks's coattails. However the arrangement was maneuvered and by whom, Fairbanks, with Beth and Doug Jr., left Los Angeles on September 28 and arrived in New York on Saturday, October 2, just in time to catch the last showing of the first Triangle program at the Knickerbocker, and from there, surely, to join their friends at the Algonquin for hot chocolate. Their corner suite was awaiting them, and so—and this is so typically Fairbanks— was a new gym and boxing ring on the Algonquin roof. He'd sent Tom Kennedy, his boxing partner in *The Lamb,* ahead to set it up.

On Monday he reported to the Triangle studios in Riverdale to begin work on *His Picture in the Papers,* directed by John Emerson, story by Anita Loos. Fairbanks had agreed on terms for a three-year contract with Triangle: $2000 per week with a $500 per week increase every six months. He would do two or three pictures in New York, then two or three in Hollywood. He'd been gone just nine weeks. Now he was back, with the best of two worlds.

And still the cycle mounted, higher, higher. One glorious night at the Sharkey Athletic Club at Columbus Avenue and Sixty-fifth Street he approached the zenith. A brief description of *His Picture in the Papers* is necessary. The picture was a typical Loos creation in that it contains a clever plot and a lot of action within a framework of satire on a current theme. The spoof is on the craze for publicity; in order to win success and the girl, the character played by Fairbanks must get his picture on the front pages of all the New York papers. He performs one herculean exploit after another, but something always happens to rob him of recognition. He challenges the boxing champion, for example, knocks him out, and is posing for the photographers when the cops come charging in and break the cameras. This is the scene that Emerson shot live at the Sharkey A.C.

To set the stage, Emerson and Fairbanks, both members of the Lambs and Friars clubs, persuaded several of their fellow members, along with a crowd of fight fans, to fill the arena. With a huge megaphone, Emerson, a ham himself, directed the crowd as the camera rolled. With his friends and hundreds of fight fans watching and shouting friendly catcalls, Fairbanks challenged the champion. The crowd watched with interest as he stepped forward, groaned as he appeared to be undersized. Then he came out stripped to fight, muscles showing, and the crowd roared with approval. Chagrin when the champ knocked Fairbanks to the canvas. Elation when he sprang up and swarmed over the champion, battering him to the floor. Fairbanks surely was high as a kite. Here he was, before a crowd of both his theatrical peers and fellow fight fans, the center of the action, with ex-champ Terry McGovern acting as referee, flailing away at a real-live opponent under the bright lights, with Emerson directing and the cameras running . . . ah, ecstasy.

Even the first showing of *Double Trouble* at the Knickerbocker could not lower his spirits. The reviews criticized the picture but not the star. "He plays the role well—that goes without saying," said the *Motion Picture World*, "but he is all alone. . . ."

It only proved that he was on the right track with *His Picture in the Papers*. His particular talent needed a special vehicle and understanding people to work with. Anita Loos, thrilled over being in New York, fed him situations and bits of business. Emerson, a subtle sycophant, walked the delicate line between director and yes-man. Thus in three films, one a hodgepodge providing an exercise in filmmaking, the second a lesson in what not to do, the third the realization and implementation of the successful formula, Douglas Fairbanks established his screen character. At a time when practically any actor was expected to play in practically any photoplay, this was not just a development in one man's career but a major contribution to the art form.

This is the significance of *His Picture in the Papers*, not some fanciful anecdote to the effect that it was shown by mistake at a time when Fairbanks was on the way out. "We were desperate for pictures from the Griffith studio," Roy Aitken said. "And I can't imagine anybody thinking we were going to drop Douglas Fairbanks. He was the best thing we had."

Nor did the *New York Times* review the film, the following day or any other day, because the *Times* had not begun reviewing films. It permitted a film enthusiast in the drama department, Brock Pemberton, to go to movies and write about them on Sunday, his day off; his gratis contributions ran Mondays, but contained no mention of *His Picture in the Papers.*

But the *Motion Picture World* and the *Motion Picture News* did review it, following its premiere on February 10, 1916, and in terms so extravagant as to demand a second reading. The reviewers may not have realized they were describing cinema history, but they were certainly impressed.

"It would be difficult to find an actor who could successfully carry those roles as does Douglas Fairbanks," said the *World.* "His personality is so all pervading that he is like the sun when it rises in a sky of morning stars. . . . In a class all by himself, at once an athlete of resource and daring and a subtle interpreter of the amusing side of human nature. . . .

"The play not only affords him just this sort of opportunity that suits his qualifications, but it is highly ingenious, clearly constructed and a work of art in itself."

In case its readers missed the point, the following week the *World* spelled it out: "Douglas Fairbanks, in the leading part, excells any impersonation hitherto attempted."

Said the *News,* "That Douglas Fairbanks has risen to the ranks of undisputed film favorites is clearly evident by the applause which heralds his appearance in a picture. Picturegoers have accepted Mr. Fairbanks as 'Doug,' the familiar nom de plume by which he is known to stage first nighters, and Doug as a screen comedian produces the feeling of familiarity that such a nickname embodies."

By the time the review appeared Doug had completed his fourth film and begun work on the fifth. As a final contradiction that Fairbanks was through before *His Picture* was shown, Aitken and Griffith had approved the final cost of that fourth film, *A Habit of Happiness;* shot in New York, its cost was $37,792.79. For the record, the cost of *The Lamb* was $40,821.66, *Double Trouble* $40,488.33, and *His Picture* $42,599.94. Earnings of the films are not available, but Roy Aitken recalls that all were profitable, especially *The Lamb* and *His Picture in the Papers.* But all this was only a confirmation anyway; while shooting these pictures Doug's self-esteem was at its zenith. He was as happy and normal an individual as it was possible for him to be.

One November Sunday during this euphoric fall of 1915, he and Beth started off on what they knew would be a fun-filled day. They were

going to a party, and Doug loved parties, given by Elsie Janis, star of
Miss Information ("A Little Comedy with a Little Music"), and Doug
loved Elsie. She always played up to him in her tomboy way; once when
he did handstands in the Algonquin lobby Elsie had fastened her skirts
around her ankles and tried to imitate him. The party was at her
country place, the historic Philipsburg Manor house at Tarrytown, and
that meant a pleasant drive through the country; Doug borrowed Roy
Aitken's sporty yellow Leon Bollée for the trip.

At a rural crossroads on the way someone in a hired, chauffeur-driven
limousine waved him down. It was Owen Moore, a fellow player in the
Fine Arts company, going to the party with his wife, Mary Pickford,
the screen star known as America's Sweetheart. Doug jumped out of
the roadster, gave Owen a big hello, and took off his hat and gave a
dazzling smile when he was introduced to Miss Pickford. The chauffeur
was lost and Doug gave him the right directions—he loved to give
people directions—and then with a wave he and Beth sped off in the
Leon Bollée.

Elsie and her mother gave great parties, with guests from both the
theater and society. Elsie led Doug into the center of the big drawing
room, and he soon became the center of the party, too, discoursing on
motion pictures, the Harvard-Princeton game (he'd gone to Harvard),
and the war in Europe (he'd lived in England). By the time Owen and
Mary arrived he was going strong.

As Elsie remembered later, she wanted to see Doug and all that
graceful energy outdoors—walking, running, climbing trees and fences.
She organized a walk through the countryside, and Doug soon turned
it into a game of follow-the-leader, vaulting fences, skinning the cat on
tree branches. Owen Moore turned back; he was far more interested
in the bar. Beth Fairbanks turned back; she had indulged her child-
husband enough. Finally only Elsie and Mary were following him, Elsie
because she was just simply enjoying it, Mary because Doug had made
a remark about ruining her new Russian kid shoes and she'd taken it
as a dare.

At a shallow place in the river he crossed on stepping stones. Elsie
followed, but Mary, halfway across, almost lost her balance and
stopped, afraid to go forward or back. The swift water looked deep and
cold.

Doug glanced over his shoulder and saw her there, tiny, beautiful, frightened. He stopped. Go back to help her? But he was playing a game! Of what consequence that she was appealing in her fear, that she was the fantasy object of millions of men. She was the very opposite of plump, bossy Beth, who knew him so well she'd left him with two women, and without misgiving.

Moving quickly over the stepping stones, suddenly he was beside her. He smiled at her reassuringly. Her head came only to his chin, her hazel eyes looked up at him. "Do you mind?" he asked.

"No," she said. "Please do."

He swept her up in his arms and, strong and surefooted, carried her to the bank. He put her down gently, and they stood for a moment, then went on after Elsie. There was no more follow-the-leader. They walked along talking quietly, crossed the river at the dam, and returned to the manor house. Though such familiarity was most unusual in that post-Victorian period, as they strolled she called him Douglas, he called her Mary. That was the way it began.

CHAPTER SEVEN

Doug and Mary:
The Courtship Years,
1915-1920

In any film produced in the teens, so dramatic a piece of action as the hero sweeping the heroine off her feet in midstream—if any writer or director was imaginative enough to concoct it—would lead directly to romance. With Mary Pickford and Douglas Fairbanks, it was instead the beginning of a friendship, a friendship as unusual as the friends themselves. For the rest of their lives, no matter what hurt and sadness each may have suffered and blamed on the other, they never lost the admiration, liking, and respect they developed during that year they were friends. It was a most memorable year, in the world, in the nation, in the motion picture industry, and in the lives of Doug and Mary. And all was intertwined, for the actions of these two people in 1916, brought on by changing conditions throughout the world, helped set the American motion picture industry on the financial and artistic course to world dominance.

Outwardly so popular and secure, in reality they needed each other. Mary had already been dubbed America's Sweetheart on a theater marquee in San Francisco, and of course her father image of the moment, Adolph Zukor, and Famous Players publicized her by that title. Nor was it just a gimmick; Little Mary *was* America's Sweetheart, and the sweetheart of most of the world. "More people look at this face every night than at any other in the world," said a caption in a family magazine. But she was a sweetheart only on the screen. In everyday life, in the routine of going to work early in the morning and coming home late at night, Mary Pickford was a sad, lonely, frustrated young woman. If she hadn't been, if she had led the popular, romantic life of a storybook movie star, she would probably not have altered the course of motion pictures.

At Mary's age—she was twenty-two in May 1915—most women of her background already had husbands, babies, friends, and a domestic and neighborhood pattern of life. Mary had none of these. She and her husband were rarely together. Though Owen Moore was well liked by other people, he seemed to be a different person around Mary. Whether he was jealous of the success of this golden-haired girl who wore the pants in the family, whether he was not growing in stature along with her, whether it was her mother or his bottle, or whether she just simply should never have been pulled into an adolescent marriage in the first place, Mary was not happy with Owen. Always prim and reserved about her private life, she gave no inkling, not even to her only close friend, Frances Marion, as to the nature of her sex life with Owen during the sporadic periods she lived with him, but Frances recalled later having the impression that whatever sexual enjoyment Mary had ever had with him had long departed.

Even if their relationship had been more affectionate, it would have had to be especially strong to withstand the stresses of her stardom. Owen was almost never mentioned in connection with his wife. Anyone with a financial interest in America's Sweetheart, including the sweetheart's mother and the sweetheart herself, had good reason to conceal her marital state. With Frances Marion's help, Mary wrote a daily newspaper column during 1916 and never once referred to Owen Moore as her husband. Most readers of newspapers, fan magazines, and trade papers, even of "intimate" articles describing Mary at home, would never suspect that she was married. Zukor, in attempting to maintain her public image as a virginal teenager, also saw to it that she did not smoke or drink in public. Once when she was idly toying with a lipstick that looked something like a cigarette, Zukor's wife quickly reached out and took it away from her. Mary didn't mind forgoing tobacco, but alcohol was another matter, for she had begun to share Owen's taste for it. Her drinking was done alone, or in the bosom of the family. According to those who knew the Pickfords—Charlotte, Lottie, and Jack—that would not have been difficult, for they all liked to drink; the difference was that Lottie and Jack did not have to be so secretive about it.

As for friends, with the exception of Frances Marion, Mary really didn't have any. Her working days began early and frequently went on into the night. She was impressed with her role as America's Sweet-

Sincerely,
Mary Pi...

"This Little Girl Earns $100,000 a Year" read a 1915 caption under a magazine portrait of Mary Pickford. It was at the time when, a film tycoon later observed, she was the focal point of an industry. *George Eastman House*

heart and terrified by her fears of losing it. With this push-pull impetus of dedication and fear, she devoted much more time to the science, art, and business of motion pictures than did most other picture people, male or female. She worked with people, to be sure, but when they went home or out to restaurants and nightclubs, Mary often stayed on with other technicians or went home to Mama. As for extramarital suitors, there seem to have been none at all. A good Catholic girl, Mary was opposed to both divorce and infidelity, and, if any man ever tried to penetrate her remote, strictly business facade—and there's no record that anyone did—she surely discouraged the attempt. She played love scenes, of course, but they never excited her. Discussing "the disillusionment of screen lovemaking," she observed that in the blinding glare of the bright-blue calcium lights a screen lover bending to kiss her had purple lips and blue teeth. "Alas for the little rainbow vanities," she wrote in early 1916. "We feminists are never happy unless miserable."

This, then, was Mary Pickford when Douglas Fairbanks came into her life. America's Sweetheart, the highest paid woman in the world, was really an uneducated, shy, insecure, lonely young woman with an unhappy marriage and few friends.

As for Doug Fairbanks, though he had neither reached the peak of success of America's Sweetheart nor accepted her loneliness, he was nevertheless a paradox in his own flamboyant way. For all his sudden success in films, he was still an uneasy, if not ashamed, participant in the movies, as he deprecatingly termed motion pictures to friends. (Picture people didn't like the word "movies." *Photoplays* was the preferred term, but most people settled for motion pictures, or just pictures.) Now that Doug had turned a lucrative summer vacation into a three-year contract, he wondered whether he had done the wise thing, the accepted thing, in leaving the prestige of the stage.

Certainly his wife Beth did not wholeheartedly accept either the films or California. She was still enamored of the theater, and she preferred New York to the sleepy little town of Hollywood and the dull metropolis of Los Angeles. How much the issue was discussed, and whether it ever reached the stage of contention, is another matter, for the Fairbankses seem to have drifted into a comfortable, placid relationship in which Beth was a combination mother and business manager to him. She took care of his finances, sending him out to play with no worries and with money in his pocket, and bossed him gently, which he liked. When Doug's mother became resentful of the way Beth took over her son the star and demanded that he pay her more attention, at Beth's expense, Doug had to make the traumatic decision to break away from his Tutu, leaving Beth in complete command. Her duties were hardly arduous, for Doug had a valet, the boy a nurse, and when in New York they lived in their corner suite in the Algonquin, but she had the comfortable satisfaction of running the show. She had no competition, and she was buxom and content with her life.

The Fairbankses could hardly have spent much time together. Beginning with his workout on the roof of the Algonquin in the early morning, during his picture-making activities in the day, ending with his jaunty table-hopping through the lobby at night, Doug seemed always to be with his cronies. It was a standing one-line joke: "Does Fairbanks go to the toilet by himself?" His range of acquaintances included such people as Frank Case, the debonair owner of the Algonquin, members of society from both his own and Beth's circles, fellow members of the Lambs Club and of the motion picture industry, hangers-on with battered noses and cauliflower ears, and jovial souls who were dependent upon him like his valet Buddy, a yassuh-boss stereotype. All the people he used to staunch his loneliness could hardly be characterized as friends. Poignant evidence of this can be seen in a conversation with cowboy Jim Kidd that took place on location in the Mojave desert. Doug made an idle comment about the God-forsaken countryside. "Oh, it don't much matter where you are," Kidd said, "it's who you're with that counts."

That casual remark appears in dozens of magazine and newspaper articles based on interviews with Fairbanks; he must have repeated it hundreds of times. He based a motion picture on it. So great was the impression it made on him that it can only be inferred that, of all the scores of acquaintances with whom he shared activities—work, boxing, wrestling, horseplay, games—only one said, as Fairbanks obviously and accurately interpreted it, "I like to be with you, Doug."

But Jim Kidd was not in New York that fall of 1915 when Doug found himself not in the middle of a desert but in the middle of a river, where the game of follow-the-leader brought him a new friend, Mary Pickford. Their next meeting was at the Algonquin, where Frank Case gave a Saturday night dance for his prize tenant, with Mary among the guests. Doug and Mary danced together, then talked. It was perfectly circumspect; if Beth noticed them at all, she probably assumed that they were talking about motion pictures.

She would have been right; that was exactly what they were talking about. Doug had plunged into his new career with his usual enthusiasm; he had seen *The Birth of a Nation* many times, as well as many other pictures, and had noticed that, of all the players on the screen, two stood out above all the rest. "Do you know who are the outstanding artists in pantomime?" was the way he began the conversation that night, according to Mary's account written forty years later, and then named them: Mary Pickford and Charlie Chaplin.

Mary had no love for Chaplin. To her he was a comedian who got hit in the face with pies, and she had turned down an offer to appear with him. But she continued to listen as Doug explained what it was he had seen in the work of two such apparently disparate screen stars. Mary, he said, had mastered the art through a great economy of gesture. "You do less apparent acting than anyone else I know," he went on, "and because of that you express more."

This was much more than a flattering compliment tossed off at a dance. Mary, her hazel eyes and lovely complexion framed by the world's most famous curls, looked up at him with pleased amazement. His very delivery was overwhelming. His strong, high-pitched voice seemed to come up from his toes, its force augmented by that compact body, and he squeezed out the words, bouncing them off the roof of his mouth. He shoved his head forward, his eyes sparkled, and he made small chopping motions with his hands. Such intensity could only come from complete sincerity—Mary did not know then that he could describe imaginary adventures with equal fervor. She was impressed with recognition from a star of the legitimate stage; she had first seen Douglas Fairbanks in *A Gentleman of Leisure* and she remembered him well. D. W. Griffith had been in the theater party with her, and had predicted that Fairbanks would "someday make a great impression in pictures." She had surely discussed the publicized entry of stage stars into films, and she knew that his first picture, *The Lamb,* was a hit. This was not some star-struck fan, but an actor of substance assessing her work.

Mary's recollection of her emotion was that it was "a breath of new life"; she was more accustomed to being belittled by Owen than to being praised. Further, Fairbanks's assessment of her art was both perceptive and correct. For seven years, from the great D. W. Griffith on down, she had resisted the efforts of directors to make her overact. She had worked hard to perfect that "economy of gesture" and she was proud of it. Few appreciated this aspect of her art; even the reviewers in the trade press, so extravagant in their praise, did not recognize the difficulty simplicity that was the hallmark of her talent.

And so, as the orchestra played and actors and actresses in tuxedos and evening gowns danced, Mary and Doug discussed the techniques of acting in the cinema. Mary wrote later that she had "hugged the echo of his words for days," remembering his approval and admiration.

They met again at the Screen Club Ball at the Hotel Astor, and again they talked. Mary had just finished *Madame Butterfly,* and was undoubtedly full of her experiences in the unlikely role of the tragic heroine Cho Cho San. Every morning before shooting began she had drawn the corners of her eyes back to give herself an Oriental look, and rinsed the golden curls in mascara. She had practiced working with Japanese cooking utensils, and concentrated, both at home and in the studio, on such mannerisms as covering her emotions in the accepted Japanese manner. The director, she felt, had demanded too much repression, and it is easy to picture her, eyes flashing, curls bouncing, as she angrily told Doug about their confrontations.

Far more to her liking was her role in *The Foundling,* which she was just beginning with another director. In it she played a twelve-year-old waif in an orphanage, a role that would produce both laughter and tears. It was so much easier, she observed pensively, to make people cry than to make them laugh; comedy had to be taken far more seriously.

Doug listened intently to this attractive savant ten years his junior. He was just as serious about acting as she, although he probably had no intention whatever of attempting to make his audiences cry. His films were joyous romps from the opening shot. By this time he had gotten used to the yellow gunk they put on his face to stretch out the wrinkles and bleach his brown skin, and to the long days of standing around between shots. Such discomforts had their compensations. He liked the money, and he liked the freshness of films. The tedium of repeating the same old lines over and over, six evenings and two matinees, in New York and Boston, Philadelphia and Chicago, was nonexistent in pictures. Do it once and forget it. "Every scene is opening night!" he said.

He could even talk with Mary about his mania for sports and physical activity, for she, because of the stunts and danger encountered in making pictures, had experienced far more real excitement than Doug. She had been riding western horses for years. At a time when few women even considered driving cars—cranking engines and shifting gears required muscle—she had driven an automobile around a racetrack, full throttle, at a speed of fifty-six miles an hour! She had flown in an airplane! A double with a blonde wig had taken her place in the open cockpit in some of the scenes of *A Girl of Yesterday*, which she had made that summer in California, but she had insisted on playing in the one that counted. Charlotte had refused to permit her daughter to go up, but the director, Allan Dwan, and the pilot, Glenn Martin, flying his own plane, had reassured her with the promise that Mary would never be more than a hundred feet from ground—they were careful not to say *the* ground. Just a few blocks north of Hollywood, up Western Avenue, was that mountain wilderness and paradise for filmmakers called Griffith Park. Dwan knew where a road followed the high ridge, and he set up the camera there. Martin flew Mary by it, well within a hundred feet of "ground" though the altitude was close to 1500 feet. Poor Charlotte nearly fainted. Mary was frightened too, of course, but it made a good story later.

There were the times, too, when Mary had been sunbaked on the desert, soaked in cold rivers, buffeted and stung by studio storms generated by huge fans blowing buckets of water. She accepted it all as part of the job; she was proud of being in pictures.

And Doug was impressed. He took her on a surprise visit to his mother in her suite in the Hotel Seymour, with a lavish tea brought in by a caterer. The two women got along famously, and visited again after that. Sixty years later Mary described Mrs. Fairbanks with affection as a southern lady, the widow of a wealthy Louisiana planter. And Ella, still star-struck and on the outs with Beth, naturally welcomed the opportunity to entertain America's Sweetheart.

Neither Doug nor Mary told the world about the visit to his mother, but aside from that each spoke openly about the other. Mary devoted an entire column to Doug. Frances Marion recalled that, even when discussing and writing the column, she saw no reason to question Mary's description of Doug as a good friend. There was no gossip about them. Beth seemed to have no objections to their talking together; she liked Mary, too. As for Owen, he was in California making films for Triangle.

When Doug and his entourage returned to California after Christmas, there was no tearful parting. Although she enjoyed her talks with Doug, Mary had other things on her mind that winter.

Focal Point of an Industry

The winter of 1915–16 was a crucial time in Mary's career, and, as a direct result, in the entire motion picture industry. At the time, she was under contract to Adolph Zukor and Famous Players, but her relationship with her little father figure was strained. He was paying her $2000 a week, an amount difficult to imagine anyone earning in that year, let alone an uneducated young woman, but the thrill of receiving it had worn off. The money itself was just not that tangible a symbol of appreciation. If Zukor had sought her out every week and handed her a little package of bills along with a small gift, a rose, or even a hug and a kiss, it might have meant something; instead it was routinely picked up by Charlotte in the form of an impersonal piece of paper with "Pay to the Order of" printed on it. Mary rarely saw the check, nor did she see much of what her money bought. Charlotte, terrified of losing it, didn't even want to invest it, much less spend it. At first she squirreled it away in banks, but finally brought herself to place some of Mary's money in what she deemed the safest investment: New York City bonds. New York was certainly one place that would never go broke.

With the money she never saw, Mary rented a pleasant but not lavish eight-room apartment on Broadway above Central Park, sharing it with her mother, of course, and a live-in maid. The drawing room was paneled with mahogany, with gray and rose the other colors. Pink was the favorite Pickford color: Charlotte's room was dark, almost rose; Mary's was light, a delicate shell pink.

Her clothes closet was far from full. Her abhorrence of debt, she admitted, was so strong that she still got along with very few clothes —"a good plain suit, never in extreme style, with a neat little hat, good gloves, clean collar and waist, and shoes well polished, are in far better taste than to dress far beyond one's means." She continued to inspect and brush her clothes regularly, just as she always had. As a result she rarely needed a new dress, and she hated to run up bills for something she did not need. Mary didn't even like to spend money for cosmetics. Before going out she brushed her hair to bring out the natural oil, instead of using brilliantine. She used neither eye pencil nor lipstick, observing primly that eye pencil "hardens the expression" and "cerise lips are neither natural nor attractive. . . . cosmetics tend to add years rather than subtract them."

It was the same when she went out to a restaurant; she still looked at the right side of the menu first. Even the novelty of her one luxury, a cream and gray Cadillac bought when Zukor had voluntarily increased her salary to $1000 a week, had worn off, and she now owned a sedate black limousine. It was all she needed to get from Upper Broadway to the studio on West Twenty-third Street and back. All in all, Mary's $104,000 a year, largely tax free, was wasted on her. It did not even give her peace of mind. Obsessed with the racking insecurity of the entertainer, fearing her popularity would collapse overnight, her phenomenal salary simply meant that she had that much more to lose.

Consider, for example, the time and attention Mary devoted outside of working hours to her outer attributes, face, figure, and those golden curls. Long before reporting in at the Famous Players studio each weekday morning, Mary had already devoted the better part of an hour to the maintenance of her assets. She began each day with fifteen minutes of bending and stretching exercises; then, first drawing a little warm water in the tub to step into, she took a cold shower, an unusual routine in those days before showers were common. She loved the pink glow the cold spray gave her skin. Before dressing she drank half a glass of water, sometimes hot, sometimes with lemon, and continued drinking water every half an hour during the day ("It keeps the stomach in good condition").

For breakfast she had fruit or fruit juice, one poached egg, dry toast, and tea. If there was time and the weather was good, she walked to the studio; this was her only outdoor exercise other than an occasional horseback ride in Central Park. Luncheon was always light, with no sweets. Mary would have liked an occasional ice cream soda, but she never had one. Dinner was also light; she always left the table hungry.

When Mary had worked hard all day and had to go out in the evening, she would come home, have a warm bath followed by an alcohol rub, then lie down for twenty minutes with a cloth soaked in a mixture of ice water and witch hazel over her eyes.

Major maintenance came just before bedtime. Some days her face would remain covered with makeup, clogging the pores, and so every night she began by washing her face well with physicians' and surgeons' soap and rinsing first with warm water, then cold. Next she rubbed in cold cream and wiped it off, repeating until the towel came away spotless. Then she proceeded, as she put it, to iron her face—rubbing a large piece of ice against her throat and face, pressing hard, stroking upward, continuing until the skin was almost crimson. If her hands showed any signs of chapping, she rubbed in a generous dab of camphor and mutton tallow. If she had been exposed to the sun during the day, she patted on buttermilk to keep her skin white.

Her hair required another full half hour every night; she brushed it two hundred strokes. With such brushing, Mary found, she needed no glycerine to keep her hair shining; a few strokes from time to time brought out the glow. Nor did she use a bleach, although she candidly reported that her golden curls were getting darker. She rolled it up on kidskin. "I would never under any circumstances touch an iron to my hair. It breaks and destroys it."

Mary shampooed her hair only every two weeks, beginning with an application of hot olive oil. Sometimes she used melted castile soap, sometimes physicians' and surgeons' soap. She went through three soapy waters, two clear, rubbed in two beaten eggs, and finished up with three rinses, preferably rain water, the last with the juice of lemon added. "This is hard work," Mary admitted, "but it pays."

Even as Mary was passing on her cosmetic schedule in November of 1915, she was becoming increasingly displeased with the amount this hard work was paying. Her concern had been building up since one hot day in August, when, on the way home from the studio, she'd noticed a double line of people waiting to get in the Strand Theatre at Broadway and Forty-seventh Street to see her newest picture, *Rags*. It was a happy sight; the Strand, the first theater built to show motion pictures, held more than 3000 people. Mary told Charlotte about the line of people waiting to see her, and the two women chattered about it happily.

The next week *Rags* was no longer playing, and there was no line outside the theater. Curious, Mary pinned her curls up inside her hat, bought a ticket, and went in. The orchestra was only half-filled and the balcony was practically empty. Same theater, same day of the week, same time—but no Mary Pickford.

If any other picture star went to the trouble to count the house at a movie she wasn't in, it has not been recorded. Mary not only checked, but asked questions. Both films were produced by Famous Players. How much, she asked Adolph Zukor, did he get for *Rags?* How much for the film that played to half-empty houses? "Oh, don't worry your pretty curly head about it, sweetheart, honey," Zukor told her, but Mary persisted. And he finally admitted that Famous Players got more rent for her pictures.

This was the second time Mary suspected that Zukor was not treating her with complete honesty. The year before Charlotte had overheard a couple of salesmen talking in the Famous Players offices. One had referred to a film as a dog. The other had said, "That's okay, we'll wrap it around Mary's neck and sell it like all the others."

Charlotte and Mary, curious and prying, had demanded an explanation of that from Zukor, too. Only through such personal, subjective concern did Mary become involved in the complicated business end of the industry. In actuality, much more than this one company was involved; Mary Pickford was bringing about a change in the entire motion picture industry.

Back during Mary's days at Biograph, producers sold film like hardware; regardless of who or what was on it, it brought ten cents a foot, about a hundred dollars a reel. Independent producers like Laemmle, Aitken, and Zukor, for whom Mary worked, exploited the value of stars and brought about some changes, which were paying off. *Tess of the Storm Country,* for example, the five-reel feature Zukor had hocked his wife's jewelry to complete, was brought back to theaters eight, nine, a dozen times. The moviegoing public had reached the degree of sophistication in which they would rather see a good feature with a beloved star for the second or third time than some motley showing of one-reelers. A system of rental developed and producers began to receive better profits from better products.

The problem was that full-length features, with stars being paid salaries of hundreds of dollars a week, required a larger amount of capital. The cost of the negative—that is, shooting the film itself—was beginning to run as high as $20,000, and the cost of the positive prints, advertising, and distribution could add another $10,000. Raising $30,-000 for so ephemeral a product as a motion picture was extremely difficult; certainly no bank would touch the project. Producers had to scrape up the money the best way they could. Considering the fact that the producer made little more money on an expensive film than on a cheap one—it was the exhibitors who profited the most from the repeat business—it was hardly worth the effort.

William Wadsworth Hodkinson, a San Francisco distributor—he got films from the producers and distributed them to the theaters, or exhibitors—came up with the idea that the distributors and exhibitors themselves, some of whom were doing very well, could get together and advance money to the producers for the better films they would then show. Coincidentally with his brainstorm, Hodkinson happened to pass by an apartment house named Paramount and borrowed the title for his embryonic enterprise. He drew his own trademark: a mountain peak in a circle.

Hodkinson's subsequent success story was somewhat unusual in that he went to New York, had no problem attracting other distributors, and got Paramount Pictures Corporation off to a well-capitalized start almost overnight. With money to advance—up to $25,000 for a five-reel negative plus costs of positives and advertising—it quickly signed up producers capable of delivering an aggregate of two pictures a week, one hundred four a year.

It was only fitting that a full 50 percent of those pictures, one a week, would be furnished by just one company, Adolph Zukor's Famous Players. Zukor had not only pioneered in better quality, longer films with accepted stars, but he had the greatest star of them all to offer, Mary Pickford. And should one of his films happen to be just slightly below average, he need not worry, for the deal worked both ways. If Paramount, or any other customer, wanted the eight or ten photoplays Mary Pickford could turn out a year, they would have to take all the other Famous Players films as well.

The system worked quite well, until Mary and her mother learned that that was what was meant by wrapping dogs around Mary's neck.

Zukor later observed that he always knew when Mary was preparing to open salary negotiations. Her shoes would pinch her feet, he recalled. Her costumes did not fit right. The directors were making unreasonable demands. The stories offered her were no good.

Zukor was right in that these manifestations of her dissatisfaction did indeed eventually result in a higher salary. But was it only money Mary wanted? Each of her bargaining sessions with Zukor was triggered by her discovery that he wasn't being honest with her, that he was taking advantage of her. Anyone would resent this; with Mary it was also a form of rejection. *If you loved me you wouldn't treat me like this,* Mary's subconscious was saying to Zukor, *Prove to me you love me*—only it came out "I've got to have more money." Then would come the bargaining sessions in the office, over dinner, at Zukor's home with his family, happy hours in which Zukor was showing by his attention, whether he realized it or not, that his self-adopted daughter was indeed loved and wanted. The final proof was, of course, more salary for Mary than for any other movie actress, or any other girl in the world, for that matter.

The money, though paid by Zukor, could come only from Paramount; indeed, Hodkinson agreed to Mary's raises in advance. He and Zukor recognized the value of their star; they could not let her get away. But as the increase in her salary increased the cost of each film by a substantial amount, the only way Paramount could get its money back was to raise the rent of Mary's films, also by a substantial amount. This resulted in an extreme variation in the marketing of a single product. It was still possible for a small-time entrepreneur in a low-income neighborhood to rent a whole week's supply of films, as many as eight reels a program, changed every day, for ten dollars a week. The price of admission at many such places was still a nickel for adults, children two-for-a-nickel—there was always a kid with two or three cents hanging around, waiting for another to show up. Bigger and better theaters paid more for their weekly supply, of course, but still there was a wide gap between the top existing prices and Paramount's new ones—$500 to $700 per week for one five-reel feature! The exhibitors protested. They would have to raise the price of admission, which, they maintained, was already at its maximum. People who could afford more than a dime didn't go to see motion pictures in the first place. Film fans—the shopgirls, the immigrants, the common people of whom God made so many and who in turn made up the great movie audience—couldn't pay any more.

Fortunately for Zukor and Hodkinson, not to mention the catalyst with the golden curls who had forced their actions, it was precisely the right moment for the cinema revolution they brought about. Interest in films had been penetrating up into the ranks of the middle class and well-to-do. An audience of millions was waiting for good photoplays shown in comfortable and pleasant surroundings. Nor were they all urban sophisticates; another revolution was underway, brought on by improved transportation and led by the most conservative elements in America, the farmer and the country doctor who were way out front in buying and using the motor car. Henry Ford sold 308,000 Model Ts in 1914; their owners, and the drivers of the dozens of other makes on the market, were driving to town and looking for something to do. Early that year Ford had raised the minimum wage in his factory to five dollars a day; though far more than other industries were paying, it was nevertheless an indicator of American prosperity. All in all, new customers were discovering motion pictures, this increasingly respectable form of entertainment, and the existing fans were capable of paying a nickel or dime more to see the better films in the better surroundings their attendance had made possible. After the Strand Theatre, built expressly to accommodate moviegoers—3000 seats on only two floors—opened on Broadway in April 1914, other showmen in cities throughout the country began building large new motion picture palaces or remodeling old theaters for films. In 1915, there were 17,000 theaters in America and the motion picture industry was taking in more than $500 million. Suddenly films were fashionable.

Mary Pickford's very salary was a factor in her popularity and in the success of her films. At first the industry had tried to conceal the higher salaries of its stars, lest the public resent them and other players demand a raise. As far as the public was concerned, it actually worked the other way. In its issue of May 1915 the respectable *McClure's Magazine,* which had previously shown little recognition of motion pictures, used Mary Pickford's salary as the reason to introduce her to its readers in a full page photograph with the heading:

This Little Girl Earns $100,000 a Year

"Mary Pickford gets more money than the President," the caption explained, "and thousands say she is worth it. . . . Mary plays to more people in a single night than Maude Adams [a popular stage actress] does in a year."

Many people went to see the girl who made $100,000 a year, and became fans of Mary Pickford. In large cities several of her films might well be showing at the same time; as large theaters showed her recent pictures, others ran her old ones. By this time Mary had made a dozen features for Famous Players, all four and five reels, and they, along with most of the 141 shorter films in which she had appeared earlier, were still available. Partly to protect the major theaters against the cheap competition of her early films, Paramount set up a system grading theaters from "first-run," comprising the biggest metropolitan houses that could pay top price for exclusive rental of each new release, down to "fifth-run," out in the boondocks. As Mary's popularity continued to increase, Paramount upped the price of her newest releases still more, renting each one separately from the regular program. It was a profitable system, and might well have continued indefinitely if it had not been for the completely unexpected—Mary went to the trouble to count the house at the Strand.

Mary's contract with Zukor was to expire on January 15. All fall Mary and Charlotte, rejected and resentful, simmered in secret. Just wait until contract time: he'd be sorry then for the way he'd treated her. If he wanted her to keep on making pictures for him, it would cost him plenty. As they continued to talk about it over the weeks and months, the figures went up and up and finally they reached a good round even sum: $1000 a day. Seven thousand dollars a week.

Reminiscing many years later, Mary mused that she had never really liked the business details of her career, but that it had been necessary for her to get involved in order to protect her pictures. Many of the industry executives who observed her participation firsthand have commented that whether she liked negotiating or not, she was certainly good at it. She was also unique in that no other actress, stage or screen, took so strong an interest either in the business itself or her own role in it. Marguerite Clark, for instance, Mary's leading rival during her years at Famous Players, did not concern herself at all with either production or business. She appeared before the cameras, playing her own charming self, and when the shooting was done for the day, so was she.

The negotiations that began in mid-January were all the more demanding for Mary in contrast to the busy months that preceded them. Mary loved to work—she liked to play with children, to be with children. In filming The Foundling she had visited orphanages, studying the boys and girls, talking with them, taking them presents, entertaining them. She quietly contributed to the institutions, and, in the case of one baby girl in particular need, supported her completely. The child was referred to as "Mary Pickford's baby" and the rumor spread that Mary had had an illegitimate child and was hiding it away. She had to make a public explanation.

For the actual shooting of *The Foundling,* child professionals were hired. They all knew full well that they were playing make-believe roles in a make-believe drama. Before shooting the scene in which Mary leaves the orphanage, the director, John B. O'Brien, called the children together and explained it, pointing out that they would never see her again. Mary had gotten close to the kids, sharing confidences, telling them stories during lunch hour, and somehow, even though surrounded by glaring lights with the heartless eye of the camera staring at them unwaveringly, Mary and the children became the roles they were playing. The little girls and boys sobbed out loud, and big, real tears trickled down Mary's cheeks as she hugged them and told them good-bye. After the shot was finished, it took longer to dry the tears and bring smiles back to the faces than it had to get ready for the scene.

Then there was the day that Mary saw a bunch of kids riding sleds in Central Park. Sledding was a part of childhood that Mary had especially poignant regrets about missing. She ran to them and asked if she could borrow a sled for a ride down the hill. The kids were enjoying the rides themselves and not a one was about to give up his sled to this stranger. Mary offered to pay, a whole nickel, and one of the boys consented. Mary groped in her purse, but all she had was a dime. The boy agreed to let her have two rides. He showed her how to place the rope on the sled so it would not get caught in the runners, how to push off and steer. Mary leaped on the sled in a bellywhopper, and down the hill she went, eyes squinched against the cold air, runners scrunching in the snow, other kids hollering as she sped by them. Oh, it was grand fun, and when the sled came to a stop she jumped off, ready to trudge back up the hill and do it all over again.

And then somebody cried out, "Hey, it's Mary Pickford!" Everybody gathered around, the older ones towering over her, looking at her, talking to her, demanding her autograph. There was no more sledding for Mary that day. She didn't even get her nickel back.

She had some fun, too, shooting *Poor Little Peppina,* the story of a little girl in Italy who, it turns out, was kidnapped from her American home when a baby. In order to escape, Mary disguises herself as a boy. What a wonderful opportunity for a great piece of business—cutting off her curls! Mary spent a whole day on the wig she would wear, getting it just right, color, curls, and all. She played the scene for all it was worth, starting to cut, hesitating, milking it dry before finally snipping off that first golden curl. Mary knew what would happen when audiences saw that scene, and she was right: all over the world an audible gasp filled the theater when Mary cut her curls.

Another scene that was fun in *Peppina* was taken on a street in the Italian section of New York on a busy Saturday afternoon. As was the custom, the whole crew simply went to a previously selected spot with no advance warning or preparation, set up, and started shooting. As usual, they finished the scene before people in the neighborhood fully realized what was going on. By then, however, Mary's fans had recognized her and spread the word, and people of all ages began swarming around. The crowd gathered between her and the automobile, cutting off her escape. She ducked her head and ran, turning the corner and slipping into a little grocery store. She hid in the back room, talking with the delighted family, until the excitement had died down outside and she could escape.

After the fun of *The Foundling* and *Peppina*, it was ironic that when the time came to confront Zukor and negotiate a new contract, Mary was making a dreary film called *The Eternal Grind* about a girl in a sweatshop.

Zukor remained calm when Mary and her mother demanded $1000 a day. At least he did not refuse, and calmed, patted, and reassured Mary to the extent that she was willing to keep on working. He talked of a salary ranging from two to four thousand dollars a week. Mary and Charlotte held to the demands of a thousand dollars a day. They continued to talk, but as the time went by, Mary and Zukor became embroiled, individually and together, in other, far-reaching negotiations that were to change the entire industry.

This was a momentous period in film history. There were some two hundred producers and distributors in the business as 1916 began, nearly all of them making money. *The Birth of a Nation* was still running on Broadway as well as in selected theaters over the country, and in New York alone had already broken all theatrical records for gross income. Although not completely successful, the Triangle program, which had opened in September at the Knickerbocker, had given an indication of the potential. Charlie Chaplin, the English comedian who had achieved a phenomenal popularity doing nothing but comedy shorts, came into New York to find a new employer. His new contract made headlines: $500,000 plus a bonus of $150,000 for a total of $650,000, just to make one-reel comedies.

Big business began looking into the film industry. Benjamin B. Hampton, vice-president of the American Tobacco Company, secured the promise of $20 million in financial backing to implement his plans for a colossal conglomerate that would bring together several large producers and distributors. By eliminating duplicating studios, laboratories, and exchanges, the proposed corporation could reduce overhead and save millions. With efficient, centralized operations it could make millions. Foremost in his proposal, naturally, were Adolph Zukor's Famous Players and W. W. Hodkinson's Paramount. Zukor listened to him carefully and, Hampton reported later, absorbed a knowledge of corporate financing and management that Hampton had taken years to learn. Zukor also spent many hours discussing the Triangle operation with Harry Aitken, ostensibly in regard to a merger. Aitken later remarked, somewhat bitterly, that all Zukor wanted to do was pick his brains.

During these hectic months Mary was pursued by practically every major producer in the motion picture industry. When Zukor continued to delay giving her the $7000 a week she had demanded, while that upstart Chaplin asked for, and got, five times her salary, she announced to the world that she was no longer under obligation to Famous Players. Aitken immediately offered her $600,000 a year from Triangle. Hampton got her to sign a letter giving him the option on her services while he put together his super-film corporation. Other film magnates, giants at the time but forgotten now, made Mary offers. It was impossible for her to continue work.

But though idle, Mary was the quiet center around which revolved maneuverings and machinations, multimillion-dollar wheelings and dealings on the part of a score or more nationally known figures in motion pictures and finance. Zukor was approached by a consortium of bankers offering him $1.5 million, free and clear, for his interest in Famous Players. Two years before he had hocked everything he had to finish one movie, and now, still in his early forties, with memories of apprenticeship at no salary whatever as a teenager in his native Hungary, he could have lived well on a million and a half net. It was tempting, but, as he said later, he had one ace, and with that one card it was more challenging to stay in the game. His ace, of course, was Mary Pickford.

Again Mary became practically a member of the Zukor family. The

quiet little schemer took her at least partially into his confidence and
made her a part of his conspiratorial plans. He, Mary, and Charlotte,
just the three of them, at Zukor's office during the day or at his home
after dinner or on weekends, worked out an agreement. It is easy to
picture Mary, now coquettish, now pouting, asking for another ten
thousand dollars here, another special privilege there, seeking further
proof that Zukor needed her, loved her, appreciated her—and was not
taking advantage of her. Whether she got all she asked for is not
known, but what she got was phenomenal. The press reported her
compensation and perquisites with an air of incredulity, but because of
the efforts made to simplify the complicated provisions of the agreement, the periodicals of the day, and film historians since, actually
underestimated her benefits. She got even more than was reported. Her
salary was given as $10,000 a week, for example. That was only her
drawing account. Here, from the contract itself, as preserved in the file
of her attorney, Dennis F. O'Brien, are her benefits:

The Mary Pickford Motion Picture Company was to be set up, with
a loan of $250,000 to get started, and "a president, a treasurer, and
other such services." (Charlotte took the post of treasurer, with a salary
of $26,000.) The company would produce motion pictures, proceeds
for which would go 50 percent to Mary, 50 percent to Zukor. Mary
would receive a guarantee, paid in advance, of $150,000 for the first
year, $150,000 for the second. Beginning immediately she would re-
ceive $10,000 every week, paid on Monday, as an advance against
earnings. On her films she would be given chief prominence, that is,
"her name shall be in larger letters than any other part of the subject
matter in which her name appears." She would be provided parlor car
transportation for herself, her mother, and her maid from New York
to Los Angeles and back, "including an auto." She would be provided
with "a first-class individual studio in which no other motion pictures
shall be made while she is working in said studio," and in California
she would be provided with an individual stage in a studio in or near
the city of Los Angeles. She would also be given a reasonable rest after
each picture—"(not to exceed one week)." She also received $25,000
in stock. Finally, and it is especially charming to picture Mary suggesting this at the last minute, she received an additional $40,000 repre-
senting $10,000 per week for the four weeks it took to agree on the
agreement.

Another suggestion of Mary's, never mentioned publicly, was also obviously accepted by Zukor. From the age of six Mary had struggled to keep her family together, and her personal success only made the struggle easier. Coincidentally with the announcement of the Mary Pickford Company, Famous Players gave contracts to her brother and sister. Jack Pickford was an engaging youngster who'd been featured in some acceptable films, but Lottie had done nothing since a blatant exploitation of the Pickford name four years before, nor was she likely to do anything in the future. However, Mary had her family together, and Zukor had Mary.

An unwritten part of the agreement was Mary's pledge to keep it confidential while Zukor scurried about on related deals. It is even possible that the $40,000 was actually a bonus for her silence. The official announcement was made June 24, 1916. Prior to that date Zukor, in his quiet way, was effecting what the trade press called "the greatest merger in film history." Next to Zukor's Famous Players in size was the Jesse L. Lasky Feature Play Company, run by the triumvirate of Lasky, his brother-in-law Sam Goldfish, and Cecil B. De Mille. Combining the two made the resulting company, known as Famous Players–Lasky, the largest in the industry by far. Its officers were Goldfish, chairman of the board; Zukor, president; Lasky, vice-president, and De Mille, director-general.

There was no question as to who ran the company, however, as was proved when Zukor, who couldn't stand Goldfish, told Lasky to show his brother-in-law the door. Goldfish received a million dollars to make the parting easier, and with it and two partners named Archie and Edgar Selwyn organized the Goldwyn Company, the name Goldfish later took as his own. (Some said that instead of taking the first syllable of Goldfish and the second of Selwyn, they should have reversed the process and called the company Selfish.) All this time Zukor was contriving his most Machiavellian venture. He quietly won over or bought three of the five controlling votes of Paramount, threw its president, Hodkinson, out, and put himself in. He brought in Wall Street with a $10-million stock issue, making it possible for Paramount to acquire Famous Players–Lasky and three other producing companies. Paramount was now truly paramount in the motion picture industry. Its producing subsidiaries were turning out two features a week, plus the specials of Mary Pickford. Its distribution companies served every state and the foreign market, and it was on its way to acquiring its own chain of theaters.

And the organization of this cinema colossus had revolved around one twenty-three-year-old woman whose reputation was based on playing roles of twelve-year-old girls. Mary has been criticized by feminist film historians for, as one put it, stultifying the growth of woman's self-image in a decade aching with feminine growing pains. She did indeed play winsome roles that hardly trumpeted the call for women's suffrage, but, after June 24, 1916, the world knew that it was possible for a woman to earn $10,000 a week.

Industry leaders respected her influence even more. The astute Benjamin Hampton, in his finance-oriented film history, pointing out that theaters, studios, and exchanges represented investments of several hundred million dollars and employed a hundred thousand people, wrote in 1931: "Mary Pickford remained the industry's most valuable asset. Woman's place in business has grown enormously in importance in the last three decades, but Mary Pickford is the only member of her sex who ever became the focal point in an entire industry. Her position was unique; probably no woman, or man, will ever again win so extensive a following."

Mary's arrangement with her own company inaugurated a new era in filmmaking. Her new productions would be so special that a separate agency, Artcraft Picture Company, was set up to distribute them. On the proven assumption that audiences would pay for better films, Artcraft charged rental fees that forced theaters to charge up to twenty-five cents admission. Receiving more money per picture, Mary was able to devote more attention, time, and money to each film. She could make fewer pictures per year, but better ones. And this increased emphasis on quality of story, casting, preparation, direction, photography, and editing affected the entire industry.

Her first Artcraft production got the new direction off to a lavish start. Mary selected the story from "a mass of scenarios" Artcraft made available to her. John Emerson was hired to direct. Though he had been in films only a year, Emerson had already directed Douglas Fairbanks and Sir Herbert Beerbohm Tree. In an industry filled with egomaniacal promoters, Emerson still stood out. With Zukor's money and Mary's talent, he ran wild. The film was laid in India and England. Emerson built an Indian village at the little town of Whitestone on Long Island and found real Indians to populate it, as well as camels. A barracks and a commissary were set up to take care of the large number of extras. Crowds came from all over the island, even from Brooklyn and New York, to see both village and filmmaking.

Mary had never been happier. For a brief summer vacation she had taken a house near Larchmont, a pleasant village on Long Island Sound north of New York, and she liked it so much she stayed on. Mornings she would get up early, drive through the lovely countryside and the little town of New Rochelle into New York City, then over the East River, past the neat little truck farms of Queens County, and on to her native village. Emerson treated her like a queen, and though she was beginning to have some trepidation about her role—would people really believe a blonde Hindu?—she must have basked in the attention she received. And at the end of the day came the pleasant drive back to be followed by the possibility of a most enjoyable evening, or plans for a delightful Sunday. For among the film and theatrical people also spending the summer near Larchmont was her good friend back from California, Douglas Fairbanks.

Fun in Film

With ten films completed, brown as a chestnut, in great physical shape, Doug was cockier, more confident, more outgoing than ever. He and Beth were staying with the Clifton Crawfords. One morning a friend of Crawford's offered to lend him his sailboat. Crawford was about to refuse, as he had to go into town to a rehearsal that day when, according to Mary's account of the day's adventures as written in her daily column, Doug spoke up.

"It's a perfectly calm, beautiful day and it would be foolish to stay at home just because Crawford is the only one who can sail the boat," he announced. Everyone agreed, so while Crawford went on into New York, the ladies packed a lunch, and Fairbanks, the only man in the group, took the boat on out into Long Island Sound. Aboard were Beth, Mary, Mrs. Crawford, and Elsie Janis. It was indeed a perfectly calm day and they had a lovely time, skimming along far from shore, enjoying the basket of food.

But the weather on the Sound has been known to change, and for all its protected appearance on the map, its waters can get rough. The sky turned dark, the wind came up, the rain came down, the calm surface turned into big waves, and overboard went those lovely lunches. Doug managed to lower the sails and keep the boat upright and afloat, but its passengers were cold, wet, miserable, and scared. Fortunately, Crawford came home early from rehearsal and went to their rescue in a motorboat. Doug was still in high spirits, joking, laughing, flashing that smile all the way in. He'd obviously enjoyed the day, storm, wind, waves, and all. It was adventure!

So was his life, and his new career in films. He was full of it. The Crawfords were of the legitimate theater and Beth wasn't really too interested in films either, but Mary more than made up for their deficiencies as an audience. She was enthralled by this man who dared to sail into a storm without knowing how, who plunged into films with the same enthusiasm. "How can I possibly convey the impact of this man's personality, the terrific vitality, the completely childlike enthusiasm?" she wrote nearly forty years later.

Earlier in the summer, at a party at Elsie Janis's, Doug had made one of his dramatic entries—with dark glasses calling attention to a black eye. As Mary looked up at him, her hazel eyes revealing her concern, he explained that he'd been shooting a chase scene in a mansion in New York. During the action, as exciting in the filming as it appeared on the screen, an extra called Buffalo Eddie Kelly had discharged a rifle in his face—"loaded with pebbles, sand, and gunpowder," as Mary repeated the story later. Actually it had been the wadding from a blank cartridge in a stage pistol, but the black eye was real enough.

He showed his thoughtful, considerate nature in the story of a big dinner he gave the cowboys who had worked with him on his first western. It was at a fashionable hotel and the cowboys were uncomfortable with the elegant dishes and the supercilious waiters. They were all watching Doug, he told Mary, and suddenly he got an inspiration. He picked up his knife and started eating with it. He leaned his elbows on the table, dunked his bread in his soup. Soon all the cowboys were eating the way they did in the bunkhouses, and everybody had a great time. Mary thought he was just marvelous to be so perceptive and to take action.

Few film fans today think of Doug Fairbanks as a cowboy star, but he loved to play Western roles, and, in one, gave a personal and poignant revelation of himself. *George Eastman House*

She loved to listen to stories about Fairbanks, too. Allan Dwan told how Doug always tipped the Pullman porters so lavishly that by the end of the first day of the five-day run to California nobody on the train could get any service—all the porters were waiting on Doug. So, Dwan said, on the last trip he had told all the train personnel that Doug was being taken to a home for incurables in California. One of the porters said that Doug had just given him a dollar. "Poor fellow," said Dwan. "There went his last cent." After that none of the porters would answer his ring, Dwan said. "By the fourth day he was as mad as a wet hen, and on the fifth day he was so pugilistic we fled to our drawing rooms and locked our doors in self-protection!"

The conversation did not flow in only one direction; Doug was a good listener, too. He had good reason to listen to Mary. Everyone in the business knew that she was more than just a pretty face, she was wise in the ways of film financing. Doug, too, was beginning to think beyond the camera and the screen, into the business end of the industry.

While Mary had been working out her financial deals, Doug had been learning how to make films. Just as she had been driven by insecurity and rejection to demand compensation amounting to overkill, so Doug's craving for notice and companionship was increasingly rewarded as he took more interest in the entire process of filmmaking, from cooking up plots to the final editing. Allan Dwan, who worked with both Doug and Mary, recalled that, while both had a thorough knowledge of films, Doug's grasp of production was deeper than Mary's. "Doug went into a new film from the bottom up," Dwan said. "He liked to begin with no story, no location, no cast, no nothing, and build from there. That's one of the reasons it was such a delight to work with him. He'd get some glimmer of an idea, turn loose all that enthusiasm, and off we'd all go on a new project."

Actually Doug made four films before building one from the bottom up. Though they covered only six months or so, Fairbanks was a quick study, was intensely curious about what was going on around him, and he had good people to observe and question. Motion pictures would have had a special, peculiar appeal to him. For years he had been practicing sleight of hand. He made up outlandish stories about himself and told them as gospel truth. While in the theater he had had a battery connected to a chair in such a way that it would administer a shock to anyone sitting in it, and he was so taken with the prank that he took the thing with him on tour. An irrepressible prevaricator who loved to trick people, he was right at home in motion pictures, the most duplicitous of all arts. That very term, motion pictures—cinematographs or cinema in Greek—is a lie, for motion pictures are absolutely motionless. The film may move through the projector, but each picture, or frame, comes to a dead stop before the lens, the shutter opens and closes, and that static image is thrown on the screen. At the rate of twenty-four frames per second, stills become movies.

The theater presents an illusion of reality; the cinema presents an out-and-out delusion. It began that way, for the very first film made in the first motion picture studio, February 2, 1893, was a deliberate distortion of the truth. It shows an office boy sneaking up behind a dozing clerk and shaking pepper on him. The man sneezes. The End.

What is false? Well, in actuality the sneeze was shot first, simply because the only talent on hand, a fellow named Fred Ott, was known for his explosive sneezes. But there didn't seem to be much point in just showing a man sneezing, so the industry's first screen writers cooked up the idea of the office boy and photographed it the next day; this scene was actually the second shot. The innocent bit of chicanery in placing it first got the motion picture industry off on a course of deception from which it has never deviated, and which is accepted without question by its devotees.

A few years later George Méliès, a French magician turned cinematographer, was shooting the Place de l'Opera when his camera jammed. He fixed it and resumed. When the film was developed Méliès saw the coach that he had been photographing when the camera jammed turn into a hearse, right before his eyes. It was the first camera trick, or special effect. Obsessed with the possibilities of cinematographic prestidigitation, Méliès made several film fantasies that still exist.

This, then, was the new art form in which Douglas Fairbanks delightedly found himself. *His Picture in the Papers* is full of little tricks. In one scene he climbs up the front of a building with amazing speed and agility, so much so that it's easy to suspect that he just skedaddled along a horizontal facsimile on hands and feet while a camera took the action from above. Rotated a quarter turn, the film shows him moving vertically.

In another scene a bad guy throws a bomb into a crowd. Poof goes a puff of smoke and bodies fly through the air. One man lands in front of a door, lies there, then pulls himself together and gets up. But there's something wrong—he gets up two feet from where he landed! So we can assume that the sequence went like this: the bad guy throws something toward the people. Cut. A smoke bomb goes off. Cut. Dummies fly through the air and land. Cut. The man takes the dummy's place and gets up when the camera starts—but he obviously didn't get the right spot.

In a fight scene on top of a railway car, photographed both from a distance to show the height of the car and close up to show the battle, Doug throws the rascal off. Who notices that this shot is from medium range, showing only the top of the car, so that the villain can land on an unseen pile of mattresses?

In the boxing scene it wasn't even necessary to do tricks to delude perception. Doug swings a tremendous haymaker to knock out Battling Burke. What a blow! Only in slow motion do we notice that it lands on the fighter's arm, and the fighter literally dives in the direction from which the blow came.

His Picture in the Papers made an impact on both Fairbanks and the cinema in that it was designed for the player. The character Fairbanks played was about 90 percent Fairbanks. Not only does his athletic ability stand out, but, more important, so does his natural charm. When a beat-up old nag he finds in a barnyard delivers him to his destination in the nick of time, for example, he gives the horse a big kiss. Whether the idea was his, John Emerson's, or Anita Loos's, it was one of several little touches that enhanced his appeal and helped establish him firmly as a popular comedian. Fairbanks playing Fairbanks paved the way for, years later, Chaplin to play the Chaplin he created in feature-length films and Harold Lloyd to play Harold Lloyd.

The next step in Fairbanks's film education was taken with Allan Dwan, the director with whom he was most in tune, and who had the most to offer. Like Doug's image of Doug, Dwan was a college man and an athlete, the only difference being that Dwan's background was real: records at the University of Notre Dame show that he did indeed letter in football, as quarterback, in 1906. Two years younger than Doug, Dwan, an electrical engineer, first became involved with films as a lighting consultant and took a job as director when it became open because it appealed to his liking for challenge, adventure, and excitement; that first stint was with a pirate company making one-reelers out in the wilds near San Diego. He and the actors were harassed, even fired on, by hirelings of the motion picture trust, but his films attracted attention. Triangle hired him in its big expansion of 1915. Like Doug, he admired the films of D. W. Griffith but found the man himself pompous. Two rebels, Dwan and Fairbanks made several films together, in Triangle's New York studio or on location in the West— anywhere so long as it was away from Griffith.

Their second film together, Doug's fifth, was a milestone in the development of Douglas Fairbanks as a film producer. Titled *The Good Bad Man*, it was also a revealing portrait of this ingenuous, appealing man who, more than wearing his heart on his sleeve, displayed his entire ego on ten thousand screens.

Later, the author of many of Fairbanks's films would be listed as Elton Thomas; it was no coincidence that Fairbanks's middle name was Elton, his saint's name Thomas. The name represented a collaboration of any number of Doug's cohorts. *The Good Bad Man*, however, bears the name Douglas Fairbanks; the revealing little film was written by Fairbanks, its location and cast chosen by Fairbanks. It is a romanticized fable, almost embarrassing when compared with the life of its author and star, of a man who finds his identity.

The hero, a picaresque character right out of a western novel, does not even have a real name; asked who he is, he replies, "Passin' Through," and it sticks. He knows nothing about his parents: they obviously deserted him; his father could have been the West's worst villain. Passin' Through is an outlaw, too, but he's a *good* outlaw; he robs not just for the poor, but for poor children, as when he holds up a grocery store for food for an orphan boy (the boy didn't have a father, either). He also robs for laughs, as when he holds up a train to get the conductor's ticket punch. After more adventures, including meeting the heroine, Passin' Through learns from a United States marshal that his father was a brave and respected leader and his mother a fine woman, both done in by the villain. In an exciting chase and fight, Passin' Through takes care of the villain and his entire gang, and rides off into the sunset, really, with his girl, his identity, and his future all assured.

It would be too much to say that in acting out his fantasy Doug stumbled onto his own therapy and resolved his insecurities. He obviously concealed his inner feelings well, but one man was close enough to him over long periods of time, and perceptive enough, to see behind the mask of flashing smiles and bouncing energy.

"Doug could be serious, moody, sensitive as any woman," Allan Dwan said. "Every now and then I'd see signs of depression coming on, something inside gnawing at him. All of a sudden he'd just disappear, take his anguish and hole up with it. He hid his black moods well. I doubt if a handful of people ever noticed it."

Making *The Good Bad Man* provided a cornucopia of adventures to serve as antidote for depression. The cameraman on the picture was a wild character named Victor Fleming. The same age as Doug, Fleming later became the sensitive director of many films including *Gone with the Wind* and *The Wizard of Oz*, but at that time he was one of the many robust adventurers discovering the fun and money in pictures. "Vic was half Indian, a guy who loved to drink and fight," Dwan recalled. "A fighter named Kid McCoy showed us his famous corkscrew punch and Vic knocked his whole damn crew cold with it. Doug wasn't that fond of fighting; matter of fact, he always walked away from trouble, but he was always eager to see new things, find new thrills. The three of us had a lot of fun."

They went all the way to Tucson, Arizona, then a small town with dirt streets and a frontier look, to film some scenes. Riding out into the desert with a group of cowboys and Mexicans, they saw an adobe hut that was perfect for an upcoming scene and rode up to ask permission to use it. A woman was alone in the cabin and, thinking they were a band of Mexican bandits, cut loose with a rifle. The bullets considerately went over their heads, and Fairbanks and Dwan dismounted and walked to the cabin to reassure her. She wound up in the picture.

One of the cowboys told Doug that a species of cactus stored water. Doug had to cut into one to see for himself. "Hey, look," he cried. "A cactus water pump." He immediately worked out a scene in which the thirsty Passin' Through gets a drink from the cactus pump.

Working with Dwan and Fleming, Fairbanks became fascinated by the tricks that could be done with a camera. Today, special effects are created by technicians using complex optical equipment: the processes are bewildering. In 1916, out on the desert, Dwan and Fleming, both interested in mechanics, used nothing but the camera and a piece of black paper. When the posse was chasing Passin' Through, for example, he escaped by leaping, on horseback, an impossibly wide ravine. Here's how it was done.

First Doug was photographed riding up to the ravine, stopping while his horse pawed the ground in obvious refusal to attempt the jump. Doug patted the horse, coaxed him, and went back for a running start. Then Fleming photographed the run and the leap—but over flat ground, not the ravine. And the bottom half of the lens was obscured by the piece of black paper—cameramen called it a matte. Next step was to wind the film back, return to the ravine, back away from it so that it became narrower in the distance, put the matte over the *top* half of the lens, and shoot the ravine. Develop the film, top and bottom, and there is Doug jumping the ravine.

Dwan had participated in track and field events at Notre Dame, and he marveled at Doug's athletic ability—"He'd have been a one-man track team at any college." In their next picture together Doug played an Indian, stripped to the waist during most of the film, and Dwan put him through several stunts. In one he escaped his pursuers—Doug got chased in practically every film—by vaulting from the ground high up into a tree. One way to do it would be for Doug to jump from the tree onto a smaller sapling, riding it to the ground. By reversing the film, he would appear to be going up instead of down.

Dwan, however, remembered how, back in college, the bamboo poles used in the pole vault had sometimes broken, occasionally impaling an athlete, and how steel cable had been run through the center of the poles for reinforcement. So now he took a steel rod, festooned it with leaves and branches so that it resembled a tree, and anchored it by the larger tree. Still it was neither strong nor flexible enough to throw Doug from the ground twenty feet into the air. So, out of camera range, he rigged up a block and tackle on a pole and attached a length of piano wire to it. In the scene Doug comes loping across the clearing, gracefully climbs up the carefully placed branches of the steel sapling and bends it back to earth, then, zingo! With an assist from the unseen piano wire he sails from the ground to his haven high above.

Even more exciting was the forest-fire scene, in which the entire Carquinez Wood in northern California appeared to be blazing out of control. The fire was genuine, but it was confined to a patch of artificial trees a good hundred yards in front of the actual forest, with scores of fire-fighters standing by out of camera range. The monoptic camera faithfully shows both fire and forest, with no indication that there is any separation.

The major difficulty this picture presented, incidentally, was getting permission to do it. When Beth heard that Dwan planned to portray her husband as a naked, dirty savage in a picture called *The Half Breed*, she informed him positively that Doug would do no such thing. Doug accepted her judgment but Dwan thought about it and came up with a suggestion.

"We begin with this lovely scene in which Doug is bathing in the river," he said. "He comes out, fresh and clean, muscles rippling. . . ."

Beth bought it completely, and that is the way the picture began. Doug laughed like a small boy putting one over on Mama.

Less than a year after first reporting to the studio, Fairbanks had made nine films, working directly with three directors and observing the work of several others, including D. W. Griffith. He knew how to make a movie, from idea to final editing. He knew how to use that knowledge to his own special advantage, too. Eager to get back to New York after six months in the West, he came up with an idea. "It's not where you are, it's who you're with that counts," Jim Kidd had said, and Doug thought about that remark often, basking in its simple warmth. One day an analogy popped into his head—it's not where you are, but *what you do*. So evolved the plot of a western-style thriller called *Manhattan Madness*. He and Allan Dwan returned to New York to make it.

That summer Doug and Mary saw each other often at Larchmont. They were at a party at Elsie Janis's and visited his mother again. Another connection was "Cap" O'Brien, the attorney who had worked out Doug's contract with Triangle the year before, and who represented Mary in her more complicated dealings with Zukor. Though there is no record of any discussion of motion picture finances in their meetings, there is good reason to believe that they did talk about money, and that Doug benefited by it.

According to the Fairbanks family history, he was then making $10,000 a week, his pictures were costing $250,000 and bringing in much more, and Fairbanks considered himself, in contrast to what Triangle was making, to be working for nothing. The figures were wrong, for the records show that he was making $2500 a week and his pictures were costing around $40,000.

But his claim to be working for nothing was, allowing for Fairbanksian hyperbole, somewhat justified. Salaries of the stars, no matter how large the headlines that proclaimed them, were peanuts compared to the unpublicized income of the men who ran the industry. Mary was Adolph Zukor's highest paid star by far, for example, but as president of the Mary Pickford Company he was splitting her income with her. Mary received only the fruits of her own labor; Zukor had many stars working for him, all for much less money. As an indication of Zukor's income, he had a 500-acre estate near Tuxedo Park with two elaborate residences, a private theater, his own personal, fully maintained eighteen-hole golf course, a yacht for the twenty-mile commute down the Hudson which also picked up weekend guests at Forty-second Street, and his own private gasoline station at the entrance; as his motoring guests arrived or departed they stopped to have their tanks filled.

The Aitken brothers, Doug's employers at Triangle, were living far less sumptuously, but that was not the fault of Douglas Fairbanks. There was no way his pictures could fail to make money. *The Good Bad Man*, for example, was shot in four weeks, from a story furnished by Fairbanks and with Fairbanks assisting the lone producer-director-supervisor, Allan Dwan. When "the temple of the motion picture," the Rialto, opened its doors in New York on April 21, 1916, the name Douglas Fairbanks and the title *The Good Bad Man* illuminated the corner of Broadway and Forty-second Street from that fabulous marquee. The program consisted of "The Star Spangled Banner" by the forty-piece orchestra; the overture, by orchestra and chorus; a newsreel; a female vocal solo and a dance solo; a scenic film; a violin solo; the feature; a male vocal solo, a song by the Rialto quartet, and a Keystone comedy. For this auspicious opening Triangle surely exacted a commensurate price as well as receiving excellent reviews; one reviewer predicted that the film "should prove a moneymaker for producers and exhibitors."

Mary, who, after all, had counted the house at the Strand several months before and was in New York at the opening, would have known the value of such a showcase, even if Doug, who was in California at the time, did not. She had found the solution to her own problem in the Mary Pickford Company, and its special distributor, Artcraft. Would she not have discussed it with her good friend? It could hardly be coincidence that about this time Doug initiated a study to look into the feasibility of forming his own company.

Adolph Zukor had helped Mary organize her company, at some benefit to himself. Doug happened to have a good businessman right there in the family, his older brother John Fairbanks. Now forty-three, John had worked himself up to a responsible position with a Denver company. Conservative and close-fisted, he responded with some reluctance to Doug's exuberant appeal to come to California to look into the production end of the business. Then Doug turned his optimism on full blast; John found himself in New York investigating possible methods of financing the venture. John's daughter, Mary Margaret, said that he spent a full year in New York making the financial study, and although the period of time was exaggerated it provides an indication of how seriously the family took the proposed venture.

It was easy to think of reasons why the project would be risky. John Fairbanks would have known that the odds were against any new company succeeding; some fifty motion picture companies failed during that period. A new company in this mercurial industry, based on one individual, would be an even more improbable gamble; everyone knew that any actor was only as good as his last hit. Douglas Fairbanks, observant, with some experience in Wall Street himself, and with many friends in finance, including his father-in-law, would have realized by this time that something was shaky even in so well known a venture as the Triangle empire. Harry Aitken had started out as a wheeling and dealing real estate salesman, showing free movies to attract customers. He had substituted companies with ringing names like Majestic, Reliance, and Fine Arts for his land developments, but he was still operating in the same old way. Records of Aitken's operations show that he was juggling amounts in the hundreds of thousands of dollars, pledging shares, filing balance sheets, putting up films as security, borrowing here to pay off a loan there. Triangle's eventual failure was primarily due to the fact that Aitken was more promoter than businessman, but at that time the picture was not so clear and must have been discouraging. If Triangle with all its apparent resources was in trouble, what chance had a company based on one grinning acrobat?

But Doug had been doodling SUCCESS for too many years to be dissuaded by mere practical considerations. Driven by the need to prove himself over and over, he had always taken chances, lived beyond his means. Now, with his ego fed by great reviews and personal appearances—in hometown Denver he'd been "dragged" up on the stage of a motion picture theater, to the cheers of the audience—his determination had a manic intensity. And there were other influences built up over the years. The simplistic activism of his hero Teddy Roosevelt still affected him: determine what you want and go get it in the good old American way. Far more paradoxical in this first-year high school dropout was his knowledge of, and conviction in, the theories of the German philosopher Immanuel Kant. Wherever he picked it up—he said it was at Harvard, in the classroom of William James—Fairbanks was surely one of the few actors, if not the only one, consciously guided by the categorical imperative. In its simpler manifestation, Fairbanks believed, or at least he told people he believed, that by calling on *the will to do* he could summon a nervous energy which, in conjunction with his muscular force, enabled him to exceed his actual physical strength. This metaphysical power thus enabled him to jump higher and run faster, for example. He was in the process, he told a reporter for the *New York Times*, who dutifully reported it, of developing this power to the point of being able to fly.

In the meantime, in a broader, pedestrian application, Kantian metaphysics reinforced his determination to go all out in following his dream, in achieving success. "I have determined to operate under my own name as far as the production of plays is concerned," he said, "and stamp them with my own individuality."

Finally, there was the inspiration of the one movie star who had gained independence, or at least 50 percent of it. Perhaps it was during this period that some major differences in the Fairbanks and Pickford personalities began to show. Mary had not set out to have her own company, but only to be rewarded. With her fear, shared by many actors, of forgetting her lines, she never wanted to depart from the safe, familiar lines of the play she had memorized, or, away from the theater, from the usual procedures of life and industry. Doug, by contrast, was afraid not to venture lest he be overlooked or fail to live up to his own estimation. Mary was satisfied with her equal partnership in the Mary Pickford Company; Doug wanted the lion's share of his.

Both wanted excellence and were willing to work for it. As the Artcraft company had been organized in connection with the Pickford company to finance and profit from a higher grade of pictures, Mary surely called Doug's attention to it. Artcraft spokesmen, in stories in the trade press, elaborated on Artcraft's philosophy and plans. The motion picture industry represents an art, explained Walter E. Greene, president of the new distributing company. Just as an artist does not turn out a painting in a specified time, neither should a director be expected to produce a masterpiece under such conditions. Thus Artcraft would give its directors—who were also producers—the stories they would film a full four weeks in advance so that they could study them fully and take the time to lay out their plans. Under Artcraft's sponsorship Mary Pickford would alternate directors, so that each could prepare for her in artistic detail.

By now Doug knew enough to appreciate the advantages of a quality operation. He always wanted to be associated with the best, and Artcraft would have attracted him on that ground alone. The campaign the new company put on for its first product, Mary Pickford in *Less Than the Dust,* was the greatest promotion up to that time. The film would open in eighty theaters simultaneously; a third of a million people would see it on the first day.

During that fall and winter, the Fairbanks brothers, together and singly, met with their attorney Cap O'Brien, with Adolph Zukor of Paramount and Famous Players–Lasky, with Walter Greene of Artcraft, and with others, including, surely, the pioneer star-industrialist, Mary Pickford. It all worked out, and the Douglas Fairbanks Motion Picture Company was organized, with financial backing and distribution by Artcraft and studio space and technical facilities furnished by Famous Players–Lasky. Harry Aitken, of course, took legal steps to hold him to his contract with Triangle, but Fairbanks had no difficulty proving that Triangle had not lived up to that important clause which provided for the personal supervision of D. W. Griffith on all his films. Only a few months later Griffith also left Triangle for Artcraft.

Completion of the formation of the Douglas Fairbanks Motion Picture Company in December 1916 wound up an active year for its patronym. His last film for Triangle, *The Americano,* which opened on Christmas Day, was his thirteenth. The pictures he made in his first seventeen months in the business amounted to almost one-third of the forty-three pictures he made during his entire twenty-year career.

His personal life, at least in relationship to the three women in it, appeared to have undergone no change. He and his real mother continued a partial estrangement, although he sent her checks and presents. Life with Beth, who served in the roles of substitute mother, business manager, housekeeper, and wife, continued on in its comfortable, placid way. His friend Mary Pickford remained his friend, listening, advising, inspiring.

Late at night on December 23, in her seventieth year, Ella died in her suite at the Hotel Seymour. Doug was en route home from California; he had no chance to reconcile their estrangement before she left him forever. Her sons gathered in New York. Douglas, though ostensibly the most emotional, was dry-eyed. After visiting the funeral parlor, he insisted that Robert accompany him to a Broadway show. "Tutu would understand," he said. He walked and sat woodenly and dry-eyed through the funeral services and interment, his face taut, expressionless.

Mary learned through friends that he was unable to express his grief, and sent him a note of comfort. He called and asked if he could see her. She picked him up in her limousine, and, in curtained privacy, they drove through Central Park together. He told her what his mother had meant to him, from the earliest days of his childhood to her encouragement in his career; he had probably never realized himself how vital her support had been. Mary touched his hand in sympathy and suddenly he burst into tears. He buried his face in her curls, she put her arms around him, and the hoarse, aching sobs came up from his diaphragm. Finally he cried himself out and sat back, still grieving, but relieved of that awful pressure. It was then that they looked at the clock on the console of the tonneau. It had stopped, just minutes before, at the moment when his grief had burst out of him. Both superstitious, they considered it highly significant. In the years to come, for emphasis in matters of extreme seriousness, one or the other might be heard to say, softly, "by the clock." Whether or not Doug's outburst of grief stopped the clock, sharing the intense emotion brought them together. They were no longer just friends.

Despair and Elation

One gloomy afternoon in late January of 1917 Mary stood by the window of her hotel suite and, alone and miserable, looked down at the snow-covered sidewalk nine stories below. In the month since she had comforted Doug her mood had changed from gentle euphoria to despair. She felt an impulse to open the window and let herself fall, turning gracefully, to end her emotional agony on the soft white pavement beneath.

But suicide was a mortal sin. Dizzy and frightened, Mary pushed herself away from the window and ran to the telephone. "Mama, I need you," she cried, and Charlotte, with her practical wisdom, first spoke sternly to her daughter, then got her hat and coat and hurried to her.

Mary dutifully waited, no longer considering suicide. But the causes of her depression were still there and America's Sweetheart, $10,000 every Monday, was just another unhappy young woman calling for her mother.

The new year had begun so beautifully. She was enjoying her work and her life. *Less Than the Dust*, which she later referred to as "a pretty darned good explanatory title", was behind her. It received good reviews, did well at the box office, and was by no means the disaster that Mary, with her masochistic inclination to disparage her less successful films, later claimed. But she was nevertheless unhappy with it, perhaps because of the sycophantic John Emerson; Frances Marion said he had a constipated brain. Her director now was Maurice Tourneur, a sensitive, meticulous artist who had made excellent films in both France and America. She had prevailed on Zukor to let Frances, her only close woman friend, do the scenario. Choosing the two people she would work with was a victory for Mary over Zukor's executives, who wanted complete control over this woman who was costing them so much money. Cecil B. De Mille, Famous Players–Lasky's Napoleonic director-general, had been insisting all along that he alone was capable of supervising such an investment.

The film was *The Poor Little Rich Girl*, and making it was a joy. A fairly successful play, it became a delightful screen scenario; free from the confines of the stage, Frances could do so many more things with it. For the first time in a feature, Mary would play a child from beginning to end; the entire action takes place around the little girl's eleventh birthday. The film has some striking similarities to *The Wizard of Oz*, which it preceded by some twenty years. The little girl is so protected from the cruel outside world by her well-meaning, wealthy parents that she is virtually a prisoner in her own home. She is unfamiliar with everyday speech, and the casual metaphors she overhears become frighteningly real in a dream sequence. She has heard the butler called a silly ass and the governess a snake in the grass, the nurse described as two-faced, the footman as having sharp ears, her mother as having a bee in her bonnet, and her father's Wall Street associates as bulls and bears, and her parents criticized for burning the candle at both ends. In her dream, a plumber and an organ grinder, her only contacts with the outside world, become her protectors against these fantasized dangers.

Frances Marion was an imaginative young woman with many memories of a happy childhood to draw on. Almost daily, as shooting went on, she'd make some suggestion that Mary thought hilarious. At the birthday party, for example, she proposed that Mary put a big piece of chocolate cake on the seat of a chair, where, of course, one of the guests, a prim and hateful little girl, sits on it. Tourneur, who liked to work from a script and had little sense of humor, was offended by such touches.

"French children are not like this," he protested. "I don't want to have anything to do with it."

"But I'm not a French child, I'm American," Mary declared, and insisted on doing the funny scenes Frances thought up.

The scene that caused Tourneur the most anguish, and gave Mary and Frances the most pleasure, was the mud fight with the gardener's boy in the conservatory. Over the director's protests—"I have had a dignified career! I don't approve of such naughtiness!"—Frances arranged the setting. "We'll do it," she said to Tourneur placatingly, "and then if you don't like it we'll take it out." Tourneur reluctantly agreed, and Mary had one of the happiest times of her life, reliving the childhood she had never had. She threw mud, was hit with mud, slipped and fell in mud, was covered with mud. When the scene was over she dragged Frances on the set and smeared her, too, as Tourneur turned away in horror. It was a gooey, sloppy, muddy day and Mary loved every second of it.

When the picture was finished Mary and Frances, giggling with anticipation, settled down in the screening room. Zukor and Lasky, surrounded by the other officers of the company and puffing their big black cigars—Zukor always handed Lasky one when he lit up—gave the signal and the film began. Mary and Frances soon noticed that they were the only ones laughing in the smoke-filled room. Zukor and Lasky sat in stolid silence, and the others followed suit. When the film was over and the lights came on, Mary saw only scowling faces. They were too stunned to remember exactly what was said, but Frances would always recall the word "putrid." The film was so bad, the bosses all agreed, that it would have to be destroyed. Frances went home and crawled under the bed, crying out, "I've ruined Mary's career." Mary went to bed without dinner and cried herself to sleep.

The next day Zukor summoned Mary to his office. She went in like a little girl who had been caught being bad, and Zukor took full advantage of her feeling of guilt and shame. He told her to go home and write out a telegram to De Mille, apologizing and promising to follow his wishes, then call Zukor and read it to him for approval before sending it. Mary followed his orders. In the telegram she abjectly agreed not to "interfere" with De Mille's choice of story or cast, or the final editing.

How could Mary, who, after all, still had eighteen months to go on a $10,000-a-week contract, be so affected by one bad film, and a rough cut at that? One factor, of course, was the sensitivity of the performer, to whom every setback is the end of the world. Another was the situation in her personal life at that time.

Mary always thought of herself as a good girl. It would be impossible, she once observed, for her to play a mean, hateful person. She just wouldn't have been able to handle the portrayal. Being a good girl also meant being a good wife; in Mary's religion there was no divorce, no adultery. Her intimacy with Doug had not reached the sexual stage, yet Mary must have been concerned about it. For whatever reason, although she no longer loved Owen Moore, he had persuaded her to live with him again. They had moved into a suite on the ninth floor of the Hotel Biltmore.

Mary referred later to unpleasant experiences with Owen, but all of those took place in public and the injuries she suffered were shame and embarrassment. What took place behind closed doors with him, sober or drunk, remained her private affair. She never spoke of her intimate life with him, not even to Frances Marion. She later professed, in her only mention of the incident, not to remember what brought on the suicidal despair that January day.

Whatever the cause, Mary's emotional condition was serious enough for Charlotte to call in a doctor, and the doctor to urge Charlotte to get Mary out of town, away from Owen. Zukor, though he was sincerely fond of Mary, seized the opportunity to arrange a trip to California—where she would make two pictures under De Mille's complete supervision.

Doug had been in New York all this time, but apparently he and Mary had not seen much of each other. He was putting together his company, renting office space and buying a studio, planning his first film, defending the suit brought against him by the Aitkens, supervising the decor of the room he donated to the Lambs Club, talking to newspaper and magazine writers, writing a book, and, of course, working out. Perhaps the most positive indication that he and Mary had no clandestine meetings was the publicity given the meeting they did have. Doug gave a farewell party at the Algonquin for her on Saturday night, February third. The party was covered in detail, including "the new frock Miss Pickford bought for the occasion." Four days later she left for California. Whether she was happier to be getting away from Owen or sadder to be leaving Doug, her spirits were surely given a welcome boost by the thousands of fans who came to Grand Central to see her off.

On her arrival in Los Angeles there was a welcoming party at the Alexandria Hotel, given by Zukor, attended by Mr. and Mrs. Cecil B. De Mille and prominent picture people, and then Mary went to work. She was terrified of De Mille, and still crushed by the failure of *The Poor Little Rich Girl* and its consequence, that abject telegram. Her first picture with him was noteworthy chiefly for bringing consternation to Pickford fans: Mary, unmarried, is seen sewing tiny garments! The hero marries her, and only then do we learn with great relief that the baby clothes were for a doll.

Between the two De Mille pictures Mary had fourteen days off, and she spent ten of them on the train in order to spend four in New York, ostensibly shopping for spring clothes. While she was in New York, *The Poor Little Rich Girl* opened at the Strand. In spite of the Artcraft executives' reaction, the film had been booked into theaters in advance and the company had to release it. Mary called Frances Marion, who was working in New York, and Frances, although she thought it was like rubbing salt into a wound, agreed to see it again with Mary at the opening performance. Mary wore dark glasses and a big hat over her curls, and they sat in the balcony, unrecognized.

In the first minute of the film the warm, haunting appeal of this twenty-four-year-old woman playing a ten-year-old girl reaches out from the screen and grabs you. So, surely, did it reach out to the packed house in the Strand that afternoon. It was not until the crowd began to giggle at the first of Frances's inventions, however, that Mary and Frances began to take heart. The laughs became louder, and, in the mud scene, in which Mary does indeed look like a little girl having one hell of a time, the theater seemed to rock with laughter.

"Frances, it's a hit," Mary cried, when it was over. "The biggest hit I've ever had." The reviews bore her out. "The best yet," said the *Motion Picture News*, "with no exceptions, buts, or howevers. . . . From first to last it is excellent." The film played to packed houses all over the country and must have made a fortune. As to its negative reception in the screening room, both Mary and Frances observed later that comedies should not be judged at a small screening, but previewed before a large audience.

Beginning right there in the theater, where her idolatrous fans tore the fur off her coat—the manager had to call the police—Mary's spirits took off in an updraft of happiness. She immediately started thinking of unloading De Mille, surrounding herself with her own favorite people, and making more films like *The Poor Little Rich Girl.* She went on an extravagant shopping spree that was most out of character. So, too, was her flustered arrival at the gates of the Twentieth Century Limited as the train was beginning to pull out. For America's Sweetheart, of course, it stopped and waited, but it wasn't like Mary to be late, let alone create such a fuss.

What else happened during those four days of exaltation? Was this the beginning of the affair?

In Love

No one knows when the close relationship of Mary Pickford and Douglas Fairbanks ripened into love, nor when that love was first consummated. Neither spoke of it, not even to their most intimate friends. Frances Marion received a hint of the difficulties involved some years later, when, one morning in Italy on their double honeymoon, Mary said, "Oh, Frances, you can't imagine the luxury of a comfortable bed after the hurly-burly of the couch."

At the beginning, in the spring of 1917, the romance was fun. Neither had ever really been in love before, and along with the fresh, adolescent joy of love came the spice of flaunting authority, of getting away with something without getting caught. The intrigue of it all— making plans for secret rendezvous, complete with disguises—was just what Doug enjoyed, and his infectious enthusiasm overcame Mary's cautiousness. She had never known anyone like Doug before, and he continued to sweep her off her feet. Mary was somewhat like her millions of fans in that she took herself and the movies seriously; the fact that Doug was now a superstar, with his own company, rivaling if not surpassing her as the highest-paid performer in the world, went a long way toward balancing her sense of morality. She was not fooling around with just anybody, but with a phenomenon.

Doug came back to California after completing the Douglas Fairbanks Company's first film in New York and moved right into the Famous Players–Lasky lot at Hollywood Boulevard and Vine Street in Hollywood. Mary also had studio privileges there, and they saw each other constantly during the day. But that wasn't all. One of their favorite escapades was to go motoring together.

No one driving along under the pepper trees lining the winding country road that was Sunset Boulevard would have given a second look at a Model T touring car, buzzing along westward out of Hollywood. The isinglass side curtains were always up, even in the bright sunshine and clear, sparkling air of Los Angeles County, but as the roads were often dusty some motorists never bothered to take the panels off. The driver of this Model T always wore a hat with a turned-down, wide brim, as did the woman by his side, who also wore a motorist's veil. In the open country between Hollywood and the Pacific, where an occasional trail led off into the wild, desolate Santa Monica mountains to the north, the car would turn onto one of those tracks, and, bouncing over ruts and rocks, climb steadily into the hills. At a point where a lone tree stood on a promontory the car would stop, looking out over the colorful roofs of Hollywood to the east and the green bean fields around the Beverly Hills trolley car station directly below them. After making sure they had no company except jack rabbits and rattlesnakes, Doug and Mary would rip off their disguises, laugh with delight, and throw their arms around each other. It was high adventure, necking like two teenagers in a Model T. This was their favorite spot and they went there often, sometimes taking a picnic; Mary pointed it out to Frances later.

Frances watched Mary bloom under the influence of love. She could always tell when Mary had seen Doug or talked to him on the phone. Doug was on location a lot that summer; he would call her long distance in the evenings and they'd talk for as long as an hour. "You never thought of Mary as being sexy until Doug," Frances said. "He was so physical. Other actors *looked* sexy, like Owen Moore, but Doug was the only one with that physique and drive to back it up. Another thing, he'd listen to Mary. He treated her like an intelligent person. Any woman goes for that."

Neither felt, then, that their romance could possibly go anywhere, and at that stage they were happy with what they had. Though Mary's marriage was definitely over, she did not contemplate divorce. As for Doug, he was just as much married as he had ever been, at least as far as Beth was concerned. Apparently she did not suspect a thing. Of course, Doug was frequently away making pictures, and Beth continued to spend quite a bit of time in New York.

Doug had another reason for not getting more involved with Mary: the Pickford family. Mary had brought them all out with her—Charlotte, Jack, Lottie, and Lottie's baby daughter. Lottie had broken up with her husband, an automobile salesman named Alfred G. Rupp. The Pickfords, as the Smiths were known by then, were always around. Doug found them vulgar when sober and impossible when drunk— which, apparently, was much of the time.

"I love to be with Mary," he told Anita Loos, his chief writer during that period, "but oh, that family." Anita explained his aversion years later, saying, "They were all alcoholics, every single one of them."

Doug had too much sense not to be polite to Mrs. Pickford, who, after all, had a laugh like chimes and only wanted her daughter to have the best of everything, but it was hard to conceal his opinion of Jack and Lottie. Jack was a likable young chap with a fair amount of talent, which made it all the more difficult for Doug, who had worked hard for his success and lived a circumspect teetotal life, to understand why he wasted it on liquor and girls. As for Lottie, who was neither pretty nor talented and was jealous of Mary's success even while living—and drinking—on her largesse, Doug couldn't stand her.

Although the romance only drifted along that spring and summer of

1917, enveloping the lovers with a sweet happiness but promising no future, it had a direct effect on Mary and her work. Loving and being loved added a new dimension to her talent. With this new inner security she was strong enough, and wise enough, to demand what was best for her, and get it. With her own team, Marshall Neilan as director and Frances Marion as writer, she made a series of films worthy of America's Sweetheart in every way. She and Mickey Neilan had worked together before, when he was an actor, and between scenes and after work they had often discussed the shortcomings of their directors and how certain scenes could be done better. Neilan was imaginative and creative, and also tractable; he made excellent suggestions but never got in Mary's way. Sometimes he even got out of her way completely. While they were on location in San Francisco that summer, for instance, Jack Pickford showed up and lured Mickey off on a three-day bat. Mary was used to men who drank, and instead of getting upset about it she took over the direction until Mickey sobered up and came back to work.

As for the other member of the team, Frances, like Mary, believed in work, and the two of them went to the studio early to check the costumes, sets, and even the lighting and camera angles, and stayed late. They rented houses only a few doors apart on Sunset Boulevard in Hollywood and spent a lot of time together off the lot as well as on. Mary spoke regretfully of her lack of education, and in the evenings, as Mary put her hair up, Frances conducted an informal tutorial course.

In one of these sessions they read and discussed the novel *Stella Maris*. It contained two teenage girl characters, one the lovely, protected Stella Maris, the other one of the most forlorn creatures in literature, ragged, undernourished Unity Blake. Frances knew Mary well enough to realize that when she played a little girl she was not pretending, she *was* a little girl, and that she would be perfect for the part of Stella. But she was totally unprepared for Mary's suggestion that she play both roles, ugly little Unity as well. The feat of one actor playing two roles was still novel in the cinema, but what really astonished Frances was Mary's courage in daring to play so unglamorous a part; Unity would remain an ugly duckling right through to her tragic end. But with that new confidence in herself, reinforced by secret trysts and lengthy telephone calls, Mary insisted on playing both roles.

To portray Unity she pasted her hair down with grease, which not

Mary herself was responsible for the artistry in making herself into this forlorn waif, Unity Blake in *Stella Maris. Mary Pickford Corporation*

only took out the curls but made it darker, and braided it in pigtails. She made her eyes smaller by putting white paint around them, even on her eyelashes, and used rouge, which photographs dark, to make hollows in her cheeks. She narrowed her nose by putting black paint in her nostrils, darkened her teeth, and practiced drawing her lips down to give her mouth the crooked, hard line of a child who has never known happiness. Because older children of poor families were always carrying a younger brother or sister around, she let one shoulder droop, looking almost deformed. Unity was not an unappealing girl, just an ugly one in a sordid role; as an orphan child placed in a private home, she is beaten with a hot poker by the drunken housewife who is actually more pitiable than villainous.

Adolph Zukor was aware of the plot of the story, for he had reluctantly approved it at Mary's insistence, but he was not prepared to see Mary in Unity's makeup with bruises and dirty bandages—he didn't recognize her at first. When he did, and learned that in the movie Mary is not only beaten but commits murder and suicide (she makes this sacrifice so that Stella can be happy), he wanted to shut down the picture immediately ("Vy must she look like that?" he asked Frances in despair). Mary insisted on going ahead with it. In the film the tragedy of Unity is balanced by a beautiful portrayal of Stella Maris. This lovely child, crippled in an accident, has been told she will never walk again. When, after surgery, she takes her first step and joy appears on her radiant face, the tears flow like basins running over.

Not only did Mary give inspired performances in both roles, she also inspired magnificent performances on the part of the other players. The camera crew responded by stretching their effects to the very limits of the current state of the art. In one scene Stella and Unity not only appear together, but one crosses in front of the other. It would be difficult to do today, even with the latest equipment; at that time it required a series of demanding procedures in each of which any mistake could wipe out the entire scene. The combination of a story containing both harsh realism and sentimental resolution, magnificent performances, and excellent technical work made *Stella Maris* one of Mary's finest films; some film students consider it her very best.

Effects of the Affair

While her romance with Douglas Fairbanks may deserve a share of the credit for Mary's excellent films in 1917, the affair was responsible for the very existence of one Fairbanks film shot that year, a film that bore promise of even greater things to come. It did not happen as early for Doug as it had for Mary, for his first pictures for his own company were not affected by their relationship. He did not have the same needs he fulfilled for her, or, rather, he satisfied his needs in different ways. While Mary was frequently lonely, and his physical presence or telephone voice brought her happiness, Doug never permitted himself to be alone. With his own company it was easier than ever before to keep people around him to ward off depression.

Mary and the motion picture art and science developed together. Her cameramen, particularly the pompous genius Charles Rosher, observed what we see here—that her hair was darkening and the left side of her face was better than the right (Rosher called her Monkey Face). In one shot we see how lighting the left side of her face drew attention from the right; in the other we see how back-lighting helped her retain the gold in those curls. *Academy of Motion Picture Arts and Sciences*

Doug handpicked the first talent hired by the Douglas Fairbanks Film Corporation not only for their ability but for their compatibility. Emerson, the company's first director, bolstered Doug's confidence in the early days through his sycophantic attitude, and he proved quite capable when operating under Douglas Fairbanks's supervision and John Fairbanks's budget. Anita Loos, barely out of her teens, thought Doug was wonderful and loved to work with him. Quick witted and imaginative, she had the knack of starting with nothing but a theme and, with everyone throwing in ideas, developing it as they went along. For *In Again Out Again* Anita began with the idea of Doug breaking into prison. Why? To call on the warden's daughter. How'd he meet her? In prison, of course. What was he doing in prison to begin with? That took more thinking; Anita tied it in with the pacifist movement just before America's entry in the First World War.

"Making pictures was child's play," Anita recalled years later. "We laughed our way through every film. Doug was just a big kid, and films a big romp."

In Again Out Again opened at the Rialto on the theater's first anniversary, and broke all records. On opening day in Los Angeles it played to a total of 12,000 people in four shows. It did top business (EXTRA BIG in the language of the trade magazines) all over the country. The Douglas Fairbanks company was off to a good start.

On completing *In Again Out Again* in April, Doug set out for California, stopping in major cities along the way for banquets and celebrations. His traveling party included eighteen people. In addition to Emerson, Anita Loos, John Fairbanks, and Victor Fleming, there were some new members of the entourage. Bull Montana, an Italian-born wrestler whom Doug had taken a liking to, was a good wrestling and boxing companion. Doug gave him a part in *In Again Out Again* and Montana went on to have a fairly successful screen career playing character parts. Spike Robinson was another ex-pug in the entourage. Least in size but of great importance over the years was Benny Zeidman, Doug's publicity man. Doug loved publicity and Zeidman delivered; in Fairbanks he had a lot to work with.

A study of the trade magazines and entertainment pages of newspapers throughout the country during that period shows that no other screen personality, or anyone in the entertainment world for that matter, received press coverage even close to that of Fairbanks. There were items about him, interviews with him, articles by him. He was easy to interview, whether discussing himself, the stage, films, or practically any subject. Interviewers were constantly expressing their own wonder, and reassuring their readers, that he was all he was cracked up to be. George Blaisdell wrote, in the *Motion Picture World:* "Take my word for it, he is every inch all that he looks—and anyone who has seen the player on the screen knows that he looks like a man—a regular fellow, one who 'belongs,' and in any company."

Doug could wring copy out of the most arcane subjects. He had a fixation on the sense of smell, for example, and columns were devoted to his prediction that, just as films were currently accompanied by orchestras or pianos, soon they would also be accompanied by different scents: during a love scene, for example, a gentle floral perfume would be sprayed over the audience, while they would be doused with stronger stuff during a fight scene. When he went fishing or hunting, news of the event was sent out to all papers. One story had him setting out across trackless mountain ranges leading surefooted donkeys in search of a suitably rugged location. Another story, still being circulated, told of a peak in Yosemite National Park being named in his honor, but the Board of Geographic Names reports that there is no physical feature named for Douglas Fairbanks in the western states. Park Curator Jack Gyer, provided sixty years later with the 1917 publicity release announcing the naming of Douglas Fairbanks Peak, discovered with some amazement that the site was none other than the famous Glacier Point. And so another Fairbanks legend bites the dust.

On occasion Fairbanks sounded a bit pontifical in the interviews, as when he related film editing to Spencerian philosophy ("adjusting internals to externals"), but in general the thousands of words printed about him pictured a good-humored, energetic young man who loved his life, his country, the films, the American Dream, and all such good things. Many of the stories poked fun at him, telling how he nearly fell overboard while playing a giant yellow-tail tuna or when he failed to hit anything on a hunting trip and had to buy a coyote hide to take home. The more serious profiles traced his background, complete with a Shakespearean-actor father named Fairbanks who was also sometimes a horseback-riding lawyer from Virginia, and attendance at Harvard. Almost all stories covered his physical activity—his stunts, especially the screen fights, and cowboy skills. One gave an eyewitness account of William S. Hart shooting a cigar out of his hand. Doug contributed to the fiction in a self-deprecatory way. "We had some professional pugs in the making of that picture," one reporter quoted him about *Reggie Mixes In,* a film with a lot of fights. "Griffith was opposed to their employment through fear of my getting hurt, but I told him I would take no chances. I told the boys in the beginning it was going to be real fighting, nothing easy about it at all. Nor was there. I got a bit banged up myself. I've been told there were one or two fellows really looking for me since, too, but I guess that's not so."

It's improbable that Doug imparted so much as a scratch to any of his screen antagonists in *Reggie,* but how could anyone doubt this modest, unassuming confession?

Doug was probably most impressed by two stories. One was a lengthy unsigned article in the *New York Times* Sunday entertainment section February 4, 1917—the morning after his party for Mary—in which the reporter did a good job of balancing his own factual material with the Fairbanks fictions, and justifiably ranked Fairbanks right up there with Pickford and Chaplin.

The other was the hokiest thing since the biography of Buffalo Bill, but it must have been accepted as truth by millions because it appeared in the respected *Everybody's Magazine* of December 1916. Its author was George Creel, a highly regarded journalist who in just a few months would be named chairman of the Committee of Public Information, the official publicity man for the United States in World War I. In "A 'Close-up' of Douglas Fairbanks," Creel helped establish many of the more improbable ingredients of the Fairbanks myth; some of his wilder excerpts live on, without attribution, in Fairbanks biographies.

Creel established Doug's character as a grinning optimist—"there isn't a minute of the day that fails to find him glad that he's alive. Nobody ever saw him with a 'grouch' or suffering from an attack of the 'blues.' Nobody ever heard him mention 'hard luck' in connection with one of his failures. The worse the breaks of the game, the gloomier the outlook, the wider his grin. He has made cheerfulness a habit, and it has paid him in courage, in bubbling energy, and buoyant resolve."

Creel has Fairbanks intending to go to Princeton, choosing Harvard on impulse, and leaving after a year to go with Frederick Warde. The movies sought him and "set the trap with attractive bait. 'Come over to us,' they said, 'and we'll let you do anything you want. Outside of poison gas and actual murder, the sky's the limit.' . . . Fairbanks got what he wanted. For the first time in his life he was able to 'let go' with all the force of his dynamic individuality, and he took full advantage of the opportunity." Creel continued:

In *The Lamb* . . . he let a rattlesnake crawl over him, tackled a mountain lion, jujitsued a bunch of Yaqui Indians until they bellowed, and operated a machine gun.

In *His Picture in the Papers* he was called upon to run an automobile over a cliff, engage in a grueling six-round go with a professional pugilist, jump off an Atlantic liner and swim to the distant shore, mix it up in a furious battle royal with a half a dozen husky gunmen, leap twice from swiftly-moving trains. . . .

In *The Half Breed* . . . amid a rain of burning pine tufts and with great branches falling to the ground all around him, "Douggie" was required to dash in and save the gallant sheriff from turning into a cinder. Hair and eyelashes grew out again, however, his blisters healed, and in a few days he was as good as new.

In *The Habit of Happiness* five gangsters . . . waylaid our hero on the stairs, and in the rough and tumble that followed, it was his duty to beat each and everyone of them into a state of coma. He performed his task so conscientiously that his hands were swollen for weeks, not to mention his eyes and nose.

In short, Creel depicted a devil-may-care super-athlete who did stunts on impulse, leaping off buildings, crashing through trees, catapulting himself by bending saplings, all without even alerting the cameraman, who apparently kept the thing running and pointed at Fairbanks just in case.

In 6000 words of gee-whiz hagiography, much of it based on his own sound assessment of Doug's dynamism, Creel concluded by saying that men and women liked him, and kids adored him. "And let no one quarrel with his popularity. It is a good sign, a healthful sign, a token that the blood of America still runs warm and red, and that chalk has not yet softened our bones."

In addition to all the stuff being written about him, Doug brought out his own book, *Live and Let Live* by Douglas Fairbanks, a combination of autobiography and inspirational advice. The project may have grown out of talking with Mary about the finances of her newspaper column and a contemplated autobiography. Doug—or his brother/business manager—had the book published in a cheaply bound edition like a dime novel, and arranged for its sale in ten-cent stores and newsstands tied in with the promotion of *In Again Out Again*. It brought in both publicity and income. According to one account the book was written by Kenneth Davenport, an actor who had once loaned Doug his overcoat and, as a result of going out in the cold without it, had come down with tuberculosis. Another source attributed the authorship to another member of the Fairbanks retinue. Perhaps both were involved, for more books were published under the Fairbanks name over the next few years. The commodity brought pleasure to many people: the hundreds of thousands of readers, mostly male adolescents; the distributors and publishers who profited from the sales; the writers, whoever they were, well-paid members of the congenial Fairbanks stable; Douglas Fairbanks, for they provided him with another reflection from his narcissistic mirror, another outlet for his generosity, and another excuse for companionship; and, finally, John Fairbanks, the practical businessman, because this strange indulgence of his perplexing brother actually made money.

Doug was the center of frenzied activity that went on, in and out of the studio, from dawn to dusk during the six working days of the week and often on Sunday, for Doug played as hard as he worked. His very arrivals and departures were turned into circuses. Arriving in Los Angeles after finishing *In Again Out Again,* in the spring of 1917, he was met by a crowd of friends, including William S. Hart and several cowboys, and, perched in a saddle mounted on the long narrow hood of a Pierce Arrow, escorted down Broadway by Hart and the cowboys firing their six-shooters. Not long after, tipped off that he was to be given a surprise party on his thirty-fourth birthday, he bought expensive presents for all the guests and turned the party into a real surprise. He organized his own Red Cross chapter and supported it by staging a Wild West rodeo in Los Angeles. It was such a success that the Red Cross prevailed on him to repeat it in San Francisco. He was master of ceremonies at the big rodeo in Cheyenne, Wyoming, and capitalized on it by signing up the winner and announcing that he would make his next movie in Wyoming. A couple of weeks later the Douglas Fairbanks Special pulled into Laramie, with two Pullman and three freight cars filled with assistants, actors, cowboys, and horses. In the film *The Man from Painted Post,* there's this bad guy who's a cattle rustler and has the pretty schoolteacher in his power; guess who rides in and saves the day. Even in this vehicle reviewers praised Fairbanks ("There is nothing to the story but Fairbanks and plenty of him"), and the film, like all Fairbanks films, packed the theaters.

Active as he was, Doug still found plenty of time for Mary—too much, as it turned out. Though no gentleman would kiss and tell (and Ella had certainly raised her boy to be a gentleman), it just wasn't possible for so attention-seeking an individual to keep his association with America's Sweetheart to himself; word got around. Somehow Beth remained unaware of the new dimension of her husband's relationship with Mary, but not Owen Moore. Owen was one of a number of picture people, particularly those in the old Griffith company, who resented the fact that Fairbanks had achieved in months the stardom they had not found in years; he was doubly jealous of his wife's lover. He first pleaded with Mary to take him back, then threatened to kill "that climbing monkey." He began brandishing a gun when he was drunk, saying that he was going to get Fairbanks. Word spread all the way across the continent; a rumor swept through the New York theatrical district one night that Moore had caught Fairbanks with Mary and killed him.

The love affair had had a salutary influence on Mary's work; now it was Doug's turn. Out of this situation grew an entire new motion picture, from idea to completion, as well as a portent of a new direction in his career. It began when Mary, afraid that Owen might possibly carry out his threat, pleaded with Doug to get out of town for a while. Doug resolved the issue in his own impetuous way. He had talked Allan Dwan into leaving New York to join the Fairbanks company. Dwan was actually en route to California when, in Chicago, he found a telegram waiting for him. Doug was headed east, it said; meet him at Salina, Kansas, and they'd ride back to New York together. Dwan, a free spirit, grinned and shrugged. Riding the train to Kansas just to come back to New York was as good a way as any to start the new association.

Doug bounced off the train in Salina and greeted Dwan in typical Fairbanks style. He shook hands like his hero, Teddy Roosevelt, grabbing Dwan's hand with his powerful grip and hauling him in like a roped calf. He was like a kid with a secret, and it was all he could do to wait until he'd dragged Dwan into his drawing room and closed the door to explain the reason for the trip.

"I had to get out of Los Angeles for a while," he whispered melodramatically. "Your friend Owen Moore says he's going to shoot me, if he's sober enough to point the gun."

On the ride back to New York, Doug proposed he and Dwan work out a scenario for a picture they could shoot somewhere away from Los Angeles. In his hurry to get out of town he and his brother John— Doug's only companion on this trip—had scooped up an armful of books, magazines, and scripts. One book was *D'Artagnan of Kansas*, about a young man whose mother had read Alexandre Dumas' *The Three Musketeers* and filled her son's head with dreams of d'Artagnan.

His adventures took him to the Grand Canyon, which sounded like an interesting place to work. Dwan observed that he had always wanted to see the Canyon de Chelly, and Doug said fine, they'd go there, too.

For the next two days, roaring on across the Midwest to Chicago and then New York, they talked out the story. It was Dwan who actually put it on paper, he said later—"Doug could never sit still long enough to write anything down"—but it became obvious to him that Doug had a special interest, personal as well as professional, in the story. He, too, had been exposed to d'Artagnan as a kid; he, too, identified with the brash lad from Gascony who became one of the king's musketeers.

Within two weeks the Fairbanks brothers and Dwan had completed preparations. The company, complete with cameraman Victor Fleming, leading lady Marjorie Daw, and other players left Hollywood on Saturday, October 27, for Arizona. It was an adventurous and productive expedition. They found a spot on the rim of the Grand Canyon that was so inviting they cooked up a scene to take advantage of it. The villain throws Doug over the rim, but he catches onto a rope and his faithful horse pulls him to safety. In the film it looks as though Fairbanks is dangling a mile above the canyon floor; actually at that point there is a ledge hidden from the camera, and Doug was in comparative safety the whole time. To make the scene doubly safe, Dwan did not secure the rope to the horse. Rather, out of camera range, six men were holding onto it; it resembles a hawser more than a lasso. While they were there, Doug stood on his hands on the rim for the benefit of the still photographer. The shots were printed around the world.

The photographer, however, missed another bit of excitement. They had set up camp under an overhanging cliff at the bottom of the Canyon de Chelly, but the resident Indians, who claimed the place was haunted, insisted that they go to the trouble of moving to the other side of the canyon. That night, Dwan said, a huge portion of the cliff fell with a roar right where their tents had been.

A Modern Musketeer is one of Fairbanks's most delightful films, fresh, exciting, and funny, with many inventive touches. Its significance in the development of Fairbanks and his subsequent contribution to the cinema lies in a prologue. As the hero, Doug dreams that he is d'Artagnan, and the resulting dream sequence is a terrific bit of costume derring-do and flamboyant swordsmanship. It was the first time he had played either a costume or a period role (cowboy suits weren't considered costumes), and the dashing hat, broad-shouldered jacket, flowing sleeves, and pantaloons tucked into boots added up to a most romantic-looking figure. Fairbanks liked clothes, and this eighteenth-century French costume surely delighted him; he would come back to it later.

The swordplay also fascinated him. Doug was an accomplished boxer, gymnast, swimmer, rider, roper, and tennis player, and now he took up fencing. To his stable of boxers, wrestlers, and cow punchers he added the suave, graceful Henry Uyttenhove, a former Belgian fencing champion. While competition fencing may be a rather dull spectator sport, to the participant it is one of the most demanding contests of all, requiring immense mental concentration, physical quickness, and stamina. With Uyttenhove's tutelage and his own natural ability, Doug quickly learned to put on the most dazzling display of swordsmanship, exaggerating the classic movements in a way that made fencing experts wince but delighted theatergoers. He worked out regularly from then on, and fencing became another sport in which he could probably have achieved world ranking.

It would be some years before he would call on either his newfound sport or his flair for costume drama. But with Dwan now his number one director—Emerson had departed—Doug developed still further in the familiar roles he played so well. Dwan, who still spoke with admiration of the superb Fairbanks gracefulness sixty years later—"He had the quality of floating through the air, like Nijinsky"—called on his own inventiveness to enhance that inherent grace. In A Modern Musketeer, for example, Doug escapes from his pursuers by running over the rooftops, leaping from house to house, and climbing up a church steeple. On the set the houses and steeple were only facades, with a four-foot-wide runway behind them. Dwan placed the houses six to eight feet apart and marked off a strip on the floor, to the same scale, for Doug to rehearse on. When Doug saw the distances, he protested, "I can jump farther than that!"

Dwan, knowing that Doug could indeed jump twice that far, pointed out that the idea was not to set records, but to look good. It was Dwan who convinced Doug to accent the ease and grace of his screen actions by doing less than he was capable of, eliminating any appearance of strain in favor of smooth, flowing, effortless movement. In keeping with this principle, Dwan placed the concealed handholds with which Doug climbed the steeple closer together than was really necessary. When Doug jumped over or onto a table Dwan first saw that it had a few inches taken off the legs, not because Doug couldn't make the height, but in order to avoid all semblance of strain. Thus, with shorter risers in the staircases, Doug could go up the stairs not two steps at a time, but three—and look natural doing it. One of the world's most agile, graceful men, on screen he looked even better than he was.

These scenes of *A Modern Musketeer* were shot in Hollywood; apparently while Doug was exploring the canyons Owen Moore had given up the idea of shooting him. But being alone with Mary became more difficult, and dangerous to her career. The possibility that the public would find out about Mary's affair with Douglas Fairbanks filled Adolph Zukor and the executives of Paramount, Artcraft, and Famous Players–Lasky with terror. As Zukor observed much later, "It was a royal courtship, and it put gray hairs in my head."

What if Owen Moore sued for divorce, naming Fairbanks as correspondent? Or Beth Fairbanks named Mary? It would mean the end of Mary's career—and of Zukor's investment. Charlotte was worried too, for, on a strictly commercial basis, her well-being and that of her two children and grandchild were largely dependent on America's Sweetheart. But even she could not control her daughter's love, and indeed there were times when she did not really want to. Those were the times when, after being with Doug or talking with him in one of his frequent telephone calls, Mary's happiness was so radiantly obvious that Charlotte was happy right along with her.

"Even when Mary's mother found out Doug was Jewish she preferred him to Owen," Frances Marion recalled. "Owen was drunk all the time. The main thing was that Mama loved for Mary to be happy, and Mary was never lovelier than when she was with Doug. That was good enough for Mama—if only they both weren't married to somebody else."

The fear that the affair would affect Mary's career if discovered was certainly well grounded. It was, after all, 1917, and the moviegoing public was not conditioned to extramarital affairs. Even Lottie, no Puritan herself, disapproved. In the fall of 1917 Beth became ill and was hospitalized. Mary would come in to see her, then go off with Doug on one of their Model T excursions. Telling her friend Miriam Cooper about it, Lottie said, "Mary's so sneaky, she gives me a pain in the ass."

Though the double standard in effect in 1917 would have resulted in more criticism of Mary than of Doug, his career was by no means impervious. Like Mary, he was still considered a Catholic, and his role was that of a clean-living, right-thinking young American. His philosophy of marriage was there in black and white, for millions to read, in his book *Laugh and Live:* "If a man is a manly man, he should marry early and remain faithful to the bride of his youth."

It was an unlikely event that provided them with an opportunity to be together: America went to war. Doug talked seriously of volunteering and becoming an aviator, bringing chills to those many dependent upon him, but army recruiters fortunately preferred younger, unmarried men. The government, however, found another wartime service for movie stars: raising money.

For the ready cash to finance the war, America went directly to the people; Liberty Loans provided the greater part of wartime expenditures. No one could sell Liberty Bonds like movie stars, especially the four leading luminaries, Pickford, Fairbanks, Charlie Chaplin, and William S. Hart. The third Liberty Loan, the biggest and most ambitious money-raising drive, began with official ceremonies in Washington on April 6, 1918, the first anniversary of the declaration of war. Hart was assigned the West, Chaplin the South, Doug the Midwest, and Mary the Northeast. There is no question that the four performers were sincerely dedicated to their task, for they knocked themselves out and raised billions. But it also provided Mary and Doug with an acceptable opportunity to be together while traveling across the country for five days on the same train to New York, then to Washington for three more days. They arrived on Friday, April 5. The next day, on the east front of the Capitol, with all of Congress in attendance, they spoke to a crowd of thousands. "I'm only five feet tall but every inch of me is a fighting American!" Mary cried, throwing out her arms, and a roar of approval burst from the crowd.

Rarely do performers get such opportunities for acclaim, and the deafening applause must have brought forth a gush of adrenalin. There is every indication, from Doug's subsequent action, that they enjoyed it together.

And still Beth did not suspect. She and Doug Jr. had come east sometime before, and were living at the Algonquin. Doug was to make

Doug and Mary, and Charlie Chaplin, too, raised millions of dollars for the war effort in 1918, but another reason for their happiness was that the bond tour gave them an unassailable reason to be together—although each was still married to someone else. Even her mother, whose only wish was that Mary be happy, appears to accept the situation. *Academy of Motion Picture Arts and Sciences*

a Liberty Bond appearance with Charlie Chaplin in New York on Monday, then proceed on to Michigan for a month of steady campaigning, and Beth expected him to stop over for a night or two. But he and Mary would also not see each other for a month, and they rode up to New York together in the privacy of the drawing room.

In New York Doug left the arms of the woman he loved, got in a taxicab, and leaned forward to tell the driver to take him to the Algonquin and the waiting arms of his wife. The words wouldn't come out of his mouth. He was genuinely fond of Beth, and he was a decent man. He went to another hotel. Later, Beth would say that she and Doug had seen each other that day and talked it all over. But after that, when she was even angrier, she said that he had *not* discussed it with her, because he always ran from confrontations. That had the ring of truth to it.

For, however she learned it, it was at this time that Beth at last realized that for months her husband had been having an affair with her friend Mary Pickford. She was wounded and confused, embarrassed to discover that everyone had known but her. Usually tolerantly calm and withdrawn during her husband's constant sessions with the press, she now called a press conference of her own to announce that she and her husband were separated.

"There has been so much gossip for the past eight months," she said, "I think the time has come to end it all with a definite statement. My husband and I are the best of friends, but we have decided there must be a definite separation. Just because we are such good friends there will, of course, be no divorce. There are no grounds for that. For twelve years I have put my husband's happiness first. Now his happiness lies in paths of his own choosing—away from mine. He has always been the kindest and most considerate of men in his home life. I can only wish happiness for him in the future."

Beth was warming up. "I cannot defend any woman with whom my husband's name is linked. I will not malign her. She is associated with my husband in business. That of course is no concern of mine. I have made up my mind I will no longer act as a shield for her—by that I mean that for the past eight months whatever gossip raised its ugly head I was the one defending and explaining. For the sake of the boy and for my sake I have come to realize that the only way to stop this gossip along the rialtos of both the Atlantic and Pacific Coasts is to plainly state that this time gossip has a foundation in fact."

The reporters asked who the other woman was. "Miss Mary Pickford!" said Beth.

No paper dared print the direct accusation, or even mention Mary's name in the story. Reporters did track Mary down, however, found her eating dinner with her mother and brother at her hotel, and asked her to comment on the separation. "If Mr. and Mrs. Fairbanks have separated it is no concern of mine or of any other person but themselves as far as I can see," Mary said. "We are simply associated together in business. And now we're working together to help put over the Liberty Loan."

Doug was in Flint, Michigan, exhorting a local theater audience to buy bonds when the reporters caught up with him. He stepped off the stage, the audience still applauding, to be hit with Beth's statement and a request for comment.

"The story is false!" he cried. "It is a piece of German propaganda! It's on a level with the report they spread that I was shot. Three times the shooting story has been started since I began work with the Liberty Loan. My wife and I have no differences whatever and the story is untrue from beginning to end."

Beth had been receiving telegrams and telephone calls ever since the news first got out. It was even worse than she had expected; everybody but her knew that her husband was having an affair with Mary Pickford. Mary's cool, what's-that-got-to-do-with-me attitude caught her off balance, and now this German propaganda bit. Before she'd been hurt. Now she was mad. She called another press conference.

"I'm not an emotional woman," she announced, "but there's a limit to my endurance. Denials don't ring true. It's not playing the game."

Mary, Beth went on, "has told all my friends, some of my relations and my representatives that she is in love with Mr. Fairbanks and I do not understand why she would deny it publicly. . . . I will not allow them to keep on with their denials!"

Still Mary's name was not printed; the papers referred to the other woman as "an actress." She and Doug wisely kept their mouths shut. But another player had to have his hour upon the stage. From his monastic dwelling, the Los Angeles Athletic Club, Owen Moore strutted out with a statement on behalf of his wife, Mary Pickford, the lady who had never been mentioned. "The 'other woman,'" Owen said, "is now ill and under great nervous stress and I feel it obligatory upon myself to save her the humiliation of making any public statement." Owen went on happily saving her humiliation with a number of innuendoes. "Mr. Fairbanks," he said, "in his days of poverty took his wife from a home of wealth and refinement. . . . Mr. Fairbanks possesses a peculiar and complex personality that has a strong fascination for women. He combines a warmth and enthusiasm and persuasiveness with the instinct for possession that doubtless came to him from his Anglo-Saxon ancestors."

Owen said that he had only recently come to a realization of actual conditions—but he was now "prepared to take action."

But the only action taken was by Beth, who went to Los Angeles, closed up the Fairbanks house at Hollywood Boulevard and Fuller Street—Doug moved in with his brother John across the street at 7254 Hollywood Boulevard—and returned to New York. Later that year, with Doug's cooperation, she was granted a divorce; John Emerson testified that he had gone with Doug to a house where there were some beautiful girls. Doug liquidated his holdings and gave Beth half a million dollars. She was planning to marry James Evans, a Pittsburgh stockbroker, and the money would certainly provide everything she and their nine-year-old-son would ever need.

Doug felt guilty for the rest of his life. As for Beth, many years later when she was happily married to her third husband, musical comedy star Jack Whiting, she was walking along with her son and his wife when an acquaintance of the younger woman called, "Mrs. Fairbanks!" It was Beth who turned around.

United but Apart

One pleasant January evening in 1919, John D. Williams, head of the huge new organization of theater owners called the First National Exhibitors Circuit, strode toward the dining room of the Alexandria Hotel in Los Angeles. Williams had many reasons to be happy. The war was over, and the country, free of wartime restrictions, was headed for prosperity. The flu epidemic, which had killed tens of thousands and closed many theaters, had ended; the theaters were filling up again. Prohibition would soon be the law of the land, leaving millions of saloon and beer hall habitués with nowhere to go but the movies. And so, anticipating the biggest boom in the history of entertainment, he and other leaders of the motion picture business were meeting in southern California, which was fast becoming the production head-quarters of the industry, with plans to make a good thing even better by putting the industry on a sound business basis. Number one on the priority list was to slash the exorbitant salaries being paid performers. It went against all business principles to pay people millions of dollars for having golden curls or being able to jump, or shoot, or look funny. It just so happened that the contracts of the very people who met those

Chaplin fans have speculated that the outgoing Fairbanks was the best, if not the only, friend the lonely comedian ever had. The three best-known performers in the world were comfortable in each other's company, and liked to clown for the camera. *George Eastman House; The Academy of Motion Picture Arts and Sciences*

descriptions—Mary Pickford, Douglas Fairbanks, William S. Hart, and Charlie Chaplin—were expiring this year. By merging the giants of the industry, beginning with First National and Paramount, Williams, Adolph Zukor, and other major executives would present a solid front against these parasites and cut them down to size.

At the door of the dining room, John Williams looked inside and suddenly felt an awful sensation in the pit of his stomach. Right in front of him at a large table in the center of the room, meeting together, eating together, and unquestionably conspiring together, were Miss Pickford, Fairbanks, Hart, and Chaplin, as well as the director, D. W. Griffith. The enemy had joined forces!

Williams retreated to the lobby and passed on the dire news to the other executives who were beginning to show up for dinner. In a scene worthy of a great comedy director, these mighty men of the industry gingerly approached the door of the dining room one by one and peered in, jaws dropping as they realized that the five most expensive talents in motion pictures were indeed meeting together, doubtless plotting a merger of their own.

At their table in the dining room, the conspirators, with the possible exception of the pompous Griffith, were enjoying themselves tremendously. They barely suppressed their giggles at the sight of each new stricken face at the doorway, and Fairbanks and Chaplin, both excellent mimics, gave hilarious impressions of the unhappy fellows. Reporters covering the convention approached the group and were told that in order to protect themselves and the motion picture public from theatening combinations and trusts, the five artists had decided to unite.

This dinner at the Alexandria Hotel was one of the events leading to the formation of the United Artists Corporation. There were others. Everyone in the industry knew that film producers paid a high cost for distribution, not only in percentages agreed upon in advance but in the actual split, for distribution companies didn't talk about their take. Cap

The four giants of the industry—Fairbanks, Griffith, Pickford, and Chaplin—made history when they created United Artists—but would it have happened if Doug, the prime mover, had not been looking for another way to be with Mary? *George Eastman House*

O'Brien, the theatrical lawyer, had discussed the problem with his clients Mary and Doug, and had recommended an artist-controlled distribution company. During the Liberty Loan drives, Doug had discussed the picture industry with both Secretary of the Treasury William Gibbs McAdoo and his assistant, Oscar A. Price; Price had suggested that he distribute his own films. Chaplin wrote later that the whole thing had begun as a bluff suggested by his brother Sydney. Perhaps the most positive proposal had come from Benjamin Percival Schulberg, a onetime Zukor assistant; Schulberg had outlined his plan to a senior executive, Hiram Abrams, who presented it to Pickford and Fairbanks.

No matter who made the original proposal, it was the artists who had to make the decision, for it was only the artists who had anything to lose. Their current associations provided them with incomes, free from money-raising and distribution worries, of hundreds of thousands of dollars. Those were expensive bridges they would burn.

From the behavior pattern already established by Mary and Doug, it seems obvious who started United Artists. The year before, Mary had undergone her periodic financial skirmish with Zukor, but with a different result. Owners of major theaters over the country, angry, among other things, over having to take all Zukor's dogs in order to get Mary, had formed First National, signed Charlie Chaplin to make eight two-reel comedies for $1,075,000, and offered a similar deal to Mary. Zukor protested that he could not match it. He and Mary were no longer close, either geographically or emotionally. In the industry, administration and finances were now located in New York, production in Los Angeles. Mary rarely saw the little man who had been her father figure, and, with Doug in her life, she didn't miss him. Zukor's final offer was a peculiar one, which showed how little he understood her: $250,000 to make no pictures at all for five years. The suggestion was upsetting. Retire at the age of twenty-five? Was she that close to giving up her public, her position, the food of her ego? "Oh, I couldn't do that, Mr. Zukor," she said. "I love pictures, and I'm just a girl. I couldn't quit now."

Mary signed a contract with Williams which, in order to top Chaplin, was publicized at $1.1 million, representing $350,000 each for three pictures a year, and $50,000 for Charlotte. She would actually receive more, for this was only a guarantee against earnings, and, further, she would have complete control over her productions. It was this happy situation that a merger of major companies would endanger. Again she was being rejected, this time by many men. Zukor's suggestion that she retire was now a real threat, and without compensation. She would of course have confided in Douglas Fairbanks; they were seeing each other both openly and covertly.

Thus the idea of controlling the distribution of her own films, born out of desperation, was nurtured by love, for Doug wanted to comfort Mary, to work with her, to *be* with her. He too was perturbed by talk of the proposed merger. He was America's idol, the ecstatic center of an adulatory group of interesting, productive people, all made possible by the Zukor-Paramount-Artcraft bankroll. He would hate to lose the connection. But Doug also saw in United Artists another step toward SUCCESS. He was already a star, with his own company; he would now be an officer, a director maybe, in a national—international!—organization. He plunged into it with all-American enthusiasm.

As for Charlie Chaplin, he, too, was concerned with what a merger might do to him, not only by curtailing his income but, equally important, by compromising the artistic integrity of his work. He had another incentive to plot and plan with Doug and Mary in their almost nightly meetings. Chaplin's early life had been unbelievably pathetic; Mary could never forget his description of walking his mother to the insane asylum when he was seven years old, as street boys jeered and threw stones at them. Doug, naturally warmhearted but also attracted by successful people, became the shy, neurotic genius's first, perhaps his only, real friend. Charlie followed him around like a puppy. When he was so discouraged over *Shoulder Arms* that he considered junking it, Fairbanks insisted on seeing it, and roared with laughter. ("Sweet Douglas," Chaplin wrote in his autobiography, "he was my greatest audience.") Thus reassured, Chaplin released the film, a three-reel masterpiece. Chaplin saw that the United Artist concept was sound, but he would probably have followed Doug into it even if it hadn't been.

In short, it was Mary and Doug who molded, out of their own fears and hopes and enthusiasm, and $100,000 each, the worldwide corporate entity that still exists, United Artists.

In an inspired effort to gain prestige for the enterprise, Doug approached McAdoo, a nationally known figure who was considered to be a potential candidate for president of the United States. McAdoo declined the presidency of United Artists, but agreed to serve as counsel; he received a share of stock and his protégé, Oscar Price, was named president. Cap O'Brien was vice-president and Hiram Abrams general manager, with Schulberg promised a position when the corporation got underway. Only one of the original five defaulted; Hart, discovering that he was expected to put up $100,000 of his own money, accepted instead an offer from Zukor for $200,000 a picture. In later developments, Price was fired, Abrams became president, Schulberg sued and got an out-of-court settlement, and McAdoo quietly resigned, selling his stock to the four founders.

When United Artists became a reality one of the industry leaders observed, "So the lunatics have taken over the asylum." The remark was sour grapes: it was later established that the Paramount–First National merger had indeed been in the planning stage when the formation of UA contributed to its demise. UA fulfilled its founders' purposes in that it provided them with a controlled distribution and an agency to secure advance financing. Griffith and Chaplin chose to have their own studios, but United Artists gave Doug and Mary, now officially business partners, the further advantage of buying a property together, the Hampton Studio on Santa Monica Boulevard in West Hollywood. A motion picture studio is a wondrous toy, and they spent hours together playing with it.

But a studio is not a home. Doug and Mary had been in love for two years now; he was thirty-six and she ten years younger, and to see each other away from the studio meant sneaking off like teenagers. There may have been some early foundation for the observation voiced by many of their friends that they had fallen in love with each other's image, but surely by now they were in love with each other as a man and a woman. They wanted to go home together at night. One day, driving to the studio with Margery Daw, Doug's current leading lady, Mary, in a most unusual outburst, said, "Just when I should be at the peak of my happiness I'm surrounded by misery and sorrow. I can't stand this strain much longer."

Much of that strain was caused by the very man who loved her. He was becoming jealous and possessive. The affair was surely frustrating to Douglas Fairbanks, actor and narcissist. Doug was not the type to hold happiness contentedly in his heart. He was the lover of America's Sweetheart and he wanted the world to know it. He wanted to tell everyone what Mary had said to him last night, what they were going to do tomorrow.

Their dates would end with bitter feelings of rejection. It was the same argument. Doug wanted her to divorce Owen and marry him. He knew that he would risk losing his popularity; Mary was the only thing for which he would sacrifice his career. But Mary could not make that sacrifice, nor did she see why Douglas would demand it. So each suffered the depression of rejection every time the subject came up— and Doug brought it up repeatedly. Both were under terrible pressure; the company they had started to produce their pictures was now dependent upon them for pictures to produce. Mary had no one to run to. Frances Marion had gone to Europe as a war correspondent, then returned to work in New York. Mama was always there, of course, but Mama could not sympathize with her dilemma. To divorce and re-marry was unthinkable for so many good reasons—her career, her responsibilities, the church.

Mary was losing weight, her full girlish cheeks beginning to look hollow. It was ironically fortunate that the film she was making, *Suds*, ends unhappily, with the forlorn little girl just sitting there, alone and miserable. And while all this was going on, she was called on to spend a weekend in Chicago. Her appearance would help attendance at *Pollyanna*, her first United Artists film. She had to go. Charlotte went with her, of course, and Frances Marion agreed to meet her there in her hotel suite. Frances later recalled that at the most hectic time, Mary tense and late for her appearance, the phone rang. It was Doug. Charlotte pleaded with Mary to have him call back later, but Mary insisted on going to the phone. He was on location making *The Molly-coddle*, and she knew that he was in some lonely little town, receiver pressed to his ear, waiting to hear her voice.

Frances and Charlotte carried on a conversation with each other to avoid eavesdropping, but each heard Mary utter a little cry. When she hung up she was sobbing.

"Douglas is going away. He says he has waited long enough for me to decide about my divorce. It's now or never, this very night, or he'll be on his way tomorrow and I'll never see him again!"

Charlotte told her daughter it was impossible, Frances tried to comfort her, as all the time Mary, sobbing, was trying to get ready to go make an appearance before her people. Once again she would be rejected—and by Douglas! That fear was stronger than anything else.

"Remember, Mary, you're America's Sweetheart," Frances heard Charlotte say.

"I only want to be one man's sweetheart and I'm not going to let him go!" Mary cried.

She went through with the ceremony, and when she returned she put in the call to Douglas.

CHAPTER EIGHT

Doug and Mary:
King and Queen,
1920–1928

Even as Mr. and Mrs. Douglas Fairbanks held each other tight in blissful legality as they sped eastward on the first leg of their honeymoon trip, they suffered moments of anguish and terror. Had they destroyed themselves? Would their public accept them or reject them? Would they fall together, or would one survive while the other perished?

Mary was the more distressed. Four decades later she gave a little shudder as she said, "The greatest menace was always the loss of popularity—more than health, more than *anything.*" She was now facing that menace. Her honeymoon trip eastward was as suspenseful as any chase scene she had ever filmed. Would her fans forgive her? Or would they turn their backs and leave her with her recurrent nightmare turned real, an empty theater? Again and again, as the rails clacked beneath them, as the train stood motionless in stations across the country, during the days and nights, she asked Douglas—she never called him Doug—for reassurance. He would hold her and stroke her and soothe her. . . . "Mary," he would say—or Hipper, or Tupper, or any one of a number of nicknames he had for her, "you're America's Sweetheart. Surely they'll let you be my sweetheart, too."

And then they'd go through the whole thing all over again. Could they have lived without each other . . . could they have continued on as secret lovers, without risking it all?

It had been so much easier for Doug. It was Beth, not Doug, who had brought suit for divorce, and her hasty remarriage had helped him in the public eye. For Mary the ending of a marriage had been an ugly experience from the beginning. First had come the necessary arrangements with Owen. Mary was fond of the Moore family—his mother Roseann, who talked as though she had never left the farm in County Meath, the brothers Matt, Tom, and Joe, all in films, and his sister Mary, who had given her life for her adopted country serving in France with the Red Cross. But when it came to negotiating over money, some of the mutual affection wore off. Frances Marion said that Owen's mother told him to "git all ye can outa Mary." Mary wrote later that on the very day her mother cashed in a stack of bonds to make the payoff, Charlotte happened to run into Owen's mother outside the bank. In the course of the conversation Mrs. Moore said, "Oh, sure, Mrs. Pickford, poor Owen must have something."

Neither Mary nor Owen ever revealed the amount Mary paid Owen for her freedom. Rumored figures were as high as a million, but persons who knew them—Frances Marion, Allan Dwan, Miriam Cooper, Robert Fairbanks—believed it to be around $100,000.

That bought only Owen's agreement to accept the papers and not contest the divorce. For the divorce itself Mary had to undergo more sordid experiences. By 1920 Nevada was already known for its liberal divorce laws and that is where her attorney, Cap O'Brien, advised her to go. But it required elaborate planning for Mary Pickford to fulfill the requirements of three months residency and the intention to become a bona fide resident of the state without interfering with her work schedule or letting the press and public know. About the middle of February, Mary, Charlotte, and O'Brien arranged to board at a ranch near the tiny village of Genoa near the tiny county seat of Minden, where, on the morning of March 2, Gladys Smith Moore appeared before Judge Frank P. Langen to request a divorce on grounds of desertion. The Nevada attorney engaged for the hearing was one P. A. McCarran, who as Pat McCarran later became an influential senator. Demurely dressed in a simple black frock, her golden curls pinned up under her hat, wearing what was later referred to as "large colored goggles," Mary softly recounted, at McCarran's gentle urging, her marital problems, beginning with the truncated honeymoon when Owen had gone off on a drunk as soon as the boat docked in Havana. One of the most discomfiting moments of the proceedings occurred when the judge leaned forward and said, "You have spoken several times of your company. What is your work?"

"Engaged in motion pictures," Mary replied, after a long pause.

The divorce was granted, but not before a heated discussion as to whether Owen Moore's presence in Nevada to sign some papers constituted collusion. After that it did not take long for the identity of Gladys Moore, and the suspicion of collusion, to reach the outside world. Mary and Charlotte eluded the press by returning home by way of San Francisco, their compartment door locked, but Mary could not hide forever. She finally held a press conference in which she denied that any collusion with Moore had taken place. She would never be excommunicated by the church, she said in answer to another question, because she would never marry again.

Not even Douglas Fairbanks? She tossed her head and put her hands on her hips in that feisty gesture the world knew so well. "That rumor is absurd," she said. "Such a thought has never entered my mind."

Her mother, her sister, her lawyer, her business advisers, her friends all warned her of the consequences that would result if such a thought did enter her mind and she actually did marry Fairbanks. Mary was approaching a state of hysteria, and came to Doug for comfort. A kind and considerate man, he tried to soothe her, but he was also impetuous, and very much in love. He begged her to marry him immediately, and when she hesitated he pleaded, argued, demanded, cajoled, fretted, shouted, and sulked. Both were finishing up their current films, but surely little progress was being made as the co-owners of the studio dashed back and forth, now ignoring each other for the benefit of visitors, now charging into each other's dressing rooms to torture themselves some more.

"What if the world doesn't approve?" Mary asked, according to her memory of one of those conversations. "Will your love be strong enough? If we both lose our careers, will our love be sufficient for our happiness together?"

"I can't speak for you, Mary, but I know that my feeling for you is not of the moment. It has nothing to do with your career or your fame, or how other people feel about you. I love you for yourself."

But in spite of all this doubt and argument, the decision had already been made when Doug had said, "If you don't marry me you'll never see me again." Such a monumental rejection was too much for Mary to contemplate. On the night of March 26, Doug gave a small dinner party for Mary at his home. Among the guests were R. S. "Cupid" Sparks, the county marriage license clerk, and the Reverend J. Whitcomb Brougher, pastor of the Temple Baptist Church. Doug was attempting to overwhelm her. But it was Friday, a bad luck day, and Mary was wearing a black dress. At last, out of all this confusion, she had something positive to center her thoughts on. If she waited until Sunday, a good day for a wedding, it would give her and Charlotte all day Saturday to get a nice dress.

Sunday afternoon, March 28, 1920, Doug and Mary—and Cupid Sparks with the secret license—met at Reverend Brougher's home in Glendale. Mary wore a simple white tulle dress and, according to tradition, one stocking wrong side out. Brougher conducted a modest ceremony befitting a Baptist pastor joining two divorced Catholics in holy matrimony, and Douglas placed a plain platinum band on Mary's finger. They went to his home for a quiet Sunday supper with Charlotte, Marjorie Daw, Robert Fairbanks and his wife, and Benny Zeidman.

"This house is yours, Mary," Douglas said. "It's my wedding present to you."

"Oh, no, Douglas," she said, "I want to feel that this is your home, and that I'm sharing it with you."

But when they sat down to dinner Douglas placed Mary at the head of the table, himself at her left. That was the way it would be from then on.

On Monday, wearing a piece of adhesive tape over her wedding ring and naively sure that no one noticed it, Mary went to the studio to finish her film. Doug, trying to control his cocky grin, headed to a location in the mountains to finish his.

They kept the secret for three days, then everything exploded at once. Reporters beseiged the studio and both the Pickford and Fairbanks residences. In Nevada the attorney-general issued a 7000-word complaint attacking Mary's divorce on the grounds that she had had no intention of residing there and that Owen's visit to Nevada represented collusion. If the complaint was upheld, the divorce, and by consequence her marriage to Douglas, would be invalid. Doug and Mary now had to call in their attorneys and fight to save the divorce in order to save their marriage. Mary, so sensitive to the press, remembered one particularly vitriolic story as being typical of the attacks on her. If a baby was on the way, it asked, would the child be named Moore, Fairbanks, or Pickford?

It would take two years of legalistic haggling before the Nevada Supreme Court finally upheld the divorce.

In the meantime, Doug had made reservations on the S.S. *Royal George,* sailing from New York on May 19. In addition to everything else, Charlotte became ill and Mary refused to leave her side. The bridegroom not only had to postpone his honeymoon, he came home to an empty house. Somehow Mary reached a compromise between her dependence on her mother and her love for her husband. Charlotte recovered and agreed to accompany the honeymoon couple as far as New York. Mary and Doug left their tangled legal affairs in the hands of their attorneys, their pictures in the hands of their directors and assistants, their studio and corporations in the hands of their executives, and headed east for the sailing of the *Lapland,* on May 29. They still had good reason to believe that they had sacrificed their careers. As the train rolled on across the continent, all they could do was hold each other and attempt to convince themselves that they were prepared for the end of their dreams, for anonymity.

As we have seen, on their honeymoon trip to New York and Europe Doug and Mary found themselves accepted to the point of danger. Though America did not match the almost-hysterical fervor of their fans abroad, as the happy couple traveled back across the country on their return from Europe they were greeted warmly enough to dispel any remaining fears about their careers. They were more popular than ever.

No speculation seems to have been advanced by Mary, Doug, or their assistants and advisers as to why their marriage increased their appeal. Certainly their fears had been valid. Both had, after all, been Catholics, and the law of the church was clear. Apart from the religious aspects, in casting aside their legally wedded mates to find happiness with each other they had definitely gone against what their associates judged to be the moral tone of the world in 1920.

Obviously the moral tone was more tolerant than they realized, and the public had grown more sophisticated. According to the historian and authority on twentieth-century America William H. Harbaugh, scholarly evidence indicates that the changes in the American lifestyle associated with the Jazz Age, or Roaring Twenties, were actually well underway even before World War I.

"The intellectual revolution wrought by Darwin's *Origin of Species* had already weakened traditional religious values," Professor Harbaugh says. "Pragmatism was challenging old standards of truth and morality, and Freudianism was already the vogue of the educated classes. Victoria was dead, and so was William McKinley! Divorce was becoming more common and more socially acceptable, and the use of contraceptives was soaring. Meanwhile technology was bringing new leisure to almost everyone, at least in the burgeoning cities. Working days were becoming shorter, and white collar jobs were mushrooming. William Randolph Hearst had made sex and scandal a daily feature of his newspaper chain, and a host of magazine publishers were catering to the mass taste for romance in weekly and monthly editions that ran into the millions."

It had been only eighteen months since the people of Europe, and, to a lesser but positive extent, the people of America had been involved in the Great War. Now, with peace, they were ready for new idols, and who could better replace warriors in the hearts of the world than sweethearts?

Thanks to the universality of the silent film, Doug and Mary were the worldwide epitome of romantic love, the modern fulfillment of every love story since Adam and Eve, the prince and the princess. How wonderful that the most popular man in the world and the most popular woman in the world had found each other at last. That each had survived an unhappy marriage made their union all the more appealing.

Idealized in public, their marriage was idealistic in private, complete with hurts and sorrows and tender forgiveness. Doug knew that he was intensely jealous, and on their wedding night begged Mary not to do any "twosing" with anyone but him. She readily promised, unaware of how strictly that word "twosing" would be interpreted. She found out in their first real fight, in Coblenz, Germany, on the Fourth of July. The commanding general of the American occupation forces gave a dance in their honor and led Mary out on the floor for the first dance. Doug was instantly furious with jealousy. He controlled it during the dance but at the end of the evening, obviously enraged, he silently took her to the door of the house where they were staying, then stormed off into the night. Mary was alone in a private house in what had recently been an enemy country—the German owners had been evicted to provide comfortable quarters for them—and she was scared and miserable. Finally Doug returned. He apologized, and she repeated the promise she had made on their wedding night. This time she realized the degree of his jealousy, and the seriousness of her promise.

For two such public personages, Doug and Mary concealed their intimacies well. Frances Marion was one of the few who realized the extent of Doug's jealousy; she saw it at the very beginning, when she and her bridegroom, Fred Thomson, joined the honeymooners in Italy. Loyal to Mary and having disliked Doug from the time he first endangered Mary's career, Frances was both disgusted by his possessiveness and baffled by it. "He was not only jealous of any man who looked at Mary," Frances recalled, "he was even jealous of *me*. He was jealous of her *mother!* It was so silly, there wasn't any reason for it."

Frances went on to explain the reason without realizing it herself. She had been abroad before, and whenever she called Mary's attention to some quaint European custom she was unwittingly threatening Doug. He needed to be not only Mary's husband and lover, which Frances could understand, but number one in her life across the board.

Mary appeared to understand this facet of her complex mate, and after that one innocent dance in Coblenz gave him no cause for jealousy. (It was not so difficult, Frances observed—"away from Doug, who really turned her on, Mary wasn't all that sexy.") On one embarrassed occasion she declined the request for a dance from the duke of York, later to be King George VI. Mary recounted the incident many times, and as for Doug, nothing could be more delightful than telling his cronies how his wife, America's Sweetheart, had refused to dance with His Royal Highness.

This one episode is typical of the first years of their marriage. They may not have understood or even identified all of each other's needs, but they certainly were fulfilling them. All the anxieties, the secret fears, the drives of quiet desperation, the anguished aspirations, so compelling that they hurt, were now being gratified. If gratification can be measured, theirs would have the highest rating on the scale, for he was the most popular man, she the most popular woman—and they had each other! It was not that love had overcome their personality problems, or that some miraculous remission had set in. Rather, they were enjoying the absence of the stimuli for anxiety and depression.

Stating it a little more poetically, but with perceptive accuracy, Edgar Allan Poe wrote of another idyllic couple in another kingdom

by the sea that they "loved with a love that was more than love." Doug
and Mary's love, too, was more than love; it was synergetic, filling their
interlocking needs, giving both repeated booster shots. In every way,
Doug and Mary brought themselves an adjuvant happiness that is a joy
to contemplate.

At Home

And so, with their return from Europe in August 1920, began the
golden years of the reigning king and queen of silent films, a realm that
covered the world.

The castle to which the king brought his queen was given the name
Pickfair by the press, perhaps with a nudge from Doug's press agent
Benny Zeidman. Later its location would be known as Summit Drive,
and sightseeing guides would tick off the neighboring estates by their
owners—Harold Lloyd, Ronald Colman, David O. Selznick, Charlie
Chaplin. When Doug had first discovered it, however, it was far out
in the wilds. The year before Raoul Walsh and his wife Miriam Cooper
had looked at it on a house-hunting expedition; Miriam heard a coyote
howling and demanded to be driven back to civilization immediately.

To reach the site from Hollywood, Doug and Mary would drive
down Sunset Boulevard, a lovely thoroughfare with a bridle path in the
middle, turn right at the stylishly remote summer resort, the Beverly
Hills Hotel, proceed northward, following Benedict Canyon up into
the hills (in this area the canyons, rather than the hills, have names),
turn right again on the dirt road making its way up San Ysidro Canyon,
following it to the last habitation. There were only two year-round
homes in the mountains at that time, one known as Gray Hall, which
has been occupied over the years by a series of celebrities, the other the
residence of the Harry W. Robinsons, built in 1911. At the top of the
ridge was a hunting lodge owned by four families from Los Angeles who
came out on summer weekends. (Then as now, currents of air move
down the canyons from the higher ridges, providing natural air condi-
tioning on the hottest days.) Mrs. Robinson remembered well when,
early in 1919, Douglas Fairbanks purchased the hunting lodge and
began remodeling it into a permanent home. "He and his wife were

nice people," Mrs. Robinson said, with the tolerance of the first settler, "but of course we never saw much of them."

The remodeling of the lodge resulted in an attractive Tudor-style house, high on a ridge dominating the eighteen-acre estate with a view all the way to the blue Pacific. No gift could have been more appropriate, nor more appreciated. Though Pickfair may have been more remote than Mary would have liked, there were always plenty of servants around; the nocturnal rustlings of the animals and the howling of the coyotes did not disturb her. What appealed to her, what fulfilled an imperative need, was the spaciousness of the house, its large rooms with light streaming through big windows. The living room, with a huge fireplace at one end, was especially inviting. For many years Mary's living quarters had been dingy, partitioned cells in cheap rooming houses. Even after she reached stardom, home was a series of apart-

Just a rustic hunting lodge—until Douglas Fairbanks remodeled it and brought home his bride. Then it became known the world over as Pickfair, and an invitation to dinner—with a printed menu but no wine— was the certificate of social success. *Charles O. Lewis*

ments and hotel suites in New York, and in Hollywood rented houses shared with Charlotte and, off and on, Lottie, Jack, and Lottie's baby. Mary had observed, with astute poignancy, the efforts of theatrical people to make a home out of a furnished room by having a pet in it. Some lucky ones might have a small dog, but to most denizens of theatrical dumps the ultimate symbol of domesticity was a lonely canary.

Another element of a home, to Mary only a wistful memory, was a big family kitchen. From way back in her childhood, Mary could remember baking days, when the kitchen overflowed with the fragrance of bread, cookies, spices, and gingerbread. Now she had her kitchen, as big as any in her dreams.

Mary never learned to cook, but both she and Douglas satisfied their cravings for a pet. Doug's was, naturally, described as the biggest

To the queen of Pickfair, who remembered too well the small and dingy quarters in theatrical rooming houses, the large and sunny rooms were especially attractive. And the table was set for fifteen every night, just in case. *Charles O. Lewis*

German shepherd in the world; it weighed a hundred pounds and cost
$5,000. Mary's wire-haired terrier, Zorro, was far more expensive,
though in a different way. Over the years she paid out a fortune in
claims, for Zorro bit anything that moved—servants, hotel maids and
bellboys, delivery men, people on the street, and even policemen; he
bit two Parisian gendarmes in one day. He bit other dogs. One day the
hotel doorman in New York brought him back after a walk around the
block, and explained Zorro's limp as the result of being kicked by a
horse. Why had the horse kicked him? Zorro had bitten the horse.
Why had Zorro bitten the horse? There wasn't anything else to bite.
Mary often took Zorro to the studio, where he not only bit people but
left his mark everywhere. No one dared kick the beast for fear that
Mary might hear about it. The happiest day in the studio was when
Zorro went up to a spider, an electrical receptacle into which a dozen
lights can be plugged, lifted his leg, and sprinkled it. The shock
knocked him across the room.

The Fairbankses also had horses, kept in a stable down the hill. They
could ride down to the bridle path on Sunset Boulevard or, more to
their liking, range over that vast, unpopulated expanse of mountains
behind them, looking west toward the sea, north over the desert that
was the San Fernando Valley, or south over the bean fields of Beverly
Hills. They had a private swimming pool, not only one of the first but
one of the largest, 175 by 200 feet, complete with a sand beach. For
a time they had a series of small ponds for canoeing, a rare sport in the
Santa Monica mountains. On Sundays they would stroll through the
vegetable garden, watching the plants grow, occasionally stooping to
pluck out an audacious weed, and discussing what should be planted
where.

In 1919, the year Doug transformed the hunting lodge into Pickfair,
building construction in Beverly Hills totaled $304,000; the next year
the figure reached almost $2 million as Beverly Hills, population 672
including the two new residents, began to grow.

The influence of Mr. and Mrs. Fairbanks reached far beyond Beverly
Hills. The only nearby town, a couple of miles to the east by motor
under the feathery leaves of the pepper trees lining Sunset Boulevard
or by trolley up the middle of Santa Monica Boulevard, was Hollywood.
The name was not yet synonymous with the cinema; the entire Los
Angeles area was still in competition with New York in film production.

The growing film industry, however, now employing thousands of people and generating millions of dollars, was bringing about major changes in Hollywood. It was no longer just another nice town blessed with warm sunshiny days and cool starlit nights, summer and winter. The population was approaching 70,000, and although its twenty-one churches outnumbered motion picture studios three to one, the influence was shifting. Aside from the weekly dance at the Hollywood Hotel there was no nightlife; music at eating places was prohibited by law and the town's two restaurants closed at nine. The Alexandria and Ambassador Hotels in Los Angeles provided the only other public functions in the area at their weekly dances.

Any organized social activity in the area excluded members of the motion picture colony, for there was still a prejudice against picture people which was not entirely unwarranted. Many were uneducated and uncultured, especially the comedians, who were the roughest and the raunchiest of the lot. The parties of Mack Sennett, the former boilermaker's helper who headed the Keystone Studio, were well known for the proliferation of alcohol and sex. As the area attracted motion picture hopefuls, so did it attract reporters to supply the moviegoers of the world the latest information and innuendo on the stars through syndicated articles and the mushrooming fan magazines.

In such a milieu misdemeanors became hot news and crimes became spectacles. The murder of William Desmond Taylor provided headlines for months, as new items about his background, and the intimate involvement of not one but two movie stars, Mary Miles Minter and Mabel Normand, came to light. Fatty Arbuckle, a popular comedian, was involved in the death of a young movie aspirant during a drunken weekend in San Francisco. Reports were printed that Arbuckle, who weighed close to 400 pounds, had raped the girl, torn her internal organs, staunched the flow of blood with a pop bottle, and then gone off and left her to die. Others held that Arbuckle was a great guy, the girl a tramp, and the death due to natural causes. After three trials with predictable headlines Arbuckle was acquitted, but so great was the feeling against him across the nation that citizen groups protested the showing of his pictures and audiences pelted the screen with vegetables. Theater owners got the message, and Arbuckle, whose guilt was still vehemently charged by some, his innocence vehemently defended by others, was through.

Another scandal was the death of Wallace Reid, one of the stars of
The Birth of a Nation, through causes related to drug addiction. These
and other affairs, actual or purported—the Pickford-Fairbanks divorce
and remarriage could be included—eventually led to the appointment
of a former postmaster general, Will H. Hays, as censor of the industry,
and to production rules that prohibited even a shot of a man and wife
in bed together.

Enough happened in the early twenties, in short, to provide adequate
ammunition for those who maintained that Hollywood was the Sodom
and Gomorrah, to say nothing of Babylon, of the world. Paradoxically,
it was during this same period that the film colony, now generically
termed Hollywood, reached a degree of acceptance and dignity. The
major catalyst was its ruling family, the king and queen of the cinema,
Douglas Fairbanks and Mary Pickford.

Just as knights and ladies had come to Camelot, so luminaries of the
world came to Pickfair. They represented an unusual grab bag—European nobility, even royalty, American millionaires, sporting figures.
What this strange assortment had in common was the Fairbankses,
Doug and Mary. It was Doug, of course, who collected them, but it
was Mary who maintained the smooth-running stability of Pickfair.
Even when in danger of being overwhelmed, she was able to keep her
perspective and her sense of humor along with a touch of awe. Once,
when playing tennis on the Pickfair court, a lady guest fell and needed
to wash off. Mary took her upstairs to her bathroom and sat outside the
door listening to the splashing inside. "Here I am, Gladys Smith of
Toronto," she told herself, "and there in my bathtub is the Queen of
Siam."

From England came Lord and Lady Mountbatten, the duke and
duchess of Sutherland, the earl and countess of Lanesborough. They
left their aloofness at home. The Mountbattens posed for a gag picture
pushing a lawnmower; King George V saw a copy and censured the
young couple severely. And the countess of Lanesborough made such
a pest of herself at the studio that Raoul Walsh promised to take her
out and drown her, leading to the inevitable phone call from a practical
joker saying he was a police officer with a drowned lady and a suspect
named Raoul Walsh. One weekend the duke of York, an officer in His
Majesty's Navy and the future King George VI, put in with his ship
and had a ball crashing through prop windows like a stuntman and

delightedly licking the resulting shards, for in Hollywood such windows are paned with fragile sheets of sugar. From Spain came the duke and duchess of Alba—and a retinue of seventeen. Fortunately, Charlie Chaplin, across the road, had some extra room.

American millionaires dropped in, too, including the best known of them all, Henry Ford, with his wife, Clara. One evening when it was time to go, Mary and Clara could not find their husbands. Outside, they heard voices. Fairbanks and Ford were up on the roof.

"Oh, Douglas!" said Mary, as she did when exasperated.

"It's all right, Mary," Doug called down. "I tested the handholds twice."

One evening at dinner, Albert Einstein grabbed a plate, knife, and fork and pushed them around the table in a show-and-tell demonstation

Doug attracted all celebrities, but sports stars were his favorites. When someone like Babe Ruth showed up, everybody got in the act—and the picture. *Charles O. Lewis*

of the theory of relativity. Only the cerebral degree was unusual, for Fairbanks customarily demanded that his guests describe or discuss some phase of their expertise. (Einstein had followed an exponent of extrasensory perception.) He would also assign a guest a role—labor leader, economist, manufacturer of some specific item, athlete—and demand a five-minute talk pertaining to the assigned sphere of operations. This erudite parlor game was taken seriously, with speaker and listeners concentrating intently, hoping to gain the approval of the master of Pickfair.

Doug balanced his intellectual stimulation with wild practical jokes. He would feign rage with his Japanese valet, then grab him by the heels and swing him around his head. (The valet was a former acrobat who saved his generous salary and returned to Japan to become a motion

Doug could have been a champion in almost any sport. Here he is, in his late thirties, competing with the champion hurdler, Charley Paddock, and a fellow with his own style, Charlie Chaplin. *Charles O. Lewis*

picture producer.) At the dinner table the most proper countess might find herself trying to eat with a flexible fork or sipping out of a dribble glass. An occasional squeal would reveal that the dinner-jacketed host had crawled under the table to bite, yes, *bite,* a shapely ankle. Miss Pickford, the hostess, seated as always at the head of the table, would give, as always, the expected reaction—"Oh, Douglas!"—with a mixture of exasperation, tolerance, and love. And perhaps a touch of envy, too, for Mary, though gracious and queenly in her role of mistress of Pickfair, had not had Doug's exposure to the haut monde and was still insecure.

The table at Pickfair was set for fifteen every night, ready for whomever Doug might bring home on the spur of the moment, from Jack Dempsey to Mitchell Leisen, a sensitive homosexual art director. His guests were usually men; Mary was often the only woman at the table.

After dinner everyone would file into the long, comfortable living room to participate in what was to become a Hollywood ritual: watching an unreleased movie. The screen was set up at one end, guests took their places in comfortable couches and chairs along the sides of the room, and the servants came in to sit at the far end. Chocolates were passed out to the ladies, cigars to the gentlemen. On less formal evenings Doug and Mary might indulge in their favorite confiture, peanut brittle. When the lights came on at the end of the film Doug would awaken from a sound sleep and proclaim, "Best damned movie I ever saw!"

By this time it would be ten o'clock, and the party was over, for Doug and Mary liked to get up at six in the morning. The guests who were leaving departed immediately, while Mary herself took hot water bottles to the beds of those who were staying. Guests retired early, cold-sober, and either with their spouses or alone. Doug slept on an open-air porch and believed in fresh air for everyone else as well, even though in the mountains it was chilly at night. Hanky-panky was frowned on at Pickfair, for with their relationship now properly established Doug and Mary had reverted to their true natures as out-and-out prudes. Charlie Chaplin, their closest friend, was always welcome, but when an internationally famed courtesan, Peggy Hopkins Joyce, who had had a sizzling affair with Chaplin, came to call, Mary sent word that she was not at home.

Chaplin also was known to include young girls among his paramours

If you can't lick 'em—invent another game. Fairbanks could never defeat Bill Tilden, the greatest player of his time, at his own game, tennis, so he invented "Dougledyas," usually called simply "Doug." *Quigley Collection, Georgetown University*

—his first two wives were each sixteen and pregnant at the time of their weddings—and the four Fairbanks nieces later realized that they had never been permitted to be alone with him. As for alcohol, though some visitors recall watery cocktails in later years, during the early twenties no alcoholic beverages at all were served. "We'd go there all dressed up," recalled Miriam Cooper, a frequent visitor at Pickfair, "and sit down at this huge table with the lovely china and servants falling all over themselves serving you, and not even get one lousy drop of wine."

The king and queen rarely went out, and when they did it was a grand occasion. Hosts lucky enough to get them willingly acceded, at the cost of great confusion in the seating arrangements, to their insistence on sitting together at dinner. Other ruling families, many of them transformed almost overnight from $50-a-week players and assistants to stars and directors with six-figure incomes, attempted to emulate the dignity and decorum of Pickfair.

With the increasing number of picture people who could be depended upon to comport themselves with reasonable sobriety, and the growth in importance of the industry, program committees began including film representatives in all major functions. Civic and industry leaders remarked on the good grace with which the Fairbankses accepted these commitments; actually, to these narcissistic refugees from the theater, a live performance was irresistible. Their advisers and assistants screened out the smaller parochial functions, but at the major dedications and cornerstone layings and banquets for visiting celebrities Doug and Mary represented the motion picture industry, just beginning to take itself seriously, with a proper sense of protocol. In many areas they were more than figureheads. They were leaders in the successful effort to keep Beverly Hills an independent community, campaigning from door to door. They were foremost in the organization of the Academy of Motion Picture Arts and Sciences, and Doug was its first president. Though Mary did not seek out the limelight to the same extent, she certainly encouraged him, standing by his side, looking up at him with sparkling eyes in time-honored fashion.

As do all outgoing people of accomplishment, the Fairbankses, together and separately, received some criticism. Mary, shy and reserved in contrast to her extroverted husband, appeared stiff and stuck-up to some. It was said of Doug that he made his annual trips abroad merely to line up titled guests for the following year. Frances Marion, loyal friend of Mary, thought that Fairbanks was both a snob and a hypocrite. "He'd kowtow to a duke and a duchess," Frances said. "When some nice ordinary people like you and me were expected he'd say, 'Why are those people coming?' and turn up his nose. But then they'd arrive and he'd swagger up, shoulders back, and put on his act."

In fairness to Doug, he may well have wished for some privacy on occasion, but once visitors, ordinary or extraordinary, came along, giving them a hearty welcome was the natural thing for him to do. As for being a snob, he was certainly impressed with dukes and earls, but he was also impressed with anybody who was successful at anything. His favorite heroes were the stars of the sporting world. Whenever a champion showed up, work was through for the day. Adolph Zukor went to see Fairbanks at his studio one afternoon, where he learned that he had already gone home. At Pickfair Zukor was directed to the swimming pool. At first he thought nobody was there—until, one after another, three heads popped up. Doug and two baseball stars, Babe Ruth and Walter Johnson, had been having a contest to see who could stay underwater longest. Even Zukor could understand Doug's adolescent delight at being host to the Sultan of Swat, the homerun king of America's national pastime. Out of the pool, Doug threw the Babe a couple of balls and, Zukor noted, watched eagerly as one took off from his bat in the direction of the upstairs windows at Pickfair. Unfortunately, it hit the side of the house and Doug could not point with pride to a window broken by Babe Ruth.

He threw passes with the Southern California football team and sparred with boxing champions from Jack Dempsey down. He loved to pose with Dempsey on his shoulders. Bill Tilden, one of the greatest tennis players of all time, was a frequent visitor to the Pickfair tennis court. Fairbanks couldn't win from Tilden at tennis, but he could beat the taller, slower champion at his own game, a souped-up form of badminton known in Hollywood as "Doug." The game required both agility and guts, for a player could block the heavy taped-up shuttlecock with his body, then hit it back before it touched the ground. Raoul Walsh broke his nose playing "Doug."

Pickfair also sported a cinder track, where Doug worked out and raced visiting Olympic champions. One of his favorite tricks was to let a guest handle a sixteen-pound shot, then adroitly switch a rubber ball for it and toss it at him.

"This is a happy house," Mary said one day in 1923. "This is a house that has never heard a cross word." She went on to give much of the credit to Doug. He was many-sided: with men he was a man, able to get along equally well with cowpunchers, athletes, and men of culture; with women he was always thoughtful and considerate. This was all true, but it was not a studied effort. Doug's real attribute was that he liked people and wanted to be liked in return. During these golden years he was successful in both.

"You wouldn't believe some of the people he put up with," said Paul D. O'Brien, who succeeded his father, Cap O'Brien, as Doug's attorney. "He even liked John Barrymore! That man was so vulgar and vicious that even his makeup man would walk away from him, but Doug thought he was great."

Doug was tolerant of other people's shortcomings and he was generous with everyone. One Sunday he drove his brother Robert and his wife Lorie to Laurel Canyon to visit some friends. No one was home, but Doug pushed open the door and led them through the new, beautifully furnished home. "It's just what I'd like to have someday," Lorie said, which was just what Doug had been waiting for. "Then why don't you move in?" he asked. "It's yours!"

Doug loved to take his four nieces, John's daughters Mary Margaret and Flobelle, Robert's Letitia and Lucille, on shopping sprees, buying toys, dolls, expensive clothes. He bought himself the finest of garments,

"Dougledyas" enjoyed such a vogue that to play it with him was an honor, to be *photographed* playing it with him a supreme accolade. Miriam Cooper, wife of Raoul Walsh, far left, saved this battered clipping for a half century. *Quigley Collection, Georgetown University*

too. At one time he had thirty-five overcoats, mostly camel's hair—he loved overcoats; seventy dress suits, most of them gray flannel, conservatively cut; ten dozen shirts, thirty-seven hats, one of which he wore most of the time, fifty pairs of dress shoes and fifteen pairs of sneakers, all alike. He had dozens of yellow pajamas, made for him in China of heavy silk. Mary and his friends knew how much he loved to receive presents, and gave him merry Christmases and happy birthdays. Christmas was a close family occasion; birthdays were bazaars. One year his presents included a gold cigarette case, a painting by Frederic Remington, a specially built Victrola, and, pièce de résistance, a .45 automatic purported to have killed twenty enemy soldiers. Another year Mary gave him a new swimming pool, oyster-shaped with a sand beach; for another she had the entire bar of an Old West saloon in a Nevada ghost town shipped in and installed.

His presents to her were less spectacular, not because of a lack of thoughtfulness, but because that wasn't what she wanted. As it was, she found her tastes changing from the simple, tasteful styles she had favored as America's Sweetheart to the equally tasteful but more expensive wardrobe befitting Mrs. Fairbanks, first lady of Hollywood. One day Adela Rogers St. John, a well-known journalist, was in Mary's boudoir as her maid was laying out Mary's gown for the evening. "It was an exquisite thing of shell-pink chiffon, the skirt made in a thousand dainty petals. Beside it lay a coat of the same color in a rich satin with a little fox collar."

Mary's maid, Madame Bodamère, an Alsatian who was with her for years, agreed that the ensemble was lovely. "Myself, I like her best in the little girl things. But she does not like to dress like Mary Pickford anymore. She likes to dress like Mrs. Fairbanks."

Mrs. Fairbanks guarded her position and image, and Doug's as well. Doug could play with his cronies, get sweaty and disheveled, and satisfy his curiosity about whatever strange event titillated him—but only up to a point. Once he proposed to a group on the beach, all sandy and smeared with sunburn lotion, that they take a peek at a dance marathon on the pier. Mary, who had just appeared, impeccable in a white sports outfit, said sweetly, "Douglas, love, you know we can't be seen in such a place."

She realized that her husband was an unusual individual, endowed with special attributes, and she was glad she had him. Decades after their period of greatest happiness she referred to him as "companion, teacher, helpmeet and guide." She could have said "father" too, for in this strong, exciting, generous man, ten years her senior, she found the reincarnation of the father who had rejected her so painfully. She also realized that he was an overwhelming man, for she established her own center of operations in a bungalow constructed to her design at the studio. One of its features was a table seating fourteen, where each day she entertained her own executives and production staff at luncheon.

Doug had his own coterie on call at the studio, too. They were more than yes-men, for some were rather independent and each made a bona fide contribution, but they were nevertheless held together by the Fairbanks payroll as well as the Fairbanks personality. Many years later another theatrical figure, Josh Logan, would discover through therapy the emotions of a man who has lost a father at an early age and describe them: he subconsciously expects every male associate to be the understanding, indulgent, permissive parent he believes his father would have been. These associates can hardly know they're expected to be someone's father, much less play the role, and the father-seeker, who doesn't know what's going on in his subconscious either, may well feel rejected by some perfectly normal action, and crack up. Fairbanks, by contrast, was for many years surrounded by a group of capable and talented men who liked him and liked to work and play with him. They laughed at his jokes and indulged his mischief. Doug had a dozen fathers.

During the twenties, as the silent film reached its most glorious apex and Hollywood became the entertainment capital of the world, Doug and Mary were rulers of their own separate operations, and shared in a third, Pickfair. They were happy people in a happy home. Under these fruitful conditions they carried on the work that made it all possible, their labor of love, motion pictures.

At Work

They had both returned from their honeymoon supercharged by their reception. Mary was especially eager to get back to work. She had spent several days in Italy discussing a story with Frances Marion

In another of her frequent attempts to get away from her "Little Mary" roles, Mary played the unlikely part of a Spanish gypsy. *Rosita* was not a successful film. *George Eastman House*

(neither considered it an unusual way to spend a honeymoon), a new project which had a special appeal for Mary. The whole world now knew she was twenty-six years old and married, and she now thought of herself as a sophisticated traveler, a citizen of the world. She would play a fitting role, a mature woman caught in the tragedy of the Great War. At the first press reception for Doug and Mary on their return to New York, Doug talked about their travels in Europe, but Mary announced her plans for *The Love Light,* to be written and directed by Frances Marion.

Frances was neither the first nor the last woman to direct a major film, and she acquitted herself well in *The Love Light,* with one qualification: she devoted more attention to the leading man in the film than to the star, Mary Pickford. Perhaps the unbalanced attention was necessary, for the young man in question, Fred Thomson, who would later be a cowboy star, was making the unusual transition from army chaplain to film actor. And he also happened to be Frances's new husband.

Actually the film was not a box-office disappointment, but neither was it the huge success Mary had hoped for. Perhaps audiences were tired of the war, or perhaps they simply wanted Little Mary to stay Little Mary.

For her next film Mary turned from her friend to her brother, who needed her badly. For all his wildness, Jack Pickford was an appealing actor in Tom Sawyer–like roles. Eddie Sutherland, a director who enjoyed the good things of life himself, looked back on Pickford's excesses with tolerance. "What do you expect from a guy with the biggest thirst and the biggest joint in town?" Eddie asked. "Join a monastery?"

Jack's marriage to the beautiful Olive Thomas of the Ziegfeld Follies was a stormy one, and the two tried to patch it up on a second honeymoon to Paris. Owen Moore, another hard drinker, was along, and there were rumors of cocaine. At their hotel after a round of cafes one night, Olive, according to Jack, took some bichloride of mercury tablets by mistake. She died in agony. Ugly rumors were whispered on both sides of the Atlantic; one was that she had committed suicide because Jack had given her syphilis, another that he had poisoned her for her various infidelities. No charges were made, however, and he brought his lovely young wife home and buried her. Mary came to his rescue and put him to work, at the age of twenty-three, as assistant director on a pleasant little comedy in which Mary plays a Belgian refugee.

While Mary was groping for a new direction in her career, Doug found his in a story in a pulp magazine, *All-Story Weekly*. Mary wrote later that she had taken the magazine to Europe, awaiting the propitious moment to give it to him. Robert Fairbanks's daughter Letitia said that it was her father who put the magazine in his hand. Richard Talmadge, Doug's stunt man at that time, years later said with a chuckle that the responsible party was really a semi-literate cowboy buddy of Doug's named Charlie Stevens. "Who else would have read it in the first place?"

However "The Curse of Capistrano" by Johnston McCulley got into Doug's hands, it happened at the right moment. No one had known how to tell Doug that exhibitors were beginning to complain about his films. John Fairbanks presented the opportunity in a letter to Cap O'Brien dated April 24, 1920, protesting that Hiram Abrams, general manager of United Artists, was giving Mary's pictures better booking than Doug's. O'Brien conferred with Abrams and replied in a long letter, dated May 7. After outlining the complicated deals with which pictures were booked—guarantees, percentages, conditions for holding them over—he got to the meat of the matter: Doug's pictures were too much alike. "Besides, the exhibitors have been complaining because you have failed to develop sufficient love interest in your pictures. . . . Women do not care to see your pictures because, as they believe, of a lack of love interest in them and a development of those qualities that attract the men, and of course, men do not go to the matinees so the afternoon business is not as big as it should be." O'Brien recommended getting away from "the type of picture you have been making. . . . do something with real dramatic values in it which you can do better than any male star in the business."

This was the information that Doug secretly carried with him as he started out on his honeymoon with Mary, assuring her that everything was going to be all right. Whether it was the dainty fingers of America's Sweetheart or the calloused paw of a bronco buster that tendered "The Curse of Capistrano," it was a desperate hand that received it. Fairbanks would probably not have gotten past the first few paragraphs otherwise, for the story was laid in the early nineteenth century, when

California was part of Mexico and men wore Spanish-style costumes and ladies wore lace mantillas and swooned. It was a common belief in the motion picture industry at that time that costume pieces played to empty theaters, and Fairbanks thought he was taking an awful chance when he decided to make one himself. Indeed, he turned it out quickly and inexpensively, and as soon as it was finished began shooting a conventional comedy.

Out of "The Curse of Capistrano" emerged that masked swordsman who came to the rescue of the weak, the innocent, and the beautiful, and who, by carving with his sharp sword his initial Z on the cheeks, face, or rump of evil men, left—*The Mark of Zorro!* The film was an immediate hit. Opening at the Capital in New York, the world's largest theater, it broke all records: 19,547 patrons paid $11,708 to see *Zorro*, the largest amount ever taken in on a single day. Police, called out to control the crowds, closed the theater after the nine o'clock show so they could shoo the people away.

In some respects Fairbanks plays his familiar character, but instead of changing from the usual unlikely hero as the story develops, he is Zorro from the beginning, playing the dual role with mask and sword. And instead of the boy next door in peaceful America, Doug is Don Diego Vega in the colorful, corrupt, colonial California of the early 1800s. Instead of just decking a few bad guys with his fists, he fights and kills with a sword. Instead of an appealing young fellow in a comedic boy-girl plot, he is, as the masked Zorro, a sizzling lover with a beautiful heroine, Marguerite de la Motte, with whom the matinee ladies could identify. True, in the truncated final love scene, Fairbanks, unmasked, holds her as though she had halitosis, but that's all right, too—Zorro is fine for a fantasy but you wouldn't want to live with him.

The Mark of Zorro marks two transitions, one in Douglas Fairbanks, one in the movie audiences of the world. It was in *Zorro*, his thirtieth film, that Doug first came on strong as the phallic symbol to which present-day students of the silent screen liken him. Part of this new sexiness is due to his use of that other phallic symbol, the sword. As he drives that magnificent body so powerfully but gracefully into rooms, over chairs and tables, and onto horses, he is also forcefully thrusting, successfully penetrating, with that sword of steel. There is more to this new Fairbanks than a mask and a sword. A marked emanation, different from that of the immediately preceding films, comes off the screen. As many critics have remarked, Fairbanks never played anybody but Fairbanks; the difference between this Fairbanks and the earlier ones was his own fulfillment as a lover. This Fairbanks had Mary.

The success of *Zorro* reflects the postwar world's search for escapism, not just by going to the movies, but by getting out of its own time altogether. Winning the war had brought peace but not contentment; the people of the United States were so disillusioned that they were turning back toward isolationism, refusing to join the League of Nations. Fears of Reds and hatred of blacks erupted in repression and violence. Wartime profiteering and increased labor strife were factors in diminishing that strange affection of the common people for the wealthy, and the war itself proved that American boys could get killed and wounded like everybody else; as a result, there were fewer heroes, fewer hero worshippers. For these and other social and economic reasons, people were eager to escape their real and current problems. A theater showing a film about far-off times and places provided just what they wanted.

Economic conditions in the very world they were escaping made it easier. The gross national product and national income were to increase 50 percent and $10 billion, respectively, during the decade. The number of automobiles almost quadrupled, and rural roads began filling in the spaces between the existing railways. Small-town theater owners began remarking that the number of people coming to a run of a show was more than the population of the town.

Theater owners accommodated their patrons by building pleasure domes beyond imagination. Across the country motion picture palaces of exotic design were built to hold a thousand, three thousand, six thousand people. The Roxy in New York held 6,272, to be exact. For twenty-five cents anyone could be treated like royalty by courteous young men in resplendent uniforms, walk on the finest of carpets amid elaborate fountains and statuary and paintings, sit in plush and ample seats in an atmosphere that was warm in winter and cool in summer, and go to a bathroom that smelled good. In the big cities audiences not only saw movies, comedies, short subjects, newsreels, and previews of coming attractions on the screen, but were entertained by monstrous pipe organs, huge orchestras, and singers presented as soloists, duets, trios, quartets, men's choruses, and women's choruses. At the Rialto in

New York, squads of ushers, wearing scarlet tunics piped in gold with gold and silver tassels looped across the front, changed the guard in ultra-military precision; at the Egyptian in Hollywood, a bearded Bedouin wearing a striped robe and carrying a spear strode across the parapet before each performance.

As the twenties began, the Federal Trade Commission estimated that there were 18,000 theaters in the United States devoted to motion pictures, attended by 20 million people a day paying some $4 million every twenty-four hours. Thus the annual gross approached a billion and a half dollars—about the same amount the American people had loaned their government at interest in the first year of the war. Though much of this income stayed in the hands of the theater owners, the remainder enabled and inspired the producing companies to make better movies which in turn enticed more of the affluent and the sophisticated to the motion picture temples.

These multimillion-dollar figures would not have seemed excessive to anyone caught in the Times Square area of New York on two evenings in the early fall of 1921, when Douglas Fairbanks's *The Three Musketeers* and Mary Pickford's *Little Lord Fauntleroy* opened within a few days of each other. Doug's film was first, and crowds began gathering early, knowing that Doug himself would be at the Lyric Theatre along with his wife, Mary Pickford, and his friends, Charlie Chaplin and Jack Dempsey. By showtime Forty-second Street was so jammed that people holding tickets had to have police escorts to get through. Doug lifted Mary to his shoulders and, as police pushed and shoved, hands reached up, and voices roared, bore her, flushed and pretty, through the crush to the theater. Inside, the picture couldn't begin until Doug had made a little speech and introduced his wife and friends. Mary smiled and waved, Chaplin did a quick little jig, and Dempsey raised his fist and scowled.

The Three Musketeers, laid in the court of King Louis XIII in the early seventeenth century, gave Doug the opportunity to wear plumed hats, flowing sleeves, a long curly wig—and his first mustache. The film reveals a giant step in the new Fairbanks trend, period spectacles. The scenario was adapted by the prestigious English playwright Edward Knoblock from the classic by Alexandre Dumas. The sets, representing d'Artagnan's rustic home in Gascony, the hovels of Paris, the splendor of Versailles, were beautifully done, at obviously great expense. Fairbanks himself, with just a touch of the appealing character of old in his gaucheries in the early part of the film and his trembling knees in his audience with the king, was more exciting than ever, agile and virile as he fought dozens of opponents with his sword and wooed the heroines with Delsartian gestures and his new mustache.

So superb was *The Three Musketeers* that no one in the audience would have dreamed of Doug's early difficulty in preparing himself for the role. Unlike Zorro, an aristocrat who fought for justice, d'Artagnan was a Gascon bully boy who fought, and killed, just for the hell of it. The romantic in Fairbanks rebelled at playing this newly discovered aspect of his boyhood hero; only after he worked in some relieving touches, justifying some of the carnage and giving d'Artagnan a bit more levity as he dealt out murder and mayhem, was Doug able to portray him.

The excitement of Doug's opening was repeated with the premiere of *Little Lord Fauntleroy,* Mary's best film since *Stella Maris.* Again she played a dual role; as Fairbanks had done in *Zorro,* she also went back to a bygone period of different customs with lavish costumes and stunning sets. Still seeking a way to grow up on the screen, this time she chose to play not her customary little girl, but a boy, the little lord, and also his mother, Dearest. The familiar story takes an American boy who has suddenly inherited an English title to the impressive halls of the huge ancestral castle. A mean old uncle exploits the humble peasants on the Fauntleroy estate, but the curly-headed little American boy, with Dearest's support in scenes reminiscent of D. W. Griffith's epics of social conscience, comes to their rescue and brings the story to a happy and teary finale.

Mary gives two of her most inspired performances in *Little Lord Fauntleroy.* She had never played a boy in films before, and in preparing for the role she was surprised to observe "the thousand and one little, intricate, difficult details of differences between a boy and a girl that I have figured out. . . . This boy part of Fauntleroy has been the most difficult I ever played." An obvious difference between boys and girls is the way they walk. "It's funny," Mary said, "but I got the walk watching Mr. Fairbanks's swagger in *The Three Musketeers.*"

Little Lord Fauntleroy was her longest film, ten reels, and playing both roles required her to be before the camera in nearly every scene; the film is also an indication of the drudgery to which Mary willingly subjected herself in her drive for excellence, her compulsion to work.

An unseen performance of almost equal brilliance and industry was given by Charles Rosher, one of the industry's greatest cameramen. Rosher had brought his talents to Mary three years before. An artist at painting with light, he used backlighting to brighten her darkening hair, a complex assortment of lights—spots, fills, gelations—to rejuvenate her complexion. After hours he went to the little laboratory of a struggling young man named Max Factor and perfected a compound especially designed for the Pickford skin; known as 7–R, it is still in use by makeup experts.

A careful study of Mary's face revealed that it was the left side which offered the beauty expected of America's Sweetheart; the right side, as he described it confidentially to associates, was "squinched." No matter who her director might be on a particular film, Rosher himself would position her so that the left side of her face, the good side, was nearest the camera. When he had no choice but to photograph the right side, he used severe backlighting as a distraction. Sometimes, too, Mary can be seen giving a quick, cute, coy look from her squinched-up side. Rosher, a haughty, disdainful Englishman, referred to Mary behind her back as Monkey Face, and she called him Lord Plushbottom. But while he was making cracks he was also making her beautiful, and while she was laughing at his conceit she was keeping him on salary the year around, with permission to shoot other films when she wasn't working.

In scenes in which the two Marys appear, Mary as Dearest wore ten-inch platform shoes concealed under her Victorian dresses in order to appear taller than her son. For the shot in which she makes an entrance down a flight of stairs, she twice lost her footing and fell. In some scenes not only does Mary appear with herself, but with other players as well; that is, Mary as the little lord is milling around with characters in one part of the frame; Mary as Dearest is with her group in the other half. This was done before the optical printer was developed to make the complex process easier; Rosher did it all within his camera. So demanding and meticulous was the process that Mary worked sixteen hours in the shot where Dearest and the little lord kiss. It takes three seconds on the screen.

Surely, now, with such elegant sophistication, with so appealing a character as Dearest, mother of that darling boy, behind her, Mary could forsake children's parts and play grownup roles. (Actually, it appeared later, audiences identified Mary with Lord Fauntleroy; that lady was somebody else.) Doug encouraged her in her wishful belief. "Dearest," he said, "is Mary as I know her—Mary with unvarying understanding, compassionate, vibrantly the woman." Nor was he flattering her, telling her what she wanted to hear. Doug was always supportive of Mary, not only because he loved her but because he recognized her talent. He had so little, he said, many times, and she had so much. Mary, in her own sincerity, praised Doug not so much for his acting ability as for his dynamism.

It was now two and a half years since they had organized United Artists in the spring of 1919. Doug had made six films for the new company, Mary five. These films were keeping UA alive, for Griffith and Chaplin, who had prior commitments, had contributed only three films and none, respectively.

While making these films and running their companies and joint studio, Doug and Mary had also taken a major part in United Artists operations. The company was set up so that the board of directors was composed of representatives of the four stockholders: Charlotte Pickford was empowered to speak for Mary, Cap O'Brien for Doug. Both took an active interest in major decisions as well as small details. Doug was especially interested in foreign expansion. A whole new market was opening up in South America. Prior to World War I American films had been shipped to Latin America through London, but now New York had replaced London, for films as well as other products, as the distributing center for points to the south as well as for Australia and Asia to the west. By coincidence the infant son whom Ella Fairbanks had left behind in Georgia now emerged as a forty-year-old named Norris Wilcox, with contacts in South America. He was sent there as United Artists' first South American representative.

The film market in the Old World was much more promising. American films represented more than 90 percent of those being shown in the 5000 theaters in the British Isles, as well as in the thousands of theaters scattered throughout Europe and Africa. A government-sponsored company in Germany was producing some unusual films, and the Soviet Union was considering film as an instrument of propaganda, but, in general, postwar recovery in Europe did not include the motion picture industry. United Artists organized Allied Artists Corporation, Limited, in the United Kingdom, and Les Artistes Associés for the continent. By the fall of 1921 money was pouring into the London and Paris headquarters from all over Europe.

It was impossible for Douglas Fairbanks to resist sticking his nose into his overseas affiliates—after all, he and Mary each had a 25 percent share in all that money coming in. For the first time in his peripatetic life he had bases in the form of offices all over the United Kingdom and Europe, with personnel eager to make arrangements and provide him with the coin of the realm. He and Mary had made three films in less than a year and he was itching to travel. This time, he told her enthusiastically, he would show her all they had missed in Europe, and North Africa as well. He leased a house in Paris until the following September; they would spend almost a year abroad. Although Mary felt that they both should remain in Hollywood and keep turning out films, she finally caught his enthusiasm. She would take Charlotte and Lottie for their first trip overseas. Lottie, for her own company, arranged to bring a friend named Teddy Sampson, a swinging young woman who had been fired by Griffith some years before after an escapade and was still going strong. By the time the party sailed from New York, following the opening of *The Three Musketeers* and *Little Lord Fauntleroy* in September 1921, the entourage, with relatives and friends and valets and maids and secretaries, required forty-three trunks.

With Paris as a base Doug and Mary opened new theaters and plugged their own films all over Western Europe. In England they saw all their old titled friends and made new ones. Though Mary was more cautious, Doug made the channel crossing by air—and the pilot let him hold the stick! In Spain Doug's old friend the duke of Alba arranged an audience with King Alfonso XIII. The king looked around, then leaned over and whispered in Doug's ear, "What is the real story on Fatty Arbuckle?"

In Germany they saw the interesting but strange films being made there. Doug took Charles Rosher through the studios in Berlin and Rosher stayed on for several months, showing the cameramen Hollywood techniques. Doug made plans for the North African trip; it was going to be a wonderful year.

It turned out to be a not-so-wonderful six weeks. Mary began losing weight; she didn't like Parisian food. Charlotte had gone home, and Mary missed her. Doing nothing was no fun for Mary; it was time to go home and go to work. Never mind that the lease had nine months to go, Mary wanted to spend Christmas at home, in Pickfair. And she did, with Doug.

New Challenges

One of the film magazines estimated in 1921 that Douglas Fairbanks and Mary Pickford each had an income of $19,230.77 a week. The figure may have been low, especially for Mary; each had been salting money away for years and although Doug had liquidated much of his holdings to make the settlement on Beth, Mary had a great deal of income property and bonds, all sagaciously administered by Charlotte. Doug also insisted on being the man of the house, which led to the somewhat bitter observation of one of his nieces: "Doug paid the bills, Mary bought corner lots."

Whatever their earnings, they had too much talent and potential to be idle. Their sudden return from Europe brought on an almost panicky eagerness to start working again—but what would they do?

If they played together, the vehicle would have to be truly colossal. They considered *When Knighthood Was in Flower* as such a showcase, but William Randolph Hearst bought it for Marion Davies. *Romeo and Juliet?* The author was acceptable, but neither wished to play in a tragedy. Plans for a double appearance were shelved. For his next film Doug chose what looked like the safest bet, a best-selling western with a respectable plot and an appealing hero, *The Virginian,* and paid $90,000 for the screen rights. In Doug's enthusiasm he managed to ignore a major part of the Virginian's appeal, the easy-going, lazy-drawl southern-gentleman characterization ("When you call me that, smile"). Thanks to Ella's fantasizing, Doug considered himself a Virginian at heart, but there was no way he could fit his energy and bounce into the character of *The Virginian.* Mary could see the incongruity of the role and commented on it.

"I can do it in slow motion," he said. "We'll shoot it fast, then slow it down."

"Oh, Douglas," Mary said, but that was the end of *The Virginian.* The company sold it at a profit, but he was right back where he started.

Edward Knoblock, knowing Doug's penchant for things English—

Doug considered himself an Englishman at heart, too—suggested *Ivanhoe,* and talk of *Ivanhoe* led to another English hero, Robin Hood. It was brought up when Doug was in a grumpy mood. "I don't want to play a flat-footed Englishman," he said. Fortunately the people Fairbanks had gathered around him were not afraid to argue, and they brought up all the romantic ingredients in *Robin Hood*—robbing from the rich and giving to the poor, the Merrie Men, the wicked sheriff and the evil king, Maid Marian. . . . Doug thought it over, discussed it with Mary, and called his staff together on New Year's Day, 1922. One of those present, Robert Florey, recalled the meeting later as a history-making event. Doug pounded the table with his fist as he announced his decision to make *Robin Hood.* It would be his biggest project, so tremendous that he intended to buy another studio, on Santa Monica Boulevard just west of Hollywood, where they could put up some really big sets, and use the empty fields surrounding it. Thousands of costumes designed from contemporary documents, shields, lances, and swords by the thousands, a tournament. . . .

"And how much is all that going to cost?" John Fairbanks asked.

"That's not the point," Doug answered. "These things have to be done properly, or not at all."

The announcement impressed not only the Fairbanks group but the entire industry. The studio had been idle for months; all Hollywood was hurting. The Arbuckle scandal had caused a panic not just in Hollywood but where it really counted, in New York, the financial center of the industry. Paramount Pictures stock had fallen from ninety to forty. Studios all over the area were closed down tight. Leading actors and directors were out of work; the lucky ones took salary cuts of up to 75 percent.

"It's hard to realize today what a shot in the arm Doug's decision to do *Robin Hood* was," Allan Dwan recalled. "I used to go over to Doug's studio to throw a football with him and Jack Dempsey, and when he said he was going to make *Robin Hood* my estimation of that guy went up a thousand percent—and it was already high. That took guts. I knew right then and there that I wanted to be a part of that operation. I agreed to work for five percent, which was unusual in those days, but I figured if I didn't make a nickel it would still be worth it."

The system by which banks financed film production had begun with the Pickford revolution and become more flexible with the organization

Allan Dwan, director of *Robin Hood*, recalled setting up this marvelous scene. Doug has taken off from a trampoline at left, and at right a landing net, covered with ivy, has been set off from the wall to soften his impact.
United Press International

Robin Hood—one of the greatest characterizations in one of the greatest films of all time. It is obvious that Doug starred in it, but how many know he financed it with his own money. *Wisconsin Center for Film and Theater Research*

of United Artists. The Fairbanks brothers, with Doug's track record of every film a moneymaker, foresaw no problem in financing *Robin Hood*. The new studio was purchased for $150,000; current city maps show it as the Goldwyn Studio at Santa Monica and Formosa. Doug had the capacity to attract the best people and get the best out of them. Famous names in film history who joined him included Wilfred Buckland, who designed the sets, Mitchell Leisen, who designed and supervised the production of costumes, and Arthur Edeson, the cameraman.

With 500 workmen, Robert Fairbanks and Dwan began building the castle. They spread out truckloads of large rocks on the ground, covered them with a netting of chicken wire and plaster, and made a mold. This was the veneer of the castle. As the castle walls reached higher and higher, they also constructed a moat, a massive drawbridge raised and lowered by a concealed gasoline engine, and cavernous interiors so huge they could be lit only by sunlight and reflectors, as in the early days of films. Meanwhile Leisen was running up the costumes. Armor, helmets, and visors were made of heavy canvas, chain mail was knitted there in the studio of coarse hemp, and all were covered with a stiff coat of silver paint.

While this work was going on, Doug was three thousand miles away,

"A-ha!" chortles Robin Hood as he dodges aside and the bad guy stops the arrow intended for the hero. Actually the arrow is stuck on with hooks. The man in the doorway is Chuck Lewis at the beginning of his lifelong friendship with Fairbanks. *Charles O. Lewis*

in New York with Mary. She was being sued by a woman who claimed to have been her agent, and Mary chose to fight rather than settle. She, Doug, Charlotte, and their retinue, including Zorro the wire-haired terror, settled in at their eleven-room suite with wood-burning fireplaces at the Ritz Carlton while her lawyers protected—with eventual success—her interests.

When Doug returned to California his smile vanished as he stared at the completed set of *Robin Hood* for the first time. Walls towered ninety feet over Santa Monica Boulevard. The interiors were immense. He would be lost in that pile of rocks. Dwan, seeing the horror-stricken look on his face, knew that something was wrong, but he didn't know the extent of it. Doug had failed to get financing, either in California or New York, and he was putting his own money, a million and a half dollars, into these very sets which he felt would detract from the only package he had to offer, his lightness, his agility, his grace. His fears were not imaginary for Charles Ray, a contemporary star of almost equal popularity, had also invested all he had in a gigantic set, a replica of Plymouth Rock for a movie called *The Courtship of Miles Standish*, and the film flopped. Ray wound up as a $7.50-a-day extra.

Dwan, a man of enthusiasm himself and proud of the sets, dragged Doug through the huge hall, up the vast spiral staircase, and stood with him at the top. "You're up here on the balcony," Dwan told him. "The sheriff's men pour in from the entrance on this side, then from the one on the other side. You're trapped. You start down the stairs—they're coming up." Dwan jumped up on the railing. "Now what do you think you do?"

"How do I know?" Fairbanks growled. "Fall on my ass, I suppose."

"Oh, no," Dwan answered. "You see those curtains?" He waved his hand toward the long dark draperies that fell the entire length of the stairway. "Watch." Fifty feet above the stone floor, Dwan threw himself off the railing, into the curtains. Instead of falling, he slid easily in a long curve to the bottom.

Doug's smile reappeared on his face, the sparkle of excitement came back to his eyes. "Hey, how'd you do that?" he asked.

Dwan pulled back the curtains to reveal what was in essence a large playground slide. He and Robert Fairbanks had worked it out; hitting a fold in the heavy canvas curtains at just the right spot funneled him into the slide. Doug, immaculately dressed in gray flannel suit and

Homburg, had to try the stunt himself. He leaped into the curtains and went whizzing down. Then, like a kid, he ran up the long stairway to do it again. He called in everybody to watch him do it several more times.

From that moment on Doug threw himself into the entire filming process with the same enthusiasm with which he had thrown himself into the canvas. There is certainly no indication in the film, and Dwan could recall no indication during all the conferences and discussions off camera, that Fairbanks was a man who stood to lose everything he had on *Robin Hood.*

"I did make sure of one thing," Dwan recalled. "In the scenes in Sherwood Forest I had those guys running around on their tippy toes. I told them I'd fire the first son of a bitch who let his heel touch the ground. There weren't gonna be any flat-footed Englishmen in that film."

The lightheartedness, the sheer exuberance that marks a Fairbanks film is demonstrated with particular effect in out-takes of *Robin Hood* —shots that were not included in the picture but were preserved for one reason or another. A series of takes shows Fairbanks jumping from a height of twelve or fifteen feet; he does it repeatedly until he lands perfectly, without teetering or grimacing. After each take a man steps in front of the camera with a clapper on which is written the number of the shot. The interesting thing is that this flunky is always laughing. In the out-takes of another film, Fairbanks is dueling with assorted villains on a sandy beach. Swords break, they slip and fall, all kinds of things go wrong, everybody breaks up laughing, and they repeatedly have to start all over again. Each time a man comes out with the clapper and a new take number, and he's always laughing. Each time another fellow comes out with a broom to sweep the footprints out of the virgin sand; he's laughing, too.

The action scenes in *Robin Hood* are by far the best of any Fairbanks picture to that time, not because Doug, at the age of thirty-nine, was stronger or more agile, but because the state of the art had improved. In one scene he makes a breathtaking leap across the moat, a distance of at least fifteen feet, to the vertical castle wall. It was a concealed trampoline that enabled him to make that distance so effortlessly, a landing net, secured some eighteen inches off the castle wall and camouflaged by ivy, which cushioned the impact and enabled him to climb so gracefully to the top. Any athletically inclined individual could have done these stunts, and indeed, Dwan recalled, some of the finest athletes in the area worked on the picture and they all tried everything. "They practically wore the slide out, and they were always sailing through the air off the trampoline," Dwan said. "We all hopped around on pogo sticks, too, come to think of it. But whatever it was, nobody did it as well as Doug, nobody had that grace, that fluid motion. Many have tried, but there has never been another one like him."

With all the grandeur of the actual sets, the castle was made to appear even loftier by the use of the now-forgotten art of the glass shot. The top of the castle and its towers is nothing more than a painting on a square of glass, done to exact scale and secured an exact distance in front of the camera lens so that it fits perfectly on the actual set in the finished film. In the opening scene, when the knights and ladies are seen cheering their heroes from two levels of the castle, in actuality there is but one level, photographed twice. On the first take a matte was placed over the top half of the lens to obscure the top half of the film; on the second take the matte protected the bottom half. Exposed together, there's a double deck of people. "I had the women be careful not to let anything drop," Dwan recalled. "If they had, it would have disappeared."

When viewed more than fifty years later, *Robin Hood* may have some draggy spots and some scenery-chewing performances; in 1922, before sound and color, presented in a three-hour show with intermission and a large orchestra playing the original score, it must have been sensational. The Academy had not been organized, and there was consequently no official best picture of the year, but it is nevertheless one of the best films of all time, a tribute to all the people who worked on it and especially to the man who made it possible through his leadership and his bankroll. He received his reward in both critical acclaim and money. Robert E. Sherwood wrote in the *New York Herald:* "It represents the highwater mark of film production—the farthest step that the silent drama has ever taken along the high road to art." *Robin Hood* netted Doug more than a million dollars.

Mary was not enjoying the same degree of personal satisfaction. Unsure of what to do, she returned to the security of a role she had played before, *Tess of the Storm Country*. She had misgivings even before the shooting began. Seven years before the film had cost a grand total of $10,000 to make; now Paramount charged her $50,000 for the story alone, a story she herself had made valuable. For the first version she and the company had simply gone to the Japanese fishing village in Santa Monica and started shooting; now it was necessary to build a village from the ground up at the Chatsworth Reservoir, a good thirty miles away from Hollywood across the Santa Monica mountains. While Doug was blazing his trail to new glories in the fantastic Robin Hood sets on Santa Monica Boulevard, Mary was trying to whip up enthusiasm for a $400,000 remake in the hovels on the lake. The second *Tess* was a good film, opened to a good crowd, and got good reviews. But it followed by just one week the smashing premiere of *Robin Hood,* which attracted such crowds that a special performance had to be given at midnight to get the people off the streets.

Only the Fairbanks influence could have inspired Mary's next venture. Doug was being praised for his boldness and daring, and he was one of the first American filmmakers to enthuse over the new German techniques. It was in this context that Mary took a bold step: she arranged to import Ernst Lubitsch, an outstanding young German who had directed two heavy historical dramas, to make her next film. Mary realized just how daring this was, less than three years after the Armistice and long before American audiences had ever heard of German films, when, with Lubitsch actually New York–bound, she was at an American Legion function and heard a diatribe against a German singer being brought to America. She contacted Albert H. T. Banzhaf, an executive in the United Artists office in New York, and asked him to meet Lubitsch's boat and get him off without fanfare. Banzhaf went far beyond the call of duty. He took one look at Lubitsch's brand-new gold tooth, yellow shoes, and peg-bottom pants and, giving Miss Pickford as his authority, proceeded to remake the man. When Lubitsch arrived in Hollywood he had neither his prized gold tooth nor much love for Miss Pickford.

Like most Hollywood legends, the versions of the impending conflict differ. Lubitsch apparently thought he was coming to America to direct Mary in *Faust;* she recalled the agreed-upon vehicle as *Dorothy Vernon of Haddon Hall.* It seems more likely that Mary, in her search for a blockbuster, had considered doing the German classic, then changed her mind. In discussing the project with Mary and Charlotte, Lubitsch said something about the scene in which Mary "stringles duh bebby."

"What?" Charlotte shouted. Lubitsch explained that, as Marguerite, Mary would have an illegitimate child and strangle it. *"She will not,"* Charlotte said, and there went *Faust.*

Dorothy Vernon of Haddon Hall was a historical novel with a complicated plot involving Queen Elizabeth, Mary Queen of Scots, the heroine Dorothy Vernon, a hero, and an imposter. It would be filled with intrigue and dueling in the great halls of a huge stone castle, all very reminiscent of *Robin Hood.* Mary delegated Edward Knoblock, who spoke German, to soothe Lubitsch, but one day after she had given him a German translation of the script she looked out of the window of her bungalow to see Lubitsch come panting across the fields on his short legs. "Oh, oh," she told Charlotte, "here comes trouble."

Mary remembered the occasion well. She had recently painted her study dove gray, and as Lubitsch shouted and paced the floor he left greasy fingerprints on the wainscoting ("He ate German-fried potatoes three times a day"). He flatly refused to do *Dorothy Vernon.* "Der iss too many qveens and not enough qveens," he said. Translation: Queens Elizabeth and Mary were too much, Dorothy not enough. The film Mary and Lubitsch finally made together was *Rosita,* a farce in which Mary plays a brunette Spanish gypsy.

The shooting was chaotic; they were either screaming with rage or screaming with laughter. The laughter began when Lubitsch, told he could take a phone call on the studio extension, said, "You mean I can have copulation here?" Angry with the entire cast one day, he gave them all a withering look. "Oh, how do you do!" he said furiously and stormed out. Another day, after Mary had pleaded with the cast not to laugh at him, they were shooting a scene in which her sweetheart, played by George Walsh, was shot and she threw herself on him, calling his name and pleading with him to answer her. "Anschver me, anschver me," prompted Lubitsch.

"Answer me, answer me," Mary said.

"No, pliss, anschver me, anschver me," Lubitsch insisted. Walsh, lying on his back, Mary's head on his chest, controlled his facial expression, but his stomach started bouncing up and down, taking Mary's head with it. "George! I'll kill you," Mary whispered, but she started giggling, too.

"Vat iss to laugh?" Lubitsch demanded.

"Nothing," Mary said. "I'm sorry."

Mary followed *Robin Hood* with a costume piece of her own, *Dorothy Vernon of Haddon Hall*. This picture, accenting the wrong side of her face, is *not* by Charles Rosher. *George Eastman House*

The next take began. "Anschver me, anschver me," Mary cried, and everybody on the set broke up.

As for the screams of rage, the entire film was shot in conflict. Lubitsch wanted to control the lighting, but Rosher was not about to let anybody else light his Monkey Face. Lubitsch wanted to end the film with a scene of tragic realism; Mary knew better. She took him aside and told him, privately and pointedly, that while he was the director, she was the producer, and he would shoot the scene her way. "I'm the court of last resort," she said. She wrote later that he tore all the buttons off his clothes in his fury, but he shot the scene her way.

Rosita got mixed reviews; some of the critics were unwilling to accept Mary as a brunette dancing girl. Lubitsch went on to become a most successful director of witty, sophisticated films. Some of his admirers sneered at Mary's effrontery in engaging him: "He was brought to this country in 1924 and, with characteristic Hollywood intelligence, put to work directing Mary Pickford ('America's Sweetheart') in *Rosita,*" wrote the erudite critic Dwight Macdonald. The union was indeed a fiasco, but the fact remains that it was Mary Pickford who first brought a German director to Hollywood after World War I. Only she could have gotten away with it.

Mary was still determined to do *Dorothy Vernon* and she and her old friend Mickey Neilan churned it out. The film proves that Lubitsch was right; there *are* too many queens. Fairbanks's fears about being overwhelmed by the huge sets are valid in Mary's case; with these massive sets and so much masculine activity, *Dorothy Vernon* is at times an imitation Fairbanks film. But *Dorothy Vernon,* and *Rosita* for that matter, weren't as bad as Mary, with her nightmare of the empty seats, thought they were. Worldwide totals are hard to determine, but United Artists' played-and-earned figures up to 1933 for the U.S.A., Canada, and South America show that *Tess* took in $1,036,424, *Rosita* $940,872, and *Dorothy Vernon* $905,944. Each made a profit of at least 100 percent in the Western Hemisphere alone. As it was a rule of thumb that any film that broke even in the United States was successful—the foreign take was gravy—Mary's films were highly profitable.

But still she was discontented. Frances Marion understood her problem. "Mary wanted to be sophisticated in Douglas's eyes," she said. "At the same time she didn't want to grow up. She was afraid people wouldn't love her, and she couldn't stand the thought of failure, of rejection."

Mary was tugged between child and woman, daughter and wife. Even before she married Doug she had once cried out in despair, "I hate these curls. I'm in a dramatic rut eternally playing this curly-headed girl. I loathe them, loathe them!" But she was nevertheless convinced that *Rosita*, with her hair up, and *Dorothy Vernon*, with her curls conforming to an Elizabethan style, were box office failures. Furthermore, she now had another dilemma: even while she was trying to be the sophisticated Mrs. Fairbanks, she was engaged in intense competition with Mr. Fairbanks. Two months before the opening of Dorothy Vernon, a steal of Doug's *Robin Hood*, Doug had taken the wind out of her sails by taking off in a new direction with the dazzling, innovative fantasy *The Thief of Bagdad*.

Mary went directly to her fans. "What type of picture would you like to see me do?" she asked the readers of the largest fan magazine, *Photoplay*, in a signed article. "In what characterizations do you like me best? What suggestions have you for my future photoplays?"

Twenty thousand letters poured into the Beverly Hills post office. When they were opened, read, translated (many were in foreign languages), and tabulated, the first six roles were *Cinderella, Anne of Green Gables, Alice in Wonderland, Heidi, The Little Colonel*, and *Sara Crewe*. The prize-winning letter, addressed to "My Dear Little Mary," concluded with a plea for child roles between ten and fourteen years of age. "These particular roles are your greatest opportunities for showing us what a wonderful actress you really are by your ability to create and preserve an almost perfect illusion. An illusion that there are such little girls and that we have one before us; an illusion that you are a real little girl in spite of the fact that we know you are a grown-up woman. Only a great actress or one who is really a child at heart, could make those little characters so natural that they become our friends."

If Mary was doomed by those who loved her to remain a little girl at the age of thirty-two, at least such adoration made it easier to accept their verdict, and to repress the next question—how much longer could she continue being Little Mary on the screen? She would play a child's role again, she decided, but in spite of her fans' suggestions, she would choose the role herself.

Many years later Mary recalled wandering alone through the deserted, make-believe streets of the lot, trying to decide what to do. She realized that although she was part Irish, she had never played an Irish role. Who did she know who was Irish? She thought of Mabel Normand, a popular star of some years before and a friend from the early Griffith days, and called her. "I'd get an Irish title," Mabel said, "and write something to go with it."

The title Mary chose was *Little Annie Rooney,* and Mary and a couple of writers, sitting on the Pickfair lawn eating sandwiches and tossing gags at each other, turned out the story in a week. William Beaudine, another friend of the early Griffith days who'd made some good children's films (and continued to make them until he died at the age of seventy-eight after completing an episode for the "Lassie" television show), was the director. *Little Annie Rooney* starts out with a long hilarious scene. The kids are having a street fight. Felt bricks bounce off their heads, plaster of paris bottles shatter, balsa wood clubs break. Right in the midst of this comedy-violence is Little Mary, as Little Annie. In between throwing missiles and having them bounce off her head, she puts her hands on her hips, pouts her famous pout, squinches up her eyes, ducks her curly head, and gives us that Mary Pickford look. From that moment on, she is no more thirty-two years old than a kitten. *Little Annie Rooney* was a box office smash.

It was a happy film to make and so was the next, *Sparrows.* The best people in the business were eager to work on a Pickford film. "We called her Miss Pickford," Hal Mohr, a pioneer cameraman, recalled fifty years later, "and I still call her Miss Pickford. She was the queen of motion pictures, and we thought of her with respect. We worked together like a big family to give her the finest artistic contribution we could create. I'll never forget Harry Oliver, that great set designer, sitting down in the swamp set, burning stumps with a blow torch. Instant aging. We had a lake three–four feet deep, with two motorboats on it—there was a moonlight chase involved. He took a lot of flax seed, which is oily-looking, and shook aluminum powder on it. Oh, the light shone like hell off it. He spread it two inches deep on a big table, and he carved a model boat, eighteen inches long, which he pulled through it with a concealed string, making a wake. We worked it out to scale, an inch to a foot, and increased the speed of the camera accordingly. I remember I hand-cranked the camera. The effect was marvelous, more like water than water. We were so proud of it. We did it for ourselves, of course, but we also did it for Miss Pickford."

Sparrows is famous for a scene that has been described not only by Mary herself but by film historians and critics as being shockingly dangerous. In the scene Mary, carrying a baby on her back, leads the escaping orphans across a fallen tree over a swamp filled with huge alligators leaping upward toward the children, huge jaws opening wide. It is a terrifying scene. There were contemporary reports that Mary had to carry the live baby across the log repeatedly, becoming exhausted, slipping several times. Mary has said that she weighed one hundred pounds, the baby thirty-three.

When Fairbanks heard what was going on, the reports continued, he ran to the set to protest. "He was a gentle, charming person," Mary recalled years later, "and he came down like a wild wounded bull. 'Don't you know you can do it with double exposure?' he cried."

Over the years Beaudine has been pilloried for endangering the life of Mary and the child. The question has been asked over and over, why did he do such a dangerous, foolhardy thing?

A viewing of the film, supported by repeated replays, backward and forward, at normal speed and in slow motion, answers the question about the baby. It's a dummy, and not even a very realistic one: the arms are straight, without elbows.

What about Mary? Hal Mohr answered that. "There wasn't an alligator within ten miles of Miss Pickford," Hal Mohr said. "Do people think we were crazy? I shot that scene myself. We had no trick department in those days. If there was a trick the cameraman put it in there. I had had some experience in cutting mattes, and this was assigned to me from the beginning. We used the log as a guideline, about three feet above the swampy pool alive with alligators. I don't know where the alligators came from—somebody picked up the phone and ordered alligators. We anchored the camera about twenty feet from the log. I cut a matte out of black fiber board to conform to the log, top and bottom, so that they would fit perfectly. We photographed the alligators first, covering the top half with the matte. I set the counter on the camera at zero, and counted out loud, two counts to the foot. The trainer walked across a platform we built over the swamp, throwing pieces of meat to the alligators. As they jumped, jaws open, the script girl made notes as to the exact count. Say the 'gator jumped at the count of thirty-seven, that's a good place to have Miss Pickford slip and almost fall. So now we get rid of the alligators, rewind and rehearse. We rehearsed two days, then shot it at the identical time of day as the first, to have the shadows conform. So you'd see Miss Pickford and the kids on that marvelous log Harry Oliver made, and at just the right moment, when we all knew an alligator was going to rear up with jaws open, she'd slip and look frightened. It was hard work for all of us, but the only thing those alligators came close to biting was a chunk of horsemeat."

One explanation for Mary's persistence in telling the story her way ("The young alligators are the most vicious," she told an interviewer thirty years later) is the mental process known as confabulation, in which an individual gradually comes to remember an event the way he wants to. The wildly exaggerated stories of dangers in *Sparrows* probably began during the shooting as a harmless bit of press agentry to rival Mary's partner at the studio and at Pickfair.

For by that time the world had come to believe the press releases on how Douglas Fairbanks risked death almost daily. The myth had been repeated so often that it was accepted as truth: Fairbanks did his own stunts. The legend persists today: "He did do them all himself, no matter what you may have heard," his son told a black-tie crowd at the opening session of the ten-week Douglas Fairbanks Retrospective in the John F. Kennedy Center for the Performing Arts in 1974.

Douglas Jr. is not too far from the truth: his father did *nearly* all his own stunts. The man in the best position to know is Allan Dwan, the director who worked with Fairbanks both when he was first beginning and again in his golden years. Dwan directed nine of Fairbanks's first twenty-nine films, the contemporary comedies, the first big spectacle, *Robin Hood,* and the grand finale of the swashbucklers, *The Iron Mask.* Indeed, it was Dwan, an athlete himself, who first recognized Fairbanks's ability.

"We didn't use a double for Doug for two reasons," Dwan said. "First, there just wasn't anyone in the world who could do things with such grace. I used tricks, shortened distances, set up trampolines, all that, to make it look even more effortless. Second, his stunts weren't all that difficult. We didn't want them to be. Look back over his films and you'll see that anything he did, or anything he did with me, could have been done by anybody, the boy next door, if he *had* to—and if he had that fantastic Fairbanks physique. But that doesn't mean we were silly enough to risk tying up the completion of a picture, with all its expenses, by injuring the star. So there were plenty of times when it was just good sense to use a double or a stunt man. You don't think he was actually riding the horse in the jousting scenes in *Robin Hood,* do you? We had him on the horse, we showed him looking grim, then pulling down his visor, then we cut away and when you next see that suit of armor hauling ass across the field with lance cocked you can bet Doug Fairbanks isn't inside it."

A few cynics believe that Fairbanks used stunt men on even more occasions. The film historian William K. Everson avers that not only did Fairbanks use a stunt man frequently, but he used one in the scene for which he is best remembered, that thrilling slide down the sail in glorious technicolor in *The Black Pirate.* Everson even named the stunt man, Richard Talmadge, one of the most famous. Others claim it was Charlie Stevens.

The definition of a stunt man is the man who doubles for the double. The double stands in for the star, gets wet, cold, muddy, pushed around. But when he's apt to get killed, in comes the stunt man. The first movie stunt men were cowboys of the 101 Ranch, a Wild West

Did Doug Fairbanks do his own stunts? Of course Doug Fairbanks did his own stunts. The man in this shot from *The Mark of Zorro,* however, just happens to be Richard Talmadge, silent film's number one stunt man, who worked for Doug for two years. *Hollywood Stuntmen's Hall of Fame*

show that wintered up the coast from Santa Monica. Out of the 101 Ranch came the cowboy star Hoot Gibson and the Fairbanks sidekick, Charlie Stevens. Stevens, part Indian, did the bump stunts, the rough stunts, in Doug's earliest movies. He got billing in later films and stayed on the Fairbanks payroll as long as he lived. He was about the same size and weight as Doug, and was an excellent rider.

As for Richard Talmadge, William Everson's nominee as the Fairbanks stunt man, Everson claimed that "you can always spot him in Fairbanks films because he was so bowlegged. You can see him dropping out of the trees in *Robin Hood.*"

Fifty-six years after first working with Fairbanks in 1919, Richard Talmadge, hearty and spry in his early eighties, chuckled and walked a few steps in exaggerated cowboy style; he wasn't all that bowlegged.

When he first started in films Talmadge's name was Silvio Metzetti. Some historians maintain that he spoke with an Italian accent, but he actually spent only one season in Italy. His real name was Sylvester Metz, top mounter and member of the famous Munich family of acrobats. They were advised to Italianize their name for their appearance in Italy, and when an American offer reached them there, they kept the name for luck. The act broke up in the States, and he became a movie stunt man in 1913. One of his first jobs was jumping seventy-two feet off a seven-story building, for which he was paid five dollars.

Recalling his stint with Fairbanks, Talmadge remained loyal to the code of the stuntman, anonymity. He admitted that he had been employed by Fairbanks, starting at $250 a week. They dressed together, worked together. But Fairbanks didn't need anybody to do stunts for him, Talmadge said, because he had such a unique personality and graceful style. He didn't want to do big stunts, anyway, but rather the kind of thing that the boy next door might do.

But wasn't Douglas Fairbanks too big a star, too expensive to risk doing his own stunts? A grin spread over Talmadge's face. "Absolutely!" he said. "I was with him for two and a half years and John Fairbanks never paid anybody for doing nothing. There's one stunt I *can* talk about. It was common knowledge at the time. I was hired to do a special stunt because Doug had gotten hurt and couldn't do it."

The film was *The Mollycoddle,* during which Fairbanks was injured when he vaulted over a horse's rump into the saddle. As was the custom, the horse's eye had been taped shut and an eye painted over it so that the horse couldn't see the rider coming, but apparently he heard Fairbanks and jerked forward. Doug sprained his wrists and it was then that Talmadge, known as Silvio Metzetti, was hired to do the final stunt in the film. This one is at least one exception to the rule that Fairbanks's stunts weren't really dangerous. Here, the result of a close study of the two-minute scene, is what happens.

The action begins with the character played by Doug, dressed in a white long-sleeved shirt, an open vest, and a broad white headband, at the top of a fifty-foot cliff. The character played by Wallace Beery— the villain—is wearing a cap, Norfolk jacket, and knickers. He is in the top of a tree, apparently spruce, some fifteen feet from the cliff. The villain has exhausted his ammunition shooting and now the hero takes the offensive. He leaps from the top of the cliff to the tree. It's daring and graceful; he sails through the air, erect, head up, chin down, arms out making pinwheel motions, feet kicking for balance. We see them grappling in the tree top, then falling, boughs breaking. They drop some fifteen feet to the rocky ground, where we see them wrestling. Now Beery tries to escape down the steep slope but Doug hurtles through the air, lands on him, and the two go head over heels. Now Doug breaks away, rolling down the slope, and Beery leaps on him. These leaps span ten to fifteen feet, and each lands squarely on the other.

They hurtle off a smaller cliff onto a mountain cabin. They crash through the roof and fight inside the cabin—Beery hits Doug with a chair. Doug throws Beery against the side of the cabin so hard that he breaks through it; Doug pushes him through the hole, then dives on top of him. They roll down the steep slope to a pool in a mountain stream, over a waterfall, and finally, in the pool beneath the falls, Doug subdues Beery and drags him to shore. Wow! You find yourself breathing harder, your pulse racing, sitting forward in your seat. It's one of the most exciting sequences in films.

But on running it again, over and over, stopping the film and examining the frames, we realize we've been fooled. In that first dramatic leap from cliff to tree, the only reason we think it's Doug is because the figure is wearing a white shirt, vest, and headband, and he's dramatic —that's good enough for us. It seems impossible for him to land in the tree after a fifteen-foot downward leap without killing himself or his opponent; running the film in slow motion we see that a split second before he makes contact the film is cut. The next thing we see is Doug and Beery, close-up, grabbing at each other. Now back to a long shot of two figures falling through the branches, and in slow motion we notice that it's a strange-looking tree and the boughs are breaking just right. As they fall to the ground the film is cut just before they hit, followed by another close-up of Doug and Beery. Down the slope they go, in a magnificent exhibition of two skilled acrobats displaying perfect timing. When Beery hits Doug with a chair in the cabin, slow motion reveals that the chair never really arrives on the target; it just disappears, and there is another cut to close-up again. Again, long shots of dangerous action alternate with close-ups of Doug and Beery grunting and tugging, until, finally, Doug sloshes out of the pool victorious.

Even with the cuts and the realization that in the first leap the Beery character catches the Doug character, that they drop out of the tree to land on an unseen pile of mattresses, that the tree was specially constructed, we can see that this was a daring, difficult sequence. The very first leap, from cliff to tree, was the real thing.

And it was Richard Talmadge, wearing Doug's clothes, leaping into the arms of his brother, Leon, in Beery's Norfolk jacket.

After *The Mollycoddle* Talmadge stayed on to be a part of the Fairbanks Fun and Games company. He and Doug were fascinated by each other. Talmadge was amazed at how easily and quickly Fairbanks could learn to do acrobatic and gymnastic stunts he had worked all his life to master; Fairbanks was equally impressed by Talmadge's training and skill. Talmadge had never seen an American football, for example, but he picked the game up so quickly that Southern California gave him a tryout. "I was too slow," he recalled later. "One thing I never learned to do was run."

Talmadge contributed a great deal to the Fairbanks style. Doug had been jumping Olympic style, taking off with one foot, bent over. Talmadge showed him how to take off with both feet, like a gymnast, to get greater height and distance, and to hold his body erect and bring his feet up for a more graceful appearance. He built a six-foot-square framework of pipe and taught Doug to do nip-ups, shooting himself back and forth on the bars. Instead of swinging rings, a standard gymnasium fixture, he put up one ring on a rope, and he and Doug competed to see who could swing out the farthest.

"I'll tell you something about Doug Fairbanks," Talmadge said. "He never upstaged anybody in his life. He was always working at having fun. He could do the damndest things—spit BB's, for instance. You'd be in a crowd, somebody would grab the back of his neck and look around, there'd be Doug with that big innocent smile and a mouthful of BB's."

Talmadge worked with Doug on *The Mollycoddle, The Mark of Zorro, The Nut,* and *The Three Musketeers,* then he was offered an opportunity to star in a cheapie turned out by an independent promoter. When the picture came out Doug volunteered, on his own, to endorse it in publicity shots of the two together, Doug saying "That's my boy." All this time he had been known as Silvio Metzetti; he was as surprised as anyone when the picture came out starring Richard Talmadge. Thus Talmadge—he kept his new name—had, before *Robin Hood,* left his mark on Fairbanks in the form of new acrobatics and gymnastics, and, he said, he never returned.

He would have enjoyed working in *Robin Hood.* Allan Dwan estimated that a hundred athletes were in that picture. One of them, Charles O. "Chuck" Lewis, was made to order for Doug Fairbanks. Chuck had been captain of his football team at the University of Missouri, had interrupted his college career to serve as an officer in the U.S. Army, was a graduate geologist, and on top of all that was pentathlon winner in the Los Angeles Olympic tryouts (the Fairbanks publicity department later promoted him to All-American and Olympic decathlon champion). He was a geologist with a Los Angeles oil company when he heard about *Robin Hood* and took the red streetcar out to see what was going on. From a $5-a-day extra, Chuck Lewis became Doug's closest friend and his companion for the rest of his life.

He was with the Fairbanks company in the winter of 1925–26, during the filming of *The Black Pirate,* in which was performed one of the most spectacular stunts of all time, the swoop down the sail. It is also one of the most discussed, if not controversial, cinema scenes, for there is wide disagreement as to how it was done—and who did it, for again a whole school of film historians maintain it was not Douglas Fairbanks. As William Everson put it, "During that entire sequence you never see his face. Now how could Fairbanks, that supreme egomaniac, have done that scene without showing us that big smile? There's only one answer—he didn't do it."

The Black Pirate opens with Fairbanks marooned on a tropical island, victim of a gang of pirates. He wears a loose-fitting shirt, open from throat to navel. "He had thick hair on his chest and they had to shave him every morning," Mitchell Leisen recalled later. In order to revenge himself on the pirates Doug joins them, promising to prove his worth by capturing a ship singlehanded. In the ensuing action he is about to be overwhelmed when he spots a line that conveniently passes through a pulley at the top of the mast. He grabs one end of the line, ties the other to a brass cannon, pushes the cannon overboard, and, whoops, up to the crow's nest. The antagonists come to get him, swarming up the mast, up the sheets from both sides. He climbs out the topmost spar, plunges his dagger into the top sail, and, holding on to the hilt, swoops down the long sail as the canvas rips, past the baffled pursuers. He repeats the stunt again on the lower sail. He thus escapes, and then captures the ship.

Is it Doug? Whoever it is, how does he do it? There are many explanations, each put forth by its exponents as gospel truth. In his memoirs the actor David Niven, mistakenly reporting that Doug plunged his sword into velvet curtains in *Robin Hood* as well as into the sails of *The Black Pirate*, quoted Doug as admitting "that on the other side of the curtains and sail the swords had been bolted into a large board."

The director Robert Parrish, in his memoirs, wrote that Doug personally showed him how the stunt was done. The dagger was actually a baseball bat attached to a pulley arrangement on the other side of the sail, Parrish said, and there was a concealed platform on the camera side, on which Doug himself rode up and down. Parrish, however, recalled Doug's smile flashing from the screen as he swooped; in current prints you can't see Doug's face, much less his smile.

Donald Crisp, just before he died at the age of ninety-four, gave a lucid if complicated account. He was the original director of *The Black Pirate*, he said, but fell out with Doug over this very stunt and was ousted in favor of Al Parker, an old crony of Doug's (Parker is indeed the director of record, but has since died). Crisp was somewhat critical of Doug in the first place. "He was always striving to be something he was not," he said. "He would have killed himself showing off. On this picture, he wanted to come down the sail himself, just stick his sword in and go. I wouldn't listen to him. We worked on this stunt for five days, planned it for two or three weeks before that. We discarded several plans. We thought of cutting the canvas, then stitching it back lightly together, using a phony knife. We tried to work out a way to wrap the handle of the knife around the hand. We experimented with sacks of sand. Parker wanted to use a dummy. When we finally worked it out Charlie Stevens wanted to do it, but as far as I was concerned it was Chuck Lewis all the way. I had it balanced so that you had to pull him down. But I wasn't taking any chances. I put a plaster cast on Chuck's arm and chest, and ran the wire through it, fastened securely. But when we tried it he kicked with his legs, which was distracting, so we ran the line down through his pants leg, secured it again to his ankle, and pulled him down that way."

Chuck Lewis didn't remember it that way. He just barely remembered it at all, for, he said, it wasn't all that unusual. "We had a place on the lot where we tried out all these things," he said. "All I remember is we got some canvas and hung it up and tried it and it worked. I did it, Charlie Stevens did it, Doug did it, everybody did it."

Authorities on textiles and sails state that it was possible to manufacture canvas of sufficient weight in the twenties, and that storm canvas could be as thick as a quarter inch, offering more than enough resistance. As for holding the sword, any of the Fairbanks group, and certainly Doug himself, was strong enough to hold onto it.

Just fifty years after the stunt Ted Galvin, Jr., a film buff of Medina, Ohio, traded a religious movie for, sight-unseen, two reels of out-takes from *The Black Pirate*. He presented them to the Library of Congress. And there may now be seen, in take after take after take, under the glorious green sky of 1926 technicolor, not Chuck Lewis, not Charlie Stevens, but Doug himself, sliding down sails again and again, using some sails two or three times, ripping them to shreds and enjoying it immensely. The sails were not on the ship, of course, but apparently on the back lot, as Chuck had said.

So Fairbanks did do the stunt on the back lot. Did he do it in the actual shooting of the film? Well, in prints available today, there is simply no way of telling. We see Fairbanks climbing around on a spar, but then the camera cuts away to a long shot and the figure on the sail can be anybody, even with a plaster cast. But the burning question raised by Everson remains: if it is Fairbanks, who was known to be narcissistic, enthusiastic, a show-off, take your pick, why didn't he show his face?

Whatever the answer, whoever the figure on the sail, it was Douglas Fairbanks who made it possible for millions of people, kids and grown-ups alike, to thrill to that marvelous stunt. It *was* done and in our hearts, Doug did it.

Auteurs

For all the fascination with Doug's stunts and Mary's curls, their roles as performers were only the iceberg tips of the activities of this energetic couple; so much of their contribution has been overlooked. The mid-1920s marked the flowering of the silent screen, but only a handful of observers the world over had come to appreciate the artistry of the cinema and recognize the complexity of the film industry. In 1916 Hugo Münsterberg, a Harvard professor, published a thoughtful book, *The Film: A Psychological Study,* in which he classified motion pictures as the most popular entertainment in the world and discussed some of its aspects. Vachel Lindsay, poet and intellectual, saw artistic merit in the new medium and shared his views with the readers of *The New Republic,* as Robert E. Sherwood did with the readers of *Life.* In the late twenties an intellectual magazine devoted to the film, *Close Up,* was published in Switzerland; its readers called themselves cinéastes. *Close Up* folded when sound wiped out the silent film.

During the transition from silent to sound a young Englishman named Paul Rotha published the first major study of the cinema, *The Film Till Now.* And in the April 1957 issue of *Cahiers du Cinéma,* a French intellectual film magazine, a theory was postulated around which the modern cinéastes, those who have finally perceived that the cinema can indeed be classified as an art form, could rally. This was the "auteur theory" which, simply put, defines the director as the *auteur,* the one individual who places his signature on a film, on whom it stands or falls. (The French word for author is used to distinguish the director from those who wrote the film.) Adherents of the auteur theory do not necessarily overlook the contributions of the producer, who may have selected and acquired the story, the writers, the production staff, the actors, and everything else that goes into a film, including money, but choose the director as their focal point for discussion. And indeed it is often the director who uses writers, actors, and technical directors as his instruments in placing his opus upon the screen.

Forty years before the term was defined, Douglas Fairbanks and Mary Pickford were, in effect, the auteurs of their films. The term producer had not come clearly into film language; in some studios the director was on his own, in others a supervisor would be assigned to one or more films. Doug and Mary really had no titles; they weren't even the presidents of the companies bearing their names. But the definition of an auteur as the one person who puts the clearly identifiable mark on a film fits them both. Mary was never the director of record on any of her films, but she was known to have taken over equably when her brother Jack or Mickey Neilan went off on a drunk. William Beaudine said that he was hesitant to direct Mary at the beginning of *Little Annie Rooney* and that Mary called him aside. "Bill, I am the producer, I am the star—do you want me to be the director, too? If I hadn't thought you could do it, I wouldn't have hired you. Now let's get back to work."

From that moment on, Beaudine said, "I really *was* her director." She had great ideas for scenes and story construction, Beaudine went on, which he welcomed. "She was a one-woman picture company."

We have seen how she directed Lubitsch to direct her the way she wanted to be directed. Allan Dwan would not work with her for the same reason. According to Dwan, he would say to her, "This is what we're gonna do today."

She'd put her hands on her hips and say, "Who says that's what we're going to do today?"

"Don't you think it would be a good idea?"

"Then why didn't you ask in the first place?"

Dwan respected Mary but didn't want her telling him what to do, and he directed no more pictures for her.

Doug did not establish his authority in the same way, but his presence was felt nevertheless. "Tell him to do something and he'd take the whole afternoon off and play Doug," Donald Crisp grumbled, referring to the racket game Doug invented. This might seem to be a reasonable excuse for the director to fall a day behind, except that it was not Doug but John or Robert Fairbanks who kept the schedules and signed the checks. Even with a friend as close as Dwan, Doug would soften any question on Dwan's direction by asking, *"Vous avez raison?"* Dwan, who liked him and put up with him, would quickly give a reason. With other directors Doug might suddenly start playing tricks, start clowning, or just take off. He would never face up to a confrontation, but he'd get his way just the same. As with Mary, directors directed him the way he wanted to be directed. Everything was worked out beforehand in a happy, give-and-take conference.

One of the flaws of the auteur theory is that some films are clearly marked with the stamp of the producer, rather than the director. This is especially valid in the cases of Doug and Mary. For them, direction was only one of many ingredients of a film. Each began at the very beginning of the creative process with story selection, a full-time operation on which a studio can prosper or collapse. One time Mary seriously suggested hiring a staff of recognized writers and sending each to some fertile spot—New York's East Side, China, Russia, Limehouse in London—to stay until he got material for a story.

Perhaps most important of all, as is true in managing any enterprise, nation, or business, Doug and Mary had what it takes to attract the best people and inspire them to do their best work. Their art directors, set designers, and costume designers knocked themselves out in pursuit of the most beautiful, the most authentic. For Mary's *Dorothy Vernon of Haddon Hall,* Mitchell Leisen fashioned costumes so fastidiously authentic that it took the actress who played Queen Elizabeth half an hour to go to the bathroom. Claude Leloir, imported for *The Iron Mask,* devoted hours to teaching featured players and extras alike the exact and most graceful fifteenth-century way of doffing a plumed hat. "I came in one day and there were thirty roughnecks learning how to curtsey," Dwan said.

Finally, both worked closely with their assistants in viewing the daily rushes, over and over, discarding thousands and thousands of feet of film so painstakingly shot, putting together the remainder in the most effective way.

Their work as auteurs, as production heads, interfered with their individual stardom. Doug poured all the creativity and technical ingenuity available into *The Thief of Bagdad* at that time, to such an extent that he sacrificed some of his own individual appeal. *The Thief* was truly the Arabian Nights of Hollywood, the most ambitious film of its kind. Illusion was piled on illusion. At the very beginning the artfully designed sets lure us into a mystical world. The castle of the caliph seems to shimmer ethereally in the atmosphere; the effect was achieved by painting the foreground black and waxing it so that the castle reflects off its surface (everyone wore felt overshoes to keep from marking it up). Doug fights a horrible gigantic sea spider, manipulated by wires, and a frightening monster, an alligator wearing a papier-mâché top and made to appear larger by double exposure—shooting Doug at long range, then double-exposing him with the monster at short range. There's a flying horse running along a treadmill in front of a black curtain while piano wires manipulate its wings. Whole armies pop up as Doug casts miraculous seeds on the ground, done by exploding flares, stopping the film, and having extras step into their places. There are two flying-carpet scenes. In one Doug and the heroine sat on a piece of painted plywood in front of a shot of moving clouds while a fan blew their hair. Much more exhilarating is the scene in which the

One of the most beautiful and elaborate sets of all time was built for Fairbanks in *The Thief of Bagdad. Charles O. Lewis*

carpet actually flies. It was hung by piano wires from a crane that actually swung it high over the crowded courtyard. The scene was shot by a camera mounted on a platform even higher, and the effect is breathtaking. Doug has some appealing scenes: he eludes his pursuers in one by jumping in and out of great urns, a trampoline stunt that took many hours to perfect. And he obviously gets a big kick out of fooling us with the rope trick. Under the power of his magic motions the rope uncoils from its basket and rises into the air. Doug motions it to stop, and it hangs there. A miracle! Doug climbs it, so gracefully. As sophisticated moviegoers we know all about piano wires; the end of the rope, of course, is attached to one, and someone above the camera range has pulled it up and secured it. And then that tricky Fairbanks grabs the top of the rope and bends it over!

The entire film is filled with marvelous effects. Doug was never more graceful; in fact, he may be too graceful, for his characterization is more like a ballet dancer than the athletic boy next door. Doug as a thief with waved hair and mustache, wearing transparent harem pajamas, golden earrings, and a head scarf, is not the Doug we identify with. The film cost more than *Robin Hood,* and runs for almost two and a half hours. The critics praised it as a masterpiece; Vachel Lindsay, in an article entitled "The Great Douglas Fairbanks," recommended seeing it, as he had, ten times. Robert E. Sherwood called it "the farthest and most sudden advance that the movie has ever made." The *New York Times* review described it as "an entrancing picture, wholesome and beautiful, deliberate but compelling, a feat of motion picture art which has never been equaled." Yet for all its outlay in time and money, its played-and-earned figures were less than other Fairbanks films that cost half as much. The star was overwhelmed by his own production.

Few stars, or directors for that matter, involve themselves in the exhibition of their own films. Again Doug and Mary were exceptions. They introduced their films by the road-show method, presenting them in gala two-a-day performances in specially chosen theaters in major cities. (*Robin Hood* ran half a year at Grauman's Egyptian Theater in Los Angeles; "All out for *Robin Hood,*" the streetcar conductors said as they stopped at the corner.) Long before their personal appearance at openings in New York and Hollywood, and as many other cities as they could get to, Doug and Mary helped plan for them in detail, down to the number of billboards reserved.

The motion picture industry has always been unusual in that its

Though *The Thief* was Fairbanks's most expensive film, it was not his
most profitable. In this fanciful costume, he was hardly the boy next door,
and in his balletic movements he was more dancer than athlete.
Charles O. Lewis

Could the movies exist without piano wire? In this snapshot Chuck Lewis
sneaked between takes of *The Thief of Bagdad,* one of the many he
provided the author from his private collection, a sharp eye can detect the
ubiquitous piano wire holding up the rope, and Fairbanks on the balcony
reaching toward it. *Charles O. Lewis*

production is so divorced from its other corporate activities. Films were
made in Hollywood, which means the Los Angeles area, but everything
else was handled in New York. The fact that somebody had to get up
the hard cash to keep a film project going until the public paid that
money back was as far from the minds of the fans as the studio was
from corporate headquarters. Both Doug and Mary knew only too well,
through the organization of their companies, how films were financed,
and Doug had personally bankrolled *Robin Hood,* at that time the
most expensive film made. It was now Hiram Abrams, as president of
United Artists, who was directly responsible for borrowing the money
from banks, but the buck came up to Doug and Mary anyway, for the
success or failure of United Artists devolved on them through default.
Of the other two partners, Griffith had begun the professional and

personal decline from which he never recovered, and Chaplin produced only two films for United Artists in seven years. Doug and Mary, Doug's brothers and Mary's mother, and their executives saw that United Artists simply did not have the production to maintain itself. One possible solution to the problem, a merger with other major studios worked out at great trouble and expense, was vetoed by Chaplin in an almost paranoiac determination to remain independent. Finally, in November 1924 all four partners did agree to bring in Joseph Schenck, a proven film entrepreneur, as chairman of the board, and Schenck brought in such stars as Norma Talmadge, Constance Talmadge, Buster Keaton, Gloria Swanson, John Barrymore, and Dolores Del Rio, and producer Samuel Goldwyn. As minutes and files of United Artists reveal, the negotiations with Schenck on United Artists and its overseas affiliates, setting up an independent theater circuit and an independent production company, and working out an arrangement to share the Pickfair studio, renamed the United Artists Studio and leased to the Art Cinema Corporation, went on endlessly. But United Artists was saved, and prospered.

Perhaps through sheer enthusiasm for the industry, or in search of additional production, Fairbanks got involved in other productions for a time. He and Chaplin saw the first print of a lugubrious film, *The Salvation Hunters,* the first effort of Josef Von Sternberg, and devoted a great deal of time to acquiring the distribution rights to the film and taking an option on Von Sternberg. Mary and Doug considered themselves representatives of the industry, with all the responsibilities their position entailed. They made appearances, issued statements, were available for interviews in which their opinions were sought. They thought creatively and instructively, and were not afraid to speak out.

Fairbanks, for example, after a dinner conversation with Winston Churchill in London, seriously proposed making films that the British Empire could use to teach the people in India and China western customs. He elaborated at length on the idea of educational films, which were not then in existence. "It's wild," he said, "but it would work out."

On another occasion, discussing the question of film censorship, Fairbanks suggested classifying films in terms of those suitable for adults or for children. Dozens of articles, some in series of up to 50,000 words, flowed out of the Pickfair studios under their names, ranging

Doug's expression shows what he thinks of Mary's high-living sister, Lottie, at her white-gowned church wedding to Allan Forrest, screen actor and second of her four husbands. *Historical Collections, Security Pacific National Bank*

After her venture into historical drama, Mary returned to adolescent roles. Here she is in *Sparrows,* saving an unfortunate baby from a wicked oppressor. *United Artists Collection, Wisconsin Center for Film and Theater Research*

Though the plot may be hackneyed, the sets of *Sparrows* were works of cinematographic art. Note the detail in this barn loft. Mary's performance was also a work of art. *United Artists Collection, Wisconsin Center for Film and Theater Research*

from personal, revealing stories of Mary's life to astute and thorough observations on the industry by Doug. In addition to these stories in major magazines, in which both surely took a time-consuming interest, fan magazines churned out stories that must have required at least some participation on their part.

Family and Friends, At Home and Abroad

It certainly isn't necessary to be a movie star to have family problems that require attention, but even in this regard Doug and Mary had unusual entanglements. Frances Marion observed that Mary saw far less of her family than she wanted to, and Doug saw far more of them than he wanted to. Mary and her mother remained as close as ever during business hours, with Charlotte still running Mary's investments. Once Charlotte returned from the safety deposit vault complaining that she had a sore finger from cutting coupons. Mary laughed. "You'd have loved it if your whole hand was blistered," she said.

As for Lottie and Jack, Mary fought with them and for them, despaired of them and supported them, and never failed them. Even after it became apparent that Lottie had little talent and that what looks she had had were gone, even after a family fight in which Charlotte and Mary took Lottie's child away from her, Mary gave Lottie another chance by setting up Playgoers Pictures to star Lottie Pickford in a film produced by Charlotte Pickford. She made a place for her in *Dorothy Vernon of Haddon Hall.* She arranged a formal wedding, with Doug in prominent attendance, when Lottie married actor Allan Forrest. Lottie's husbands numbered four in all. It was said of one that although he purported to be an undertaker, what he transported in his hearse was bootleg whiskey. Donald Crisp, outspoken in both his affection for Mary and his dislike for her siblings, said, "Lottie was a tramp."

Lottie's daughter, Mary Pickford Rupp, was the issue of her first marriage, to Albert Rupp. During a period of Lottie's misbehavior, Charlotte adopted the child and changed her name to Mary Charlotte Rupp, then to Mary Pickford II. Mary later declared that two Mary Pickfords were too many and the name was changed again, this time to Gwynne Pickford. She was always welcome at Pickfair, and went back and forth between her aunt and her grandmother.

As for Jack Pickford, who was in some ways Mary's child as much as he was her brother, Donald Crisp summed him up with "He was a drunk before he was a man." He must have set some kind of record when he lost his driver's license in 1921. Mary's efforts to help him establish a career either as an actor or as a director were not successful. Jack didn't like work. "One thing he could do," the lawyer Paul O'Brien said, "he could marry beautiful women." Jack's wives, all former Follies girls, were Olive Thomas, Marilyn Miller, and Mary Mulhern. In between binges on his own stomping grounds, Jack would often show up at Pickfair, charming and drunk. Once he and Bea Lillie, the English musical comedy star, appeared at a formal party, beautifully dressed, and, arm in arm, walked with dignity into the swimming pool.

Mary was often embarrassed by Jack, but for Doug it was worse. It was emotionally necessary for him to be number one in Mary's life, and being pushed out of that position, no matter how temporarily, for someone he detested must have been galling. On one occasion when he and Mary had planned a short trip to Mexico, Jack got sick and Mary refused to go so that she could stand vigil outside his door. Lottie also needed, or took, attention from time to time. But it was Charlotte who was Doug's chief rival. If he hadn't known it before his marriage, he learned it quickly enough when Charlotte's illness caused Mary to postpone their honeymoon. A couple of years later, after reservations had been made for the entire Pickfair retinue on an Italian luxury liner, Charlotte again became ill. There was talk of postponing the trip, but at the last moment Charlotte was rolled up the gangplank in a wheelchair.

A constant irritant in his growing schism with the Pickford clan was Doug's phobia, alcohol. Not only did Jack and Lottie drink excessively, but associates of Charlotte have said that she liked her share of the bottle, too. Doug had reason to fear that when Mary was with her tippling family she would join them.

If Doug had Ulman relatives, he kept quiet about them. A book published in July 1922, *Young Lawyer U.N. Truth's First Case* by Emory Washburn Ulman, has a glowing foreword by Douglas Fairbanks. Written in doggerel, the book is atrocious; there must have been some connection.

In his first years of marriage to Mary, Fairbanks saw little of Doug

Jr. He and the boy had never been really close and the divorce and
Beth's remarriage had pushed them even farther apart. Then suddenly
Doug Jr. came back into Fairbanks's life with a shock. Jesse Lasky,
Zukor's old partner, offered the thirteen-year-old boy a picture con-
tract.

The immediate result was a shouting match in the Fairbanks suite
of the Hotel Crillon in Paris, where Doug and Mary met with Beth and
Doug Jr. to discuss it. No one really understood the issues, a situation
always conducive to shouting louder. Doug Sr. bitterly opposed the
prospect of his son going into films. He and Mary both believed that
Lasky was seeking to exploit the Fairbanks name, not only to make
money in a cheap movie but to get even with Doug and Mary for past
differences. Doug wanted his son to have the education he himself had
never had. He could go to Harvard, play football; money was certainly
no object, for four years earlier Doug had settled half a million on Beth
and she was the only child of wealthy parents. Underlying everything
Doug said was his unspoken fear that this tall, handsome boy would
become a threat to his career and to his marriage. Doug felt young, he
looked young, he acted young. He was at the peak of his career. But
he had not reached that peak without fears and insecurities and this
was, after all, the spring of his fortieth year.

As for Doug Jr., he may have suspected that Lasky may have had
some exploitation in mind, but he was a poised, self-confident youth
—"I did have some precocity," he said a half century later—and he
truly believed that he could make good on his own. As far as education was concerned, he had attended good schools and been in-
structed by excellent tutors, and he was convinced that he could continue his education informally. He told his father that he did not
want to go to college, but what neither he nor his mother could bring
themselves to admit was that he couldn't afford to go to college.
They were broke. Beth's second husband had run through her settlement and then departed. The reason, in fact, that she and Doug Jr.,
were living in Paris was because the exchange was favorable and living was cheap. As for Beth's father, he had lost his last fortune; indeed, it wouldn't be long before Doug Jr. would be supporting him.
Finally, the boy, who idolized his father then as he would throughout
his life, could never understand, then or later, how this magnificent
individual could feel threatened by an adolescent son. The argument

went on for days. Fairbanks threatened to disown his son, to cut him out of his will. He finally lost the decision without knowing that his son had no other choice, and his son won without knowing that his father considered him vain and thoughtless. In this atmosphere father and son renewed their relationship in the same town, in the same business.

"I would go over to Pickfair and just hang around, hoping to be asked to dinner," Doug Jr. recalled. The memory still hurt. Sometimes he would be asked to stay, but more often he would not.

He still could not believe that he posed any threat to the great star, his father. He did not know that Doug once took aside his director, Henry King, and told him, "Don't let Doug Jr. look too old." He realized that he was taller than his father, inexorably pushing up to five ten, six feet, but he could not perceive that his father, under five eight and sensitive about it, resented this young giant towering over him. Doug Sr., never an unkind man, would occasionally be stricken with pangs of conscience and buy the boy presents, including a pony and a small automobile that actually ran. One day when Doug Jr. came home the pony was no longer there. It was of no comfort whatever to learn that the person who had admired it and to whom his father had given it away was Prince Hirohito of Japan.

A handsome youth with a familiar name and willing to work, Douglas Fairbanks, Jr., made several films playing, as he said later, big roles in little pictures and little roles in big pictures. When he was seventeen he gave a good account of himself in a stage production of *Young Woodley*. His father came to a performance, and word got back to the proud boy that his proud father had told Mary, "He's good, he really can act."

Then he brought about another crisis at Pickfair. At the age of nineteen, lying about his age in order to get the license, he got married. His bride was a brash, energetic dancing girl named Joan Crawford who had attracted sudden attention as a flapper in a film called *Our Dancing Daughters*. At the time Doug and Mary sincerely believed her to be an opportunist, snatching the boy with the famous name from the cradle, and incidentally making his father look older than ever. Actually the young couple were very much in love. Miss Crawford later looked back on her brief marriage with understanding for everyone concerned, including herself. She recounted an occasion when, descending a long staircase at a formal ball, she felt the train of her gown rip as someone behind her stepped on it. "Uncle Douglas," she wrote, "never missed a step. He leaned back, swung my torn train over his arm and kept right on, suavely guiding me down through the long line of guests. This man became my close friend and I loved him."

So did the five nieces—four of Doug's, one of Mary's. Doug put on a show for them, gave them presents, took them on shopping sprees. When Gwynne's grandmother and legal guardian died, Doug put his arm around the child and promised her, "You will always have a home here at Pickfair with your Aunt Mary and me."

No matter what exigencies of family or work, Doug and Mary still found time for travel and recreation—or, rather, Doug found the time and Mary put up with it. Their days began as early as six in the morning, when they would study the horoscopes especially prepared for them. Doug tended to laugh off the dire predictions, but on one occasion Mary was so concerned about her astrological forecast that she got off a plane in Kansas City and continued on to New York by train. Sometimes in the morning they would take a ride together; if not, Doug would run a couple of miles. Each would dress fastidiously; then, in their Rolls Royce, followed by an automobile containing his valet, Rocher Valente, and Mary's maid, Bodamère, they would proceed to the studio only to dress all over again in the costume of the day. At the end of every working day, six days a week, came the period Doug liked best, when from four to seven he and the fellows gathered together on the playing court and in his combination gym and dressing room. The masseur, Abdul the Turk, gave rubdowns, mixed drinks, and fixed scrambled eggs and coffee for anyone who wanted them. Doug had many of the chairs wired so that by pushing a button he could administer a shock to anyone sitting in them. When it got to the point that nobody would sit down when he was around, he had peepholes drilled in the wall and switches installed and continued his electrical prank on the sly. He loved to take a visitor into the steam room for a long sweaty stay and then push him into a pool of ice water. Doug always jumped in after him, of course.

Doug loved the beach. He would lie in the sun, his skin becoming even darker, while Mary of course shielded her fair complexion from the sun. Few people, especially women, wanted to be suntanned in those days. Fairbanks, who let himself photograph dark in films, even

darker in newsreels and newspaper pictures, certainly had some influence in making suntans popular. To enable Doug to have his sun, sea,
and sand, Mary to have a degree of comfort, and both of them to have
their retinue of family and friends, they acquired a quarter-mile cres-
cent of beach near the village of Laguna and set up a group of colorful,
elaborate tents. Later they built a large, comfortable white frame house
on the beach at Santa Monica, where Doug would occasionally startle
strollers by walking out into the waves on his hands.

Every trip abroad contained adventures, often more than they had
bargained for. Just the plans were exciting, as when Doug chartered a
Japanese ship, signed up a group of Hollywoodites, and began refurbish-
ing it for a round-the-world cruise of a year or more. This one fell
through, but there were others. Mary reported with some amazement
in 1929 that they had made seven trips to Europe together.

Even in the drab and dreary Russia of the first decade of the revolution, Doug and Mary were greeted with overwhelming response when
they visited Moscow in 1926. Doug had at first been told they would
never be permitted to enter and then, when not even the Kremlin could
deny the leading citizens of the world, that it would be too dangerous.
That made it all the more appealing to Doug, and Mary dutifully went
along. They made the long trip from Warsaw to Moscow in a huge
railroad coach that had once been the czar's. In the Soviet capital they
encountered the familiar pattern of unruly crowds and unprepared
authorities. On their arrival Mary was dragged away by two men who
half-carried her, screaming for Douglas, the length of the train. Two
armed guards took over and hurried her to a wooden gate where
another car awaited, filled with gifts of flowers and strawberries. They
took her through the gate and closed it behind them, just as Doug came
charging up. He climbed the gate and leaped into the car, right into
the strawberries. He saw with horror that Mary's dress was splotched
with red.

"Where are you hurt?" he cried. "What's all that blood?"

"Oh, Douglas," Mary said, "that's only strawberries."

After a few days in Moscow the heavy schedule and constant clamor
from ever-present crowds caused Mary to collapse. She lay exhausted
but unable to sleep as outside the hotel the crowd shouted, "Marushka,
Marushka." Doug found an American correspondent who spoke Russian and the two went out on a balcony to explain that Marushka was

ill and needed to rest quietly. The thousands of men, women, and children listened, then began applauding, but silently, not quite bringing their hands together. They went away, and Marushka slept.

The Fairbankses' trips abroad paid for themselves in publicity, of course, and combined business with pleasure, but they were always willing to do what they could to reciprocate. In Moscow they met Sergei Eisenstein, considered by some film scholars to outrank Griffith as the greatest film director, and arranged to bring both him and his films to America.

And although it was difficult to keep a level head when thousands of Greeks, Chinese, Swedes, Arabs, Indians, or Japanese were screaming their adulation, Doug and Mary always tried to remember that they were more than film stars, that they represented both America and the

Even travel to Laguna Beach was an adventure. The Fairbankses set up a tent city on the beach for an extended party. *Charles O. Lewis*

motion picture industry. They knew how powerful was the influence of the industry abroad, and they never relaxed. Doug would go anywhere, do anything, *eat* anything; Mary was more cautious, but she too was a conscientious ambassador. Only once did their popularity backfire. A few days before Doug and Mary arrived in Madrid the king and queen of Spain had returned from a trip abroad to be dutifully welcomed by a handful of subjects. Doug and Mary, by contrast, were greeted by what seemed to be the entire population. Embarrassed officials asked them to leave the country. The lesson was clear. Even a real king and queen took second place to the king and queen of the world.

Royalty has both its responsibilities and its rewards. When Doug's friend Henry Ford replaced the Model-T, he personally saw to it that the Fairbankses got one of the first, and Doug and Mary in return stepped out of their Rolls Royces and into their new Model-A for the benefit of the photographer. *Ford Arhives, Henry Ford Museum*

They had everything—each other, Pickfair, and probably the only canoe in the Santa Monica mountains—but yet their love was slipping away. *Historical Collections, Security Pacific National Bank*

CHAPTER NINE

Doug and Mary:
The Bittersweet Years,
1928–1936

Some time before Mary ascended to the throne at Pickfair, Charlotte Pickford had suffered a critical illness. She recovered, but not before Mary cried out that if her mother were to die she would go to France, drive a Red Cross ambulance, and pray for death herself. Her reaction may have been melodramatic but her anguish was real. Ever since her father had died, Mary had had a terrible fear that her mother would also die and leave her. Often, apparently out of nowhere, triggered by something deep in her subconscious, this dread would surface and leave her terrified and sobbing.

The fear that had lurked within her became real sometime in late 1925, when it was determined that Charlotte had cancer of the breast.

Mary tortured herself with the thought that she was to blame: she and her mother both believed the cancer was caused when Charlotte was looking in a trunk for a dress Mary could wear in *Little Annie Rooney* and the lid fell and struck her (in the twenties trauma was commonly considered a cause of cancer). The lump enlarged and grew painful, but Charlotte refused to have surgery. No other remedy was effective, and Mary saw her mother grow weaker and weaker, the pain increasing, over a period of more than two years. Mary often gave in to her grief, going into the bathroom and running the water so no one could hear her sobs, then placing cold wet cloths on her reddened eyes.

In late 1927, toward the end, she moved in with her mother. For more than four months she was self-imprisoned there, reading to Charlotte from the Bible, attending her around the clock, grieving. Doug lived there, too, during the entire period, though between Mary's solicitude for her mother and her preoccupation with grief there were many times when he might as well not have been there at all.

When the end finally came, on March 21, 1928, Mary cried out and fell backwards. Doug caught her in his arms, as he had once before when he carried her to safety, but this time she hit him in the face with both fists. For hours she was out of her mind, raving, abusing everyone, saying things she regretted later. She never really overcame her loss. She could not bear to pass her mother's house, for example, and always went out of her way to avoid it. She came to believe in spiritualism, and conversed with her mother "on the other side." Thirty years after Charlotte died, Mary, preparing for a lengthy recorded discussion of her life in films, carefully arranged pictures of her mother, Lottie, and Jack on the table by her, explaining that it was important for the four of them to be together for the occasion. (Jack wasted away from dissipation five years after his mother's death, at the age of thirty-five, and Lottie died of a heart attack two years later.)

In thinking back over her marriage years later, Mary said that she began to sense a restlessness in Doug as early as 1925. Nothing satisfied him, she said; he would want to drop everything and go somewhere, anywhere. It apparently did not occur to her that her own emotional state could have been affecting him. She had always known, although she didn't understand it, that Doug was jealous of her mother and that her mother was jealous of him. She scrupulously avoided giving him any real cause for jealousy as far as other men were concerned, living a strangely cloistered life for his benefit, but she could hardly be so considerate about his feelings in regard to Charlotte. During her mother's long illness Mary attended her with far more care and time than most daughters would have, and the final eighteen weeks of almost total absorption with her mother, climaxed by blows in Doug's face when Charlotte died, must certainly have had a strong impact on Doug. One of Mary's disjointed memories of her collapse at that time was of Doug's white lips. He was obviously near the breaking point himself.

Thus began the bittersweet years, in which the world's most-loved lovers found their love slipping away. The end of the romance was a great public spectacle in some respects, its dramatic scenes reported on the front pages of newspapers all over the world. But as in a motion picture, much of what was reported and gossiped about in Hollywood and elsewhere was speculation, illusion, and delusion. For as a wise observer of the human scene once said, marriages break up in the bedroom, and only the participants themselves know what goes on in there.

Mary was probably more attached to her mother than to her husband. With Charlotte on the scene her life was balanced. She could put up with Doug's inconsistencies, feed his narcissism, and enjoy the constant three-ring circus he provided, because her mother was providing her with the warm, emotional support she herself so very much needed. She had stability. But with the death of Charlotte that balance was disturbed. Doug would continue to demand attention, but to whom could Mary turn?

No difficulties appeared immediately after Charlotte's death. Like the trouper she was, Mary pulled herself together after her wild display of grief. She supervised the funeral, served as executor of Charlotte's estate. (The bulk of it, more than a million dollars, went to Mary; Lottie and Jack received trust funds of $100,000 each.) Then Doug charged back into her life. What she needed, and, just incidentally, what he needed, was a trip. Again he swept her up, along with valet, maid, and buddies, and took her to Europe. First stop was New York, where they allotted two weeks to attend to all the business details that had piled up during their absence. Doug discovered, to his surprise, that the New York office of United Artists had operated quite well without them. The two weeks' work was finished in two hours.

"What's holding us here?" Doug cried happily. "Let's go to Europe!"

Now came the frantic telephone calls to cancel their reservations two weeks hence and get on another liner departing earlier. A German vessel, the *Albert Ballin,* was sailing that very day. The royal suite was occupied by an official of the line, who offered to vacate it for Hollywood royalty, and accomodations were found for the rest of the Pickfair retinue. But they had just unpacked! An emergency plea went out, and the hotel maids ran to the Fairbanks suite to pack their trunks. Doug, of course, quarterbacked the operation, barking words of encouragement, darting from room to room. In a fleet of taxicabs they arrived at the ship just in time to get everybody on board. As friends and members of the UA New York office waved good-byes from the pier, and servants and shipboard personnel looked at the trunks to be unpacked for the second time that day, Doug and Mary set off on Mary's rest cure . . .

Mary: Portrait on Screen

As throughout their careers, Doug and Mary revealed much of themselves on the screen. The last picture Doug had made before Charlotte's death was *The Gaucho*, the story of an Argentine Robin Hood, with typical Fairbanks action. In it is an intimate revelation of one of Doug's images of Mary. Woven into the plot is a mystic shrine where the Madonna, Our Lady of the Miracles, appears to heal the

In her last film before the death of her mother, Mary's leading man was Buddy Rogers, who, some say, bore an uncanny resemblance to Charlotte. Charming scenes took place in the piano box. *Mary Pickford Corporation*

crippled and the sick. Filmed at a time when Mary was praying for her mother's life, the setting could not be coincidence. For plainly recognizable as the Madonna in this brief, exquisitely photographed scene is Mary Pickford.

As Doug was enshrining his wife before an audience of millions in 1927, Mary was filming her last picture before her mother's death and, coincidentally, giving an indication of her reaction to being placed on a pedestal by the overwhelming older man in her life. In *My Best Girl* Mary plays a girl of about eighteen, a ten-cent store clerk, a girl of the masses, a girl Mary, her mother, and her fans knew and loved so well. It was good therapy, for in addition to the show business tradition that the show must go on and the Pickford tradition that money must be made, it recalled Mary's own adolescence, when small pleasures could bring so much delight. The plot could not be more Hollywood: the son of the millionaire owner of a department store falls in love with the little clerk, and it goes on from there. A new young director, Sam Taylor, brought to it tricks and gimmicks reminiscent of Mickey Neilan at his best. But it is the leading man, Charles "Buddy" Rogers, selected by Mary, who attracts our attention. He is young and appealingly handsome, and with his crisp black curly hair, brown eyes, and soft, kind expression he bears an uncanny resemblance to Charlotte Pickford.

Buddy Rogers, son of a Kansas judge and Sunday school teacher, a college boy—he even belonged to a fraternity!—was a genial, relaxed, comfortable young man. "Buddy was as straight and square as they come," said a classmate at the University of Kansas. "Falling in love with a married woman was the only unlikely thing Buddy Rogers ever did in his whole life."

The married woman was Mary Pickford. She was secretly pleased by his lovesick glances, his eagerness to play the love scenes. "I think he's got a crush on me," she told Frances Marion, giggling with pleasure like the shopgirl she was playing. One of the many appealing features of the film is a delightful setting that appears in several scenes, a piano box in which the two young sweethearts meet. The story is still being told in Hollywood today that Mary and Buddy were seen practicing their love scene in the piano box for their own pleasure when they thought they were alone. Unlikely as this may be, there was nevertheless an exceptionally warm rapport between the two, and they shared a long screen kiss, unusual in a Pickford film. Doug Fairbanks is reported to have come on the set one day, watched Mary and Buddy together for just a moment, and then hurried away with a strange sense of foreboding.

Whatever the relationship between them in *My Best Girl*, it faded away as far as Mary was concerned while she devoted her full attention to her mother. Then came the rush-rush trip to Europe.

Mary returned with a new determination; the accolades given the king and queen of the cinema always elevated her self-esteem. She was now a woman, mature, secure in her talent. She would prove it, and in the most dramatic way. She would sever, permanently, those golden shackles to childhood roles, even before her return to California. One historic day in June 1928 she left Doug at the hotel in New York—he could not bring himself to accompany her—and went to a hairdresser where she calmly ordered the barber to cut the eighteen golden curls that fell almost to her waist. Flustered, the barber destroyed most of the curls by cutting along the cylindrical edge, but six were saved, to be preserved forever in museums. With her new short bob, shingled in back, she returned to Doug. She reported later that he was speechless, and tears came into his eyes. She took the six curls out of her purse and the two of them stood quietly together, looking down at the end of Little Mary.

Mary also determined to find a new, challenging role to further mark her liberation, and she acquired it that same week. Playing on Broadway was *Coquette*, an appealing, powerful, tragic drama; its star was Helen Hayes. Mary bought the rights to the play and began studying the part. Not only was she taking on a most challenging role, but for *Coquette* a new, major ingredient would be added: Mary would talk in the film.

Modern film historians discuss the advent of sound in the cinema primarily in relation to those unfortunate players who, because of unsuitable voices—too high, too low, too heavily accented—were forced out of films. But the advent of sound affected far more than a few dozen actors; it extended across the entire spectrum of the film world; English production, for example, was paralyzed for a year. As microphones were not sensitive enough to pick up voices from more than a few feet away, actors were rooted to their positions, speaking into microphones concealed in flowers or lamps. Paradoxically, this

Sincerely yours
Mary Pickford

Mary cut her hair! *Charles O. Lewis*

same equipment was sensitive enough to record the sound made by the whirring cameras. Thus sound wiped out much of the artistry that was reaching a state of perfection in silent films: the lovely glass shots, for example, and tricky double exposures made in the camera. In the first few years, until new techniques were perfected, sound recording governed photography.

The problems, frustrations, new rivalries and bickerings all fell on Mary Pickford as both star and producer of *Coquette,* and she was alone. Mama was gone, and Doug was having the time of his life making his own film.

To prevent the recording equipment from picking up the sound of

The Academy Award for Best Actress went to Mary for her performance in *Coquette,* a deep, moving tragedy which brought stars to Mary's crown as well as tears to the eyes of millions. *Wisconsin Center for Film and Theater Research*

the camera, it had to be enclosed in a soundproof booth with glass two inches thick in front of the lens. Because the booth was stationary and the lens was fixed, a separate camera was required for each shot. Charles Rosher, Mary's cameraman, was expected to shoot the opening scene with three enclosed cameras, one close, one medium, one long. For reasons dictated by the sound engineers Mary had to make her opening appearance from the wrong side—exposing her "monkey face" to the cameras. Even the lighting was controlled by the sound men, which meant that Rosher was unable to follow Mary from camera to camera with his special lighting effects. The first rushes were terrible; Mary, at thirty-five, did not look like a young college girl. Nor could Rosher improve upon them. So, in addition to all the obvious problems a star would have in her first talking, short-haired, dramatic role, Mary the producer had to dismiss the great Charles Rosher and find a replacement who could do what he, with all his genius, could not. She called Karl Struss, who had worked with her before; he was in New York but came to Los Angeles immediately, arriving on Sunday and going straight to the set.

"I had a light I called a wrinkle eradicator that I used just below the lens," Struss said. "It gave a softer light to the eyes. I also had special brown reflectors that I could turn to create special effects. Mary's cousin was flitting around wringing her hands. 'Just tell Mary to relax,' I told her. 'Sam Taylor will direct, she will act, I will set the lights, and everything will be all right.' "

For the dramatic courtroom scene of *Coquette*, Struss set up six cameras at different distances and angles, each with 990 feet of film. As none of these could handle a close-up, Mary repeated the scene for a special camera manned by Struss himself, with an assistant ("When I crawled out of that hot box, I couldn't stand myself"). For every foot of the nine-minute scene, there were seven choices. The scene, shot in the fall of 1928 when sound techniques were in their infancy, compares favorably with modern cinematography.

Many people who saw *Coquette* in 1929 still remember it today. "I couldn't tell you what it was about," one woman remarked, "but I remember coming out of the theater with my eyes red and my hankie soaking wet, and I could hardly wait to go back the next day."

The film opens with a long shot of Mary coming down a staircase, approaching us—with bobbed hair! It is most becoming, too; Mary's just as pretty as a picture. But in a matter of seconds we forget that she is Mary Pickford. She is instead an engaging but shallow, spoiled southern flirt. She is convincing, her accent is convincing—after all, she had worked hard to attain it for *The Warrens of Virginia,* and even harder to perfect it for *Coquette.* In *Coquette* Mary is a girl of good family; her sweetheart, played by Johnny Mack Brown, is handsome and honest, but a redneck. Her father erroneously believes the worst and shoots the boy; in the dramatic courtroom scene Mary, grief stricken but loyal, lies to save her father. In the film Mary changes before our eyes from an empty-headed little flirt into a young woman tenderly in love; then she grows with tragedy and duty into a fully defined, beautiful woman to whom we give our heart and our tears. Her performance in *Coquette* won, and deserved, the award for best actress given by the Academy of Motion Picture Arts and Sciences of which she had been a prominent co-founder two years earlier.

Together and Apart

Another co-founder and the first president of the Academy, Douglas Fairbanks, also made one of the finest films of his career that year, *The Iron Mask.* Dispensing with new-fangled sound in a tossed-off epilogue, the film represented the ultimate in the then-disappearing art of the silent film. Allan Dwan returned to the Fairbanks stable to direct it and, he recalled later, "we could do all the things we had done before only so much better." He was referring to technical effects, but he could also have been speaking of Doug. For a shot in which Doug catapults out of a tree onto a windowsill Dwan had calibrated the distance and amount of drop from an equation containing Doug's height and weight, forward velocity, and gravitational pull, but it was Doug who did it. A gymnastic coach observing the stunt—Doug had obviously swung from a horizontal bar concealed in the branches—gave a little whistle and said, "That's one hell of a move. It would challenge a champion gymnast today." Doug was forty-five years old.

And Mary was ten years younger. At last the time had come for the king and queen of Hollywood to appear together. They had talked about it for years—the entire industry had talked about it for years—

Doug loved the romance of the Old West, when California was a colony of Spain. He extended the film role of a Spanish grandee into real life, buying the immense acreage of Rancho Santa Fé with dreams of developing it. *Charles O. Lewis*

but they had never come to an agreement on a vehicle. Joe Schenck, president of United Artists, and Sam Taylor, the young phenomenon who had directed *Coquette,* urged them to do a Shakespearean play. Doug went along and, by elimination as much as anything else, the choice was *The Taming of the Shrew.* Mary, discussing it later, implied that the decision had been made before it was presented to her.

The very smoothness with which *The Taming of the Shrew* was put into production sets it apart from such epics as *Ben Hur, Gone with the Wind,* and *Citizen Kane,* films about which millions of words have been written. Those pictures have been discussed in terms of all phases of production, *The Taming of the Shrew* only in terms of the relationship between its stars. All accounts describe it as something of a battleground in which Fairbanks was a cad, a wastrel, and an irresponsible performer who was cruel to Mary both on- and off-camera. This interpretation could be expected from the students of Mary's films, all of whom seem to be unabashedly in love with her, but it also comes from Fairbanks's biographers as well. Even Douglas Fairbanks, Jr., who had first sprung to the defense of his father, rescinded his support following a discussion of the matter with his stepmother—forty-three years after the film was made.

A study of the accounts indicates that Mary Pickford was the sole source of information. Over the years she has referred to the filming of *The Taming of the Shrew* in many ways, but her last autobiography gives a good summary of her complaints. During the production, she wrote, Doug played the role of the man who tamed the shrew in real life as well as before the cameras. He would dawdle and delay shooting schedules, costing a lot of money. He failed to learn his lines. He demeaned her. "My confidence was completely shattered," Mary concluded, "and I was never again at ease before the camera or microphone."

Mary also criticized her own performance, berating herself, as she did so often. Thirty years later, still brooding over it, she recorded some of her lines the way she thought she should have spoken them in the first place. Delivered with great theatricality, this version was really no improvement, but the intensity of her delivery showed its importance to her ego. In this same recording session, incidentally, she complained that Doug had taken advantage of her, in a sense—he had been a Shakespearean actor, while she had not. It was a strange admission in view of the general feeling that Fairbanks, for all his success as a juvenile in light comedies, did not have his wife's acting talent.

Despite Mary's unpleasant memories of *The Taming of the Shrew*, they are not shared to the same extent by other members of the company. Lucky Humberstone, then at $250-a-week the highest paid assistant director in Hollywood, remembered some disagreeable moments on toward the end of the shooting, but he blamed them on the director, Sam Taylor. "Taylor had been wonderful on *Coquette*," Humberstone said, "but by this time he was beginning to get a big head. You know he demanded special credit—it read by William Shakespeare with *additional dialogue by Samuel Taylor*. Once I referred to him to the crew as Sam. He called me in and raised hell— he wanted to be called Mr. Taylor. Anyway, the only disruptive influence I saw was the director. You know Doug loved to sneak up behind people and goose 'em. He kept a guy on his payroll, a fat Mexican cello player, just because he put on such a big act when Doug would goose him. Well, one time I was checking things out on the set after everybody else had gone, and there was Mary, waiting for Doug. Neither of them saw me. He snuck up behind her and goosed her. She let out a yelp and then they both nearly died laughing."

Karl Struss, director of photography during the entire production, remembered it as a happy experience. "We went into it with such meticulous preparation," he recalled. "Long before the actual shooting began, for example, we shot hair tests—Miss Pickford with short hair, long hair, all kinds of hair. The final decision was curls. During the filming I do recall that Doug's characterization was different from hers —he treated her in the roughest possible way. But that was before the camera, of course, and it was a legitimate interpretation of the role. I do recall one afternoon when who should appear but Doug's man, his valet, with a tray of sandwiches and a pitcher of lemonade. He passed it all around as though he were serving at a formal lawn party. Everything stopped while we nibbled on our sandwiches and sipped our lemonade. Miss Pickford was aghast at this waste of time."

Some purists may object to the liberties taken with Shakespeare, but from the standpoint of sheer cinema entertainment, to say nothing of Shakespeare's own admonition "the play's the thing," the adaptation is highly effective. Whereas Shakespeare takes many pages to get underway, for instance, Taylor opens the film with Katherina the hellcat putting on a wonderful show. Nor did Shakespeare's Petruchio leap on a horse with Katherina on his back, but when Doug does it with a rag dummy slung across his shoulder and two men jumping on the other end of a seesaw off-camera, it's good theater.

Shakespeare's Petruchio breaks Katherina's spirit so that she becomes a dutiful wife. Doug does this in the film, too, but with a most important qualification: thinking himself alone, he soliloquizes on how he's going to do all these mean things and we see Mary eavesdropping. From this point on, therefore, everything he does is all right, for, as only Mary and the audience are aware, he is doing it with her permission. Every woman knows that Mary is in complete control of the situation, and, just in case we miss the point, in the closing scene she gives us a big wink.

However the play is staged, the tone is set by the performances of the two main characters, and no two combinations could possibly play it the same way. This production, for example, is totally different from that in which Franco Zeffirelli directed Elizabeth Taylor and Richard Burton. Miss Taylor, a full-blown woman with a big voice, comes through as a stronger shrew than Miss Pickford with her cute little mouth, but Fairbanks, virile and vital, is a far more forceful Petruchio than Burton.

It is easy to understand how Mary, plunged into this vehicle for her first appearance opposite her husband, could come to resent the whole thing. Her performance is by no means as bad as she has complained, but it is obvious that if she wanted complete equality with her leading man she is in the wrong vehicle with the wrong guy. Doug is overwhelming. As Paul Rotha, the perceptive English critic, wrote: "His Petruchio in the *Taming of the Shrew,* clad in rags, applecore in hand, jackboot on head, propped against a column of the church, was to me a symbol of the romanticism of Fairbanks. It needed a brave man, a born hero, to carry off that crude costume. Nobody can deny that Fairbanks was magnificent. I can think of no other actor in the cinema who could have achieved so much bravado with so little concern."

Rotha went on to discuss the thoroughness of all Fairbanks productions, the Fairbanks principle of surrounding himself "with persons who make claim to artistry," and getting the most out of them. Mary, for all the excellence of her films and the loyalty of her assistants, was never in such complete command. In this co-starring vehicle she found herself not only dominated before the cameras but relegated to a lower place in the production hierarchy.

Further, although she had shared the same lot with her husband since before their marriage, she had never before worked with him on the same production, same set, day in, day out. She was shocked by his working habits. Mary had always come to work early in the morning and plugged on through the day. If things went wrong, she kept trying to make them right. She was afraid not to work; she didn't know how to play. Doug's work habits, like his attitudes and personality, were completely different. Making pictures was fun for him. But if things weren't going well, if there were disagreements and confrontations, if it wasn't fun, then he had his own ways of dealing with the situation. He might practice a stunt, do some sleight of hand, organize a game, quit and go home, go off and sulk, or send in the lemonade. The one thing he would not do was stubbornly hang in there.

To Mary, with her industrious, frugal nature and her thorough knowledge of just how much it cost to have people standing around doing nothing, it was an affront when her partner fooled around. When Charlotte had been looking after Mary's interests, soothing and complimenting her, she could put up with her husband and his unusual approach to business. With Mama no longer there, and with Mary dominated by Doug all day on the set as well as at Pickfair, it is no wonder that she remembered their one co-starring film so unhappily.

At the completion of the film, however, in the fall of 1929, her feelings were not so bitter, for she willingly agreed to a vacation in Europe. They would take Gwynne, Mary's niece, to school in Switzerland. But if Mary thought they would deliver Gwynne and then turn around and come home, she was mistaken. In Lausanne, Doug suggested that they return home from west to east. He probably did not bother to tell her, if he realized it himself, that the distance would be three times as great.

It took four months; Chuck Lewis, Doug's shadow, recalled it as a happy trip. "Every day was an adventure," he said. "Doug loved humanity, he wanted to get out in the countryside, or on the streets of the city, be with the people, live the way they lived. Funny thing, though, Mary wanted to stay in the hotel."

They took the train across Europe, through the Balkans, and then went by ship to Egypt. They camped on the desert in colorful tents on

the bank of the Nile, rode camelback, climbed the pyramids. They ate
with the tribesmen, Doug plunging the proper hand into the couscous
and the goatmeat stew, shoving the food into that happy smiling
mouth. Mary couldn't even watch, much less eat anything. On around
the world they went, by steamer through the Suez, on to India, Southeast Asia, China, Japan. It was the same everywhere. Doug had the
time of his life, mixing with the people, seeing the sights, eating
whatever was put before him and thriving on it. Mary enjoyed the
sightseeing and the recognition, but the food made her ill; often, she
said, she subsisted entirely on soda water and crackers that smelled of
cockroaches.

They received a cable that *The Taming of the Shrew* was not doing
as well on the second run; apparently Shakespeare, even with Sam
Taylor's assistance, was too highbrow for the audiences of the period.
That was bad news, but the reports that reached them in late October
and November, halfway around the world and incapable of taking
prudent action even if there were any to take, were catastrophic: the
stock market had collapsed. Doug's losses were estimated to be in the
millions. Mary's money was primarily in real estate, but in those confus-
ing days she could well fear that she, too, was affected. And it would
not be so easy, now, to recoup.

Mary was already perturbed and fearful of the future when they
arrived in Japan, there to undergo the worst physical fear of her life.
In Tokyo some ten thousand people met them at the railroad station.
The crowd broke through the lines and, out of control, the ones in front
pushed by those in the rear, came close to trampling to death the
objects of their adulation. Doug and Mary, badly scratched and bruised
and really scared, were jammed up against the wall of a warehouse.
Chuck Lewis, with them then as always, spotted a window high off the
pavement and hoisted Doug to his shoulders. Doug got in, then pulled
Mary up.

Mary was still frightened, her stomach was upset, and she was several
pounds underweight when the party at last boarded a ship for the last
lap home. Christmas, the holiday she loved to spend quietly at Pickfair
with Doug and her family, came in the middle of the Pacific on the
Asama Maru. It was the longest, most miserable trip she had ever
made, and all across the Pacific she had plenty of time to brood. She
recalled how Douglas greeted crowds with his expansive wave and

happy smile and regaled the press with wildly exaggerated yarns, while she tried desperately to tell her own tales, made increasingly fanciful in sheer self-defense. In press conferences Doug was always lavish in his sincere praise of Mary; he told everyone how wonderful she was, what a great actress she was, how proud he was of her. He meant every word, too, but Mary was beginning to realize that in making her look good he was also calling attention to himself. And when they were being photographed together for newsreels, Doug would whip out a gleaming white handkerchief, ostensibly to wipe his face, but actually stealing a scene from his own wife.

Mary could also recall many days when Doug went out for a round of golf or some other pastime, leaving her in her room with only her queasy stomach for company. Mary never learned how to play. One of her activities, while Doug was out having fun, was to study French; she became accomplished in the language.

By the time the *Asama Maru* docked in Los Angeles on January 3, 1930, Mary had made up her mind. She was no longer interested in long trips all over the world. Doug could gallivant around all he pleased. She would stay home, tend to her business and her financial holdings, and make motion pictures.

Mary: Problems at Home

The agreement that Mary would stay home while Doug traveled was supposedly made with loving understanding, but it did not work out that way at all. Doug went to England with Chuck Lewis in the spring of 1930 for the Walker Cup golf match, and rumors of his separation from Mary began immediately. According to one widely printed account, Doug was involved with "a lady of title." Mary, susceptible to the press, was hurt and angry. Now she had neither Charlotte nor Doug. Nor could she retreat happily into her work, for her current film was the classic drama *Secrets*, a story full of both challenges and difficulties. Its selection by Mary is indicative of her emotions during this period, for the theme of *Secrets* is the indomitable strength of woman in preserving the family, bedrock of civilization, throughout history. The play covers three generations, and thus provided a virtuosic opportunity for Mary to play three matriarchal roles and to age with power and dignity on the screen.

Unfortunately, this very feature of *Secrets* makes it awkward to film. She struggled on with *Secrets* for several months. She had chosen her old friend Mickey Neilan as director, but Mickey could no longer shake off his hangovers and keep things bubbling along. Mary did not photograph well and her leading man, Kenneth McKenna, photographed *too* well, and too young. She had problems with Doug and Joe Schenck over the financing of the film, and the structure of the operation set up to fund it was changed several times. In August, Mary abandoned the project. She burned the film that had been shot. The cost was estimated at $300,000.

The blame for the *Secrets* fiasco has been placed on various shoulders: Mickey Neilan, said to be over the hill; Douglas Fairbanks, said to fail in giving her the support she needed; the headaches caused by the problems of sound, especially in a film with outdoor scenes. Another speculation was made by Paul D. O'Brien, who had succeeded his father, the legendary Cap O'Brien, as Mary's and Doug's attorney. From the time Cap had first brought the glamorous stars home with him in 1920, Paul O'Brien had a warm, personal affection for Doug and Mary. But he also saw them as they were—extraordinary persons with extraordinary characteristics—and he felt that Doug's image had received some unwarranted blemishes over the years.

According to his recollections of that frantic period, the abandonment of *Secrets* could not be attributed to either Fairbanks or Neilan.

"I have had some personal experience with alcoholics," O'Brien said, "and I have found that one of their characteristics is that when they get to drinking they change their mind. Then they change it back. It gets so that people working with them never know what to expect, and there's no stability, no confidence. Everybody's morale is shot, and the whole project—film business, marriage, whatever it is—goes to hell."

O'Brien did not specifically make reference to Mary in this regard. Rather, in the lawyer-like characteristic of making his point from what is omitted rather than from what is said, he remarked, "If you had seen Mary Pickford before noon in those days you would have thought her still the beautiful, intelligent, clear-minded woman she had been for so many years."

It was about this time that Mary's friends began noticing a difference in her. Strangely, there were actually very few of them; Mary was close only to her family and, to an extent, Frances Marion, who was busy with her own family and career at that time—besides, she couldn't stand Doug. One person who persisted in attempting to be friends with Mary was May McAvoy, the lovely blue-eyed brunette who had become an overnight star with her performance in *The Enchanted Cottage.* May had been an ardent admirer of Mary's and, now that she had achieved stardom herself, she dared to approach her. Mary was gracious, if not effusive, and May went further. She organized Our Club, composed of young motion picture actresses like herself, and asked Mary to be honorary president. Mary invited the young women to dinner at Pickfair for the first meeting, and they were all impressed by the palatial splendor and service. After that Our Club met in the less inhibiting atmosphere of the Biltmore, the girls gossiping and giggling over dinner, but Mary never attended.

"She explained that she never went out without Doug," May said. "It was a shame, too, because now I realize that she was very lonely. She was almost a prisoner. She needed Our Club more than we needed her!"

One afternoon May visited Harold Lloyd's wife Mildred at the sumptuous Lloyd estate near Pickfair, and on the spur of the moment they decided to drop in on Mary. They found her sitting by the pool alone—Doug was probably out playing golf. "She asked us if we'd like a drink," May said, "and Mildred and I said that would be fine, and she asked the butler to bring it. The butler refused! He wouldn't bring her a drink in her own home! He said that Mr. Fairbanks had given express orders that no drinks were to be served. Mary was so embarrassed. What right had that man to treat her so? Did he think she was a drunk? Mary used to take a drink with her mother—her mother loved to drink—but that didn't make her a drunk. Mary got around it in her own way. My husband, Maurice Cleary, was vice-president of United Artists, and we used to go to dinner at Pickfair occasionally. After dinner the men would go off by themselves—I thought it was rude and crude—and Mary would take us up to her room. She'd go in the bathroom and take a big slug of something, then rinse her mouth out with mouthwash."

Eddie Sutherland, a popular director and fun-loving, hard-drinking character right out of a Hollywood novel, reported a firsthand knowledge of Mary's well-stocked bathroom. The man who supplied her, he said, was her brother, Jack Pickford. "One time Jack and I were on a drunk and we ran out of booze," Sutherland said. "Jack said not to worry, and we drove over to Pickfair. Mary wasn't home and Jack went right on in the front door, didn't even knock, and we went straight up to her room and into her bathroom. 'Gin or whiskey?' he asked. 'The hydrogen peroxide bottle's gin, the Listerine bottle's scotch.' We sat down in the bathroom, Jack on the tub, me on the commode, and finished off both bottles. I was worried about Mary. I know what it's like to go looking for a drink and not find it. But Jack said it was okay, there was plenty more where that came from."

Mary's drinking was for years one of the best-kept secrets in Hollywood; no mention of it was ever made in the press. At that time only a very few suspected it at all. Certainly no one, least of all she herself or the starry-eyed critics of her films, ever connected it with her work.

But why would a beautiful, intelligent, clear-minded woman turn to drink at such a time? One answer, hazarded by a few persons who knew the Pickford family, was that she had been drinking for a long time, with both her family and Owen Moore. As Anita Loos, who had known Mary for sixty years, practically shouted: "All the Pickfords were alcoholics! All of them! They were all drinking when I first met them. That was the only trouble with Mary's career, her marriage, everything else."

For all Miss Loos's certainty, alcohol was probably only an occasional irritant during Mary's golden years, the twenties. Only after losing her mother was it more likely for Mary to attempt to deal with her depression with alcohol. Another cause for depression could have been Doug's overpowering personality, which made it difficult to actualize her own individuality. And though this is sheer speculation, we have seen that the teetotaler Doug placed Mary on a pedestal; the sight and sound of her under the influence of alcohol would be a shocking blow, and a powerful weapon in her hands. She could strike back at his terrible dominance and possessiveness simply by having a few drinks.

Whatever her motivation, Mary certainly managed to tear up Douglas Fairbanks. He never complained, never spoke of Mary's drinking to anyone else, not even to his son, his brother, or his best friend, but some of those who were close to him sensed his inner torment, and the cause. "One night in Paris Mary had a little too much to drink," Chuck Lewis said, "and she got mad at Doug, screamed at him and flounced out. Doug sat there stewing for a minute, then turned to me and said, 'Chuck, please follow her and make sure she gets back to the hotel all right.' It was not the last time he asked me to follow her home, either. He never said anything else, I knew how much it bothered him."

It would not have been the rare overt occasions as much as the more frequent evenings of covert drinking alone or with her family, whom he detested, that tortured Doug. One of the worst things about closet drinkers is that there comes a time, after the guests go home or they reach a saturation point, when they relax their control, and then they're just like other drunks. And that, too often, is how Douglas Fairbanks must have seen the woman he loved. It must have been especially harrowing to a man who had signed the temperance pledge when he was twelve, convinced that drink and drunkenness were disgusting, and who had never been even a little tipsy himself.

Breakup

Whatever the cause of *Secrets'* abortion, Doug responded in his typical way. After telling reporters that it was all his fault, he took Mary off on a short vacation in nearby resorts, then returned to throw himself into his next film, *Reaching for the Moon.* Again, the reasons for Doug's choice of a vehicle are almost pathetically transparent when we consider his situation at the time. Here he is, forty-seven years old, combing his hair carefully to cover his bald spot. Though he makes brave jokes about his stocks having fallen arches, he is nevertheless hurt financially by the decline of the stock market, and bitterly disappointed, too, for it has shaken his simplistic, Teddy Roosevelt–inspired belief in the American dream. He is beginning to have serious problems with his wife, America's Sweetheart, whom he still loves. He has mastered both his art and his business, one of the few in the history of entertainment to do so, but now he finds himself in a whole new ball game! Sound, with its ubiquitous microphones and boxed-in cameras, has placed restrictions on the very phase of filmmaking at which he excels.

And so, for his next picture Doug went to the popular musical

Doug and Doug Jr., after bouncing in and out of each other's lives, came to appreciate each other as Doug Jr.—and perhaps Doug as well!—reached maturity. *Wisconsin Center for Film and Theater Research*

comedy writer and composer Irving Berlin for a story with music, adapted and directed by the highly respected Edmund Goulding. In *Reaching for the Moon* Doug plays a young, fantastically successful stockbroker who manipulates the market like a game. He falls in love —for the first time—with a girl who is even more of a fantasized image than he is: she is a beautiful, wealthy, socially prominent aviatrix who is always winning airplane races and getting her picture in the paper. Through twists of plot Doug finds himself on an ocean liner when the stock market, out of control due to his absence, crashes and wipes him out. Next he discovers that the girl has been toying with him. So what does he do? He takes on the entire ship in a great free-for-all, a marvelous fight scene in which he shows off that bronzed muscular body in a violent ballet of strength and grace. After he beats up everybody the girl flings herself into his arms and challenges him to win his fortune back for her. "I will! I will! I will!" he cries. The film is excellently staged and directed and has a fine cast, including the beautiful star Bebe Daniels, and a young singer, Bing Crosby, making his film debut. But it is still obviously a vehicle for Douglas Fairbanks to act out a bucketful of fantasies.

While Doug was attempting to recapture his rollicking, frolicking youth in *Reaching for the Moon*, Mary was making a desperate attempt of her own. Her new film was *Kiki*, in which she plays a French chorus girl who chases a married man, even spends a night in his apartment (his wife is cheating on him, which is supposed to make it all right). The film has one delightful and hilarious number, directed by Busby Berkeley, in which Mary, playing a chorus girl pretending to be a chorus boy in top hat and tails, with frozen expression and Chaplinesque movements, gets mixed up in an unfamiliar routine. But more typical of the picture, unfortunately, is one of the first scenes Mary plays with the leading man, Reginald Denny, in which we find ourselves watching Miss Pickford with her hand inside her décolletage, fondling her left breast. After too many moments, she pulls out a brassiere. "I busted my brassiere," she says in her French accent. "It is most annoying to have these men attack you. I have to buy a new one practically every week."

It is obvious that Mary is trying to be modern, sexy, brash. She succeeds only in being embarrassing. If Charlotte had been alive, she would never have let Mary make that awful film.

Mary as Kiki, a chorus girl with a French accent. *Academy of Motion Picture Arts and Sciences*

After these individual blatant efforts to portray their fantasized images of themselves, early in 1931 they took their first trip to Europe together in more than a year. On the Riviera, Doug ran into an old friend from the early New York days, Lorillard S. Tailer, an heir to the Lorillard fortune and a cousin of Griswold Lorillard, with whom, Tailer was convinced, Doug had attended Harvard.

"Doug was as crazy about golf as I was," Larry recalled. "He'd paid a golf pro $10,000 to get his handicap from seven to two. He seemed to be having wife trouble—I was too—we just said to hell with them and played thirty-six holes a day. Then we entered an international match scheduled for Easter Week in Rome. Mary wanted to go home, but Doug wasn't about to—'We're going to Rome!' he kept saying to her. 'Come with me.' He was awfully perturbed at the thought of her leaving, but she did go without him, and my wife went without me, and after that we didn't think about them one damn bit! So off we went to Rome.

"Next morning I went to Doug's suite for breakfast. All of a sudden out of the bedroom comes this beautiful Italian girl with nothing on but her fingernail polish, and practically choked him to death. He said, 'Excuse me, Larry, I'll see you a little later.' And I said, 'But Doug, we've got thirty-six holes to play today!' He said, 'I'll be all right.' He was, too. I'll never forget the tremendous drive he made to birdie the thirty-fifth hole—we won the match! We went on to play in Prague, and Troon in England, and there were other beautiful women chasing him, and sometimes he let them catch him. I got to thinking, what about Mary. He'd never cheated on her before that I knew of. But he frowned and said, 'The ball is out of bounds.' She'd left him and gone home, and when the ball is out of bounds you play another."

Accusations of infidelity had been made before, but this was the first confirmed case of it. Doug's friends agreed that he had never been a woman chaser, that he had long remained faithful to Mary in a quaint old-fashioned way unusual to Hollywood. "It was when they began spending so much time apart, Doug traveling all over the place, Mary staying home, that Doug began seeing other women," Paul O'Brien said. And Chuck Lewis, asked about it point-blank, said, "Well, he was human, and there were lots of women willing to play. But that was when Mary wasn't around. He never hurt anybody, he was always discreet."

Though there was never any doubt as to Mary's glamor and beauty, her public just simply wanted her to remain Little Mary. *Charles O. Lewis*

So was Mary. Indeed, so discreet were both that it is a question as to which one strayed first. Certainly Mary's need came first. Charlotte's death deprived her of the support she had had for so long. Doug gave her Rolls Royces and trips around the world—which she could well afford herself—but he was hardly the kind of person she could plug into for the quiet loving tenderness she needed. That kind of person was right there waiting. He was Buddy Rogers.

Whatever the relationship between them while working in *My Best Girl*, it was enhanced in their subsequent meetings. Buddy was one of the young bachelors often summoned to Pickfair as extra men. In contrast to the host and husband at Pickfair, exuding vitality and demanding attention, Buddy, with his haunting resemblance to Charlotte, was considerate, solicitous, and secure. And in love. When did Mary first accept that love? A friend of Buddy's said that he knew something was going on as early as 1929, when Mary was filming *The Taming of the Shrew*, but it was not until two years later, after Mary's return from Nice, that their relationship became public knowledge. It was rather embarrassing, too; they were alone in a motorboat on the Hudson River some miles above New York when the engine failed, and Buddy had to get help to make shore.

Paul O'Brien felt it his duty to report the event to Doug when he returned from Europe. "I expected him to be angry, or hurt," O'Brien said. "Instead he laughed like hell. He thought it was a big joke."

Fairbanks may have laughed like hell, but probably not because he thought it was a big joke. After twelve years of jealousy, at last he had something to be jealous about. He couldn't let O'Brien see him cry, so he laughed. And it could hardly be coincidence that he left almost immediately for a long tour of the South Seas, the Philippines, Southeast Asia, and Japan. This time, along with Chuck Lewis, he took with him director Victor Fleming and cameraman Henry Sharp. They brought back some fairly interesting travel shots that Doug and Fleming put together to make *Around the World in Eighty Minutes*, for which Robert E. Sherwood wrote the commentary. The film was pleasant and profitable, and had given Doug an excuse to run away. But he was home to spend Christmas at Pickfair with Mary. Even with alcohol and infidelity between them, they were happy enough together to plan an extensive addition to Pickfair. The 1932 Olympics were to be held in Los Angeles that summer, and they anticipated many visitors.

As he and Mary saw less and less of each other, Doug traveled the world over in search of new thrills. Here he is enjoying that new sport, skiing, in Switzerland with Charlie Chaplin. *Charles O. Lewis*

In his restless search for new adventure Doug took up big-game hunting. He was successful, though he actually hated killing. *Charles O. Lewis*

Here is more of Douglas Fairbanks—and Chuck Lewis— than most people have seen before. They are cooling off themselves and an elephant in a stream in Cooch Behar, India. *Charles O. Lewis*

Doug took off for Tahiti shortly after the new year began to make *Mr. Robinson Crusoe.* Hollywood buzzed with stories of his conquests with the Polynesian maidens. But, said Eddie Sutherland, the director, "That wasn't Doug, that was me. The girls there were very friendly, which meant that most of them had the clap. I made friends with the doctor, and he told me which ones didn't. All Doug did was walk on the beach and look at the sunset with them. Doug was too square to fool around."

On the first day of shooting Sutherland discovered the sound equipment wasn't working and it would take weeks to get another set. Everyone was disconsolate. "I had an idea," Sutherland said. "We shot

When he wanted a vacation in the South Seas, Doug simply packed up a boatload of friends and technicians and shot *Mr. Robinson Crusoe* in Tahiti. Here is one of the sets. *Charles O. Lewis*

the whole film, everybody saying the words, then when we got back to Hollywood we dubbed in the sound. It worked perfectly for everybody but Doug, he was always a frame off. I finally gave up trying to make his voice fit the film, and cut the film to make it fit his voice. It was a fairly good picture. It made money. *All* Fairbanks pictures made money."

It was ironic that, for all his travels, Doug made more films and brought in far more revenue to United Artists than Mary. She was doggedly making a second effort on *Secrets*. She had appealed to Frances Marion to do the scenario: "You're the only one who can write for me," she said. Frances hated the story—she had written it once before—but she understood Mary's desire to make the film.

"Mary saw herself in those costumes," Frances explained. "She saw herself in a great dramatic role, making an impact on Doug as well as on her public. She would be faithful to one man on the screen, through three generations. She felt it would be the vehicle through which she could prove herself all over again. I'm a woman, too. I understood."

But *Secrets*, with a good portrayal of a frontier woman by Mary and a strange performance by the fragile English actor Leslie Howard as a rugged pioneer, was an unhappy choice for Mary's last cinema appearance.

The Olympics came, and Pickfair was crowded and happy that summer of 1932. Then came the letdown and again Doug fled, this time to the Gobi Desert, in an unsuccessful attempt to hunt giant panda in Nepal with the famous naturalist Roy Chapman Andrews, and finally to England with Chuck Lewis for golf.

But again he was home for Christmas. He and Mary came together, then separated, like the ends of an accordion. Impossible as their situation had become, their love for each other was still so strong that it kept pulling them back together. But more forces were introduced to keep them apart. In London, Doug met a woman who fulfilled many of his fantasies, just as Buddy Rogers provided the emotional security Mary was seeking. One evening, in the swank Trocadero restaurant, Doug noticed a most attractive young woman, slender and blonde. He arranged to meet her, and liked her high expressive voice, her quick happy laugh, and as an anglophile impressed by titles, he liked her name, too. Though she was a former chorus girl named Sylvia Hawkes, the daughter of a livery stable employee, and though she was estranged from her husband, Lord Ashley, heir to the ninth earl of Shaftesbury, she was still known as Lady Ashley. She was attracted to the famous American movie star, too, though he was fifty and she twenty-nine. Her sister said many years later, after Sylvia's fifth marriage, that "Doug was the only man she ever really loved."

Practically everyone in the London social set, and their friends in New York and Hollywood, knew about Doug and Lady Ashley before Mary, who learned of the romance only when a bracelet ordered for Sylvia was delivered to her by mistake. It was now Mary's turn to be jealous with good reason. She demanded an explanation, and in his infatuation, with a continent and an ocean between them, Doug replied too frankly. He was thinking of staying in England permanently, he cabled. He no longer intended to pay for the upkeep of Pickfair.

It could have happened only in Hollywood; one day in July 1933, Mary and Frances Marion had lunch with Louella Parsons, the columnist, and showed her the cable. Louella broke the story under headlines of the size usually reserved for war, and papers around the world followed the example. The long-whispered rumors of trouble in the Pickfair paradise were now substantiated. Though the strange magnetism pulled them together again for a brief spell in the fall of 1933, and though Doug recanted his threat about Pickfair, Mary filed for divorce in December. For the first time, Mr. and Mrs. Fairbanks spent Christmas apart. Mary was finding temporary solace in work, making appearances across the country and playing in a radio drama; Doug was traveling restlessly.

Torn between Mary and Lady Ashley, between California and England, Doug was an easy mark for a Hungarian-born British producer, Alexander Korda, in Korda's efforts to tie in with United Artists. An expansive, enthusiastic entrepreneur who seemed to perceive the fading anglophile's weaknesses, Korda built a film around Doug and enticed him to appear in it by arranging for him to live beyond his dreams. While making the picture he would stay at a magnificent country estate so huge that twenty-six gardeners were required to maintain the beautifully landscaped grounds. Every weekend the house was filled with guests, including Lady Ashley.

In the film *The Private Life of Don Juan,* Doug is surrounded with English beauties—Merle Oberon, Benita Hume, Binnie Barnes. Although the picture is beautifully photographed and well directed, it is, at least for those who remembered and appreciated Douglas Fairbanks, depressing and embarrassing. In a scene that goes on interminably the aging Don Juan, played by the aging Fairbanks, cries out again and again that he really is Don Juan, really, really. The disappointment of the film is somewhat eased by the assurance of Doug Jr. that his father didn't care about the project and was happy with his perquisites.

While making *Don Juan*, Doug was served a legal document that shocked and angered him: Lord Ashley was petitioning for divorce, citing Doug as corespondent. Furious as he was, he thought of Mary and realized how the headlines would affect her. He called in an effort to prepare her. "I'm afraid we're in a little trouble, Hipper," he began, but Mary was not amused. She took this public disclosure that her

Fairbanks played an aging Don Juan in an embarrassing film, but with an English estate at his disposal he lived the life of a lord and was happy. With him are Joan Gardner, Elsa Lancaster, Benita Hume, and Merle Oberon. *George Eastman House*

husband—the divorce was not yet final—had been intimate with another woman as a personal blow. Still, even after Ashley had been granted his divorce on the specified charges, even after Doug had chartered a yacht and taken Sylvia and her friends on a four-month cruise from the Virgin Islands to Singapore, Doug continued to be pulled back to Mary, often with the connivance of friends and relatives. Joe Schenck, the head of United Artists, tracked Doug down in Spain and brought him back to Hollywood in an effort to get them together again. Mary's family, Doug's family, and many of their business associates and friends tried to effect a reconciliation. Cap O'Brien, who always referred to Sylvia as Lady Ashcan, commissioned an investigation of her past history in the hope that its results would turn Doug against her. Chuck Lewis, though loyal to Doug and convinced that he was the more aggrieved party, always believed that he would be happier back with Mary. "All Doug ever wanted," he said, "was a sober Mary."

Their love refused to die; neither could kill it. Each had now hurt the other in the most sensitive, vulnerable areas. Doug, since boyhood offended by alcohol, had had drunkenness thrown in his face. A romantic Victorian bearer of the double standard, pathologically jealous, he now had to live with the knowledge that his wife had been intimate with another man. Mary, herself susceptible to jealousy, now knew that her husband had had an affair with another woman, but—and this is what really hurt—the world knew it too.

"I was sick of the whole thing," Frances Marion said. "A reconciliation didn't have a chance. Doug wasn't big enough to forgive and forget, and Mary knew it. And still, she'd ask me, her eyes brimming with tears, if I didn't think she could find happiness with Douglas again."

Doug, after the divorce became final in January 1936, put on one more campaign to win Mary back. He was staying with his brother John's daughter Mary Margaret, and every day he tried to arrange some kind of meeting with Mary—morning, luncheon, afternoon, dinner, evening, it made no difference. Sometimes she would agree to see him, and he would go off, eyes sparkling, teeth flashing. Even when he could not see her, he put on a good front as he went off to talk business or play golf. One day when a forest fire was raging nearby, he chartered a plane to get a close look at it, taking Mary Margaret and some friends along. After seeing the fire, he was restless—did they want to go south

A new element came into Doug's anglophile life when he met in London a beautiful woman with a prestigious name—Lady Ashley. He chartered a yacht and took her on a cruise—destination, Japan. *Charles O. Lewis*

Lady Ashley discovered that life with Fairbanks would not be all glamor, as when they stopped in the New Hebrides. But the romance continued. *Charles O. Lewis*

to Mexico, east to Arizona, north to San Francisco? San Francisco won, the pilot radioed ahead, and when the plane landed limousines were waiting to take the party to a sumptuous dinner in a private dining room at the Mark Hopkins Hotel.

"But there were many nights when we'd sit at home, just the two of us, playing double solitaire," Mary Margaret recalled. "I wound up owing him two hundred and fifty dollars. He'd talk about settling down in a villa in Rome and reading books. 'When you've been every place, seen everything, there's nothing left to strive for,' he said. That just wasn't like Uncle Doug. I didn't realize it then, I was so happy to be with him, but he must have been miserable."

And Mary was unhappy, too. Although, Frances Marion recalled, Mary's eyes always lit up when Doug called her, she could not bring herself to welcome him back, not after just receiving her final decree. Imagine the headlines! Doug, perceptive in his desperation, told Mary that he would get out of her sight, leave southern California, and if she wanted him back, she would not have to say anything that would embarrass her, only "Come home for Christmas dinner." Then, with Doug Jr., with whom he was finally developing some rapport, he took the train east. For probably the first time in his life, he revealed his deepest feelings to another male: all across the continent he wrote long telegrams to Mary, showed them to Doug Jr., and frankly discussed them with him. "I don't remember the exact wording of any of the messages," Doug Jr. said later, "but I do recall the tone. He was pleading, beseeching, he crawled. He was prepared to take all the blame, not only for his own indiscretions but for hers."

In New York Doug went to the Waldorf Astoria, and Doug Jr. stayed in his mother's apartment. They saw *The Postman Always Rings Twice* together and agreed to have lunch the next day. But the next morning a mutual friend told Doug Jr. that his father had sailed for Europe and wanted him to pick up his mail. At the hotel the room clerk apologetically handed him a telegram that had been placed in the wrong box. It was for Doug, from Mary. She had telephoned but had not been able to reach him.

The night before, after seeing the depressing play, Doug had gone back to the hotel alone and left word not to be disturbed. Rising early, as always, he asked the clerk to check his box: nothing, no word from Mary. Despondent, he turned to the familiar solution: running away.

A liner was sailing for Europe that very morning and there was always a cabin for Douglas Fairbanks. To make sure that he would receive a welcome on the other side of the ocean, he put in a transatlantic call. Yes, said Sylvia, she would marry him. Doug boarded the ship. It was out of sight of land when the ship-to-shore call from Doug Jr. came in. There was a message from Mary, he shouted. She wanted him to call her.

It had been a bad day for Douglas Fairbanks; he refused to believe his son, who then called Mary in California and told her the whole story. She was at first reluctant to do any more; sending the telegram had taken a lot out of her. Doug Jr. quietly persisted and she finally agreed to call Doug at sea, waiting while the operators went through the lengthy procedure. Finally, via telephone wire and radio link, accompanied by squeals and static, Doug's voice came on the phone. Embarrassed and shy, he asked if what she wanted to tell him was what he had hoped.

Anyone overhearing her answer on the air must surely have wondered about the urgency of her call, for she said, "Yes, Douglas, I wanted to ask you to come to Christmas dinner."

There was a long pause. "It's too late," Doug Fairbanks said. "It's just too late."

CHAPTER TEN

Doug and Mary:
The Final Years,
1936–

Douglas Fairbanks and Sylvia Ashley were married in Paris on March 7, 1936. Doug had turned over his share of Pickfair to Mary Pickford as part of the divorce settlement, and he brought his bride home to the beach house in Santa Monica. All Hollywood chose up sides, with the great majority favoring America's Sweetheart, the wronged little woman. Stories were told of Doug introducing the new Mrs. Fairbanks as "My wife, Lady Ashley," and buying her a Rolls Royce with the Ashley coat of arms emblazoned on the door.

Some of Doug's friends and relatives continued to resent her, and have described her as cold and mercenary. Although over the years she had an unusual list of husbands, consisting of two English lords, two Hollywood kings (Fairbanks and Clark Gable), and one Russian prince, she preferred privacy and was never known to the public. But many of the people who visited her and Doug felt that they were happy together. Thirty-five years later her niece would recall happy visits to the beach house. "Aunt Syllie and Uncle Doug just did all kinds of fun things," she said.

With a base in the area once again, Doug resumed an active life in Hollywood. He looked into motion picture ventures and played golf nearly every day, sometimes thirty-six holes. But a new element was added to his life: Sylvia liked to stay up at night. "That woman will kill him," Mary said.

Mary married Buddy Rogers in June 1937. "I have never been so happy, I never expect to be so happy again," Mary said after the lovely ceremony, and many members of the film colony approved. "We were all glad to see Miss Pickford find happiness with Buddy," Hal Mohr explained. "Doug was just too much Doug."

"I have never been so happy, I never hope to be so happy again." *Mary Pickford Corporation*

With natural beauty and a delightful sense of humor, Sylvia brought Doug
happiness. They are with Fred and Adele Astaire, left, and David Niven
and Norma Shearer, right. *Charles O. Lewis*

Beaming with pride, Doug brought his new English bride home to
America, where they were met at the pier, as usual, by photographers.
George Eastman House

The happy couple talked of finding a new home, but Buddy gradually settled in at Pickfair. While Mary remained active at United Artists, Buddy continued in films, then organized an orchestra. Mary went with him as he played engagements in major cities. They were in Chicago in December 1939 when Mary heard the tragic news from Hollywood.

On Saturday, December 9, Doug and Sylvia went to a football game, then to Douglas Jr.'s birthday party. At the party, late that night, Doug's niece Mary Margaret saw him lean his head back against a chair for a moment and close his eyes. "Are you all right?" she asked.

"I'm tired," he answered, "so tired."

The next morning he had a pain in his chest, severe enough for him to agree to see a doctor. The doctor came and arranged for an electrocardiogram which revealed that Doug had suffered a heart attack. He prescribed a sedative and the standard treatment of the day: bed rest for months, if not longer.

Doug had several visitors during the day; his son came in to read him some poems, and Sylvia was in and out. A male nurse was retained for the night but stayed outside Doug's room. As had been Doug's custom for years, he did not want anyone to see him asleep; when taking a nap he always put a handkerchief over his face. About midnight he called the nurse and asked him to open the window so that he could hear the surf. To the routine query he barked out, "I never felt better in my life!" Sometime later, all alone, he quietly died.

Throughout Hollywood lay diagnoses were made that are still being repeated: Doug exercised too much, he was musclebound and the blood wouldn't circulate properly, he couldn't stand the thought of remaining inactive so long and drifted away through choice. We know today, of course, that far from contributing to his death his constant exercise and excellent physical condition may well have postponed it. His heart attack could rather have been attributed to inheritance, tension, rich food, lack of sleep, excessive smoking, and his age; heart attacks at fifty-six are not unusual. And his death, following the initial attack by some eighteen hours, was again, unfortunately, not unusual. The danger period lasts for forty-eight to seventy-two hours after the coronary occlusion; if Fairbanks had spent that period in a modern intensive care unit and, after recovery, had modified his lifestyle to continue his exercise but not his diet, his late hours, and his cigarettes, he might well have lived to a ripe old age.

Some of the old effortless grace might be gone at the age of 56, but the strength and desire were still there. Doug Fairbanks never quit trying.
United Press International

Mary, in Chicago, was told of his death by telephone. Buddy Rogers, a kind and considerate man, offered to comfort her, then left her alone to cry.

Over the years Buddy remained gentle, loving, and permissive. He was not excessively jealous, nor did he have any hangups about alcohol. "That little devil," Eddie Sutherland said Buddy told him once, affection in his voice, "she gets to drinking and she just can't stop."

Few others knew of this side of Mary, however, and as her loyal friend Frances Marion demanded in a conversation just before Frances's death in 1974, "Why should they? What's that got to do with the happiness Mary Pickford brought the world?"

Mary continued to bring happiness to the world long after she ended her film career. She made personal and radio appearances. She remained active in United Artists, finally selling out her interests in 1956, and was active in many philanthropies. She struck terror in the hearts of the increasing numbers of those who consider the film America's greatest art form when she announced that she was going to destroy all her old films; she did not want Little Mary to be ridiculed, shown as campy slapstick. Influenced by the pleas of Buddy Rogers, Lillian Gish, and Matty Kemp, managing director of the Mary Pickford Company, she not only relented, but provided a $250,000 fund for the restoration and preservation, under Kemp's direction, of as many films as could be saved. Most of her films are available, from the earliest flickering one-reelers to *Kiki,* including her superb characterizations in *Tess of the Storm Country, Stella Maris,* and *Coquette.*

Douglas Fairbanks still lives on film, too, from the earliest comedies on into technicolor and sound.

In the early 1970s Mary Pickford, approaching eighty, retired to her large, sunny bedroom overlooking the green lawn of Pickfair, and remained there, seeing only Buddy and a few old friends and servants. In 1976 she was presented a special award by the Academy of Motion Picture Arts and Sciences, and, still beautiful and articulate at the age of eighty-three, she was seen and heard for the first time by millions.

The television cameras also gave a quick glance at Pickfair, and lingered on a portrait of Mary with her golden curls, painted during those golden years when she and Douglas Fairbanks were the most recognized, the most loved couple in the world. Those days were gone, of course, like the golden curls and the silent screen. So was that powerful, romantic, idyllic love that she and Doug had shared. But while they shared that love they also nurtured the growth of America's art form and gloried in the love of millions of people all over the world. No other couple ever reached that popularity; no other couple ever will. No matter what happened later, for a glorious decade they enjoyed a happiness that surpassed their dreams.

COMMENTARY ON SOURCES

This book began in the spring of 1972, when my wife Bonnie, who was writing a book with Miriam Cooper, a silent screen star and a friend of Mary Pickford and Douglas Fairbanks, went to the library to get a book on the famous couple and found that there were none. We immediately set about the job of providing one. Five and a half years later, what started out to be a popular biography of two entertainers has become an exhaustively researched study of two complex personalities and the industry and art form in which they were inextricably involved. As the book is still directed more to readers than scholars, I have not burdened them with notes, but for those serious students of film history —and 800 American institutions offer 10,000 courses in film and television —here are some comments on the sources of information.

Researching a book dealing with motion pictures presents an unexpected and unusual challenge. For almost every subject there exists written material providing a reliable background, as well as a circle of knowledgeable persons. In film history, particularly biography, however, the researcher finds himself in a whole genre of substandard literature—slap-dash, poorly researched, full of inaccuracies, distortions, and fantasy. As Arthur G. Lennig, professor of cinema at the State University of New York at Albany, wrote to me, "One kind word of advice. ALL, I repeat, ALL books are inaccurate on the movies." Authors themselves do not protest too much. Ralph Hancock, co-author of *The Fourth Musketeer*, when asked about a seeming discrepancy in the book, said, "Look, I had to fill those pages in some way. If you have a different version, I'd advise you to go with it."

And Anita Loos replied to a question about an apparent variance from fact in one of her books: "I think you're taking the whole thing too seriously. Who cares about the movies?"

Just as biographies and memoirs of film people can be distorted, so their recollections in interviews may also be misleading. They are, after all, entertainers. The very qualities that enable them to reach the eminence in which their statements and observations matter also impel them to tell their interviewers what they think their interviewers want to hear. The best example was Judy Garland, on the way to her analyst, making up exciting dreams to tell him.

These are also imaginative people. A highly respected director told me at length of going to a Rose Bowl game with Mary Pickford, calling her attention to a player named Johnny Mack Brown, and taking her to the dressing room after the game to sign him up to appear with her in *Coquette*. Brown had indeed played end for Alabama in the Rose Bowl game, but had gone back to Alabama for a year and then appeared in several films before *Coquette*. The director, apprised of this in a subsequent meeting, looked at me perplexedly and muttered, "Could I have dreamed it?" I did not answer him, for the answer would have been yes, he did dream it. He was only one of many who told me their dreams, or made up entertaining stories when I was hoping for facts.

Both Douglas Fairbanks and Mary Pickford were also prone to repeating dreams as facts, though in different degree. Attempting to find the real Douglas Fairbanks was frustrating in that he rarely talked about his early days, and much of what he or his press agents did say was obviously fanciful. On the other hand, an enormous amount of copy on Mary Pickford, beginning with her birth, was turned out under her name, all apparently earnest and sincere. With her the question is, *which* Mary Pickford, *which* version of the of the same event?

It would be difficult, if not impossible, for an ordinary person to understand these extraordinary people. Of all the individuals interviewed, therefore, even those closest to Mary and Doug, none was a more indispensable key than Dr. Seymour Rabinowitz, psychoanalyst and professor of psychiatry. Dr. Rabinowitz read many drafts of the manuscript, participated in hours of discussion, and, in effect, served as a guide through the labyrinths of two fascinating personalities.

I was also fortunate in being able to talk to those people who, outside of their families, were probably the most intimate with Mary and Doug during their peak years. It's doubtful if Mary had any close friend other than Frances Marion. In our sessions, which to me were delightful, Miss Marion, though in her late seventies and in the last few weeks of her life, was most perceptive and obviously accurate in her recollections, for we both had voluminous material to back them up. Others who talked to me of Mary personally, each contributing importantly to the mosaic of her personality and her career, included her contemporary actresses Lillian Gish, Blanche Sweet, Miriam Cooper, and May McAvoy, and Donald Crisp and Allan Dwan. As noted in the text, my audacity in contradicting Miss Pickford's accounts of *The Taming of the Shrew* grew from interviews with others on the set—Lucky Humberstone, Karl Struss, and the charming Dorothy Jordan, Mrs. Merian C. Cooper. The second generation Fairbankses, of course, have long known Mary well, and in recent years others, such as her cousin, producer John Mantley, and the sensitive and capable managing director of the Mary Pickford Company, Matty Kemp, have been close to her and have spoken frankly.

In the case of Douglas Fairbanks, I interviewed many responsible people who knew him personally. His son and I have talked for many hours, and corresponded at length. Letitia Fairbanks Smoot, daughter of Robert and the family historian, repeated or corrected and augmented much of *The Fourth Musketeer.* Lucille Fairbanks Crump, her sister, confirmed most of what she said, and Mary Margaret Chappelet, daughter of John Fairbanks, discussed her Uncle Doug from her own and her father's viewpoint. All of this adds up to a composite of recollections referred to in the text as family legend.

I had the good fortune to talk with the two men who knew Douglas Fairbanks best, Chuck Lewis and Allan Dwan. Chuck Lewis, a prosaic man, gave straight answers to straight questions. To the reports that in his last years Douglas Fairbanks was a tormented, demented man in need of psychiatric treatment, Lewis gave a hearty laugh. Doug's breakup with Mary had indeed affected him deeply, Chuck said, but he was never in danger of losing his sanity. Chuck, himself still happily married to his college sweetheart of nearly sixty years before, did not approve of Sylvia Ashley or Doug's marriage to her, but he still believed Doug to be happy with her, his golf, his friends, and his many ventures.

Allan Dwan had worked even more closely with Fairbanks, from his first months in films, and was more perceptive as to his complex character. Contemporary reports proved his reliability. Well worth the effort of seeking out were Richard Talmadge in Carmel, Paul O'Brien in Sarasota, and Roy Aitken in Wisconsin. Although it was easy in Mary's case, somehow it was difficult to visualize and hear Douglas Fairbanks off screen. William Bakewell, who played the dual role of the princes in *The Iron Mask* and who was a frequent guest at Pickfair, overcame that difficulty by mimicking Doug's mannerisms —the energetic bounce, the way of forcing out his words.

One mystery remains: How in the world did the story ever get started about "Roxy" Rothapfel showing *His Picture in the Papers* under duress? The strange thing is that although Anita Loos had it happening at the Roxy (which would not open for ten years) and Richard Schickel at the Strand (which Roxy had just left), Roxy was in fact the manager of the Knickerbocker Theater for about three months, during which time the premiere of *His Picture in the Papers* occurred.

There is absolutely no question but that the premiere was previously announced and publicized—Elsie Janis, Irving Berlin, and John Barrymore were invited—but there must have been some basis for the rumor somewhere. Anita Loos, of course, can hardly be blamed for parlaying the event into her story of how she saved Doug from oblivion, but very little of it is true.

Lady Ashley, as she began calling herself again four husbands later, has unfortunately for film biography clung to her privacy over the years. The belligerence of her representatives has boomeranged, in effect, in that some writers have taken potshots at her in retaliation. I was at least able to get from her sister, Mrs. Vera Bleck, and her niece, Mrs. Lauretta Bleck Edlund, a more sympathetic portrait. Both were convincing in their belief that she married Douglas Fairbanks because she loved him and that they were happy together.

Two other questions which less accepting readers may ask are: Did Doug actually sweep Mary off her feet in the middle of the river, and did the clock actually stop in Mary's limousine when Doug burst into tears? Well, Mary wrote about the river episode in her column that year, Elsie Janis referred to it in her book, and Frances Marion, who was at the party, told me it happened. As for the clock, all that can be said is that the Fairbanks nieces report having heard Doug and Mary say to each other, softly, "by the clock."

These and other individuals consulted personally gave a depth to the biography that could not otherwise have been attained. The basic framework, however, came from the printed word—millions of printed words. A complete bibliography follows, but some sources are particularly noteworthy.

Books consulted come under the classifications of those on films, film history, and the film industry; those on or under the byline of Mary Pickford or Douglas Fairbanks; and those by or on other personalities in which there is material pertinent to either or both. Generally speaking, I found in film history that the closer the book to the period, the more complete was the information. Examples are Benjamin Hampton's *History of the American Film*

Industry, first published in 1931, and Paul Rotha's *The Film Till Now,* 1930.

Books on or by Douglas Fairbanks and Mary Pickford all contain valuable information, but practically everything must be checked for accuracy. So, too, is there information which is sometimes pertinent, sometimes erroneous, in many of the books on or by other film personalities. Some listed are obvious, such as Robert M. Henderson's biographies of D. W. Griffith, but why should William O. Douglas's *Go East Young Man* be included? Because it presents a particularly poignant insight into the problems of a fatherless youth who, like Doug, knows he must tear himself away from the security offered by his mother.

Many periodicals published major articles by or about Mary and Doug. Again, some of the earliest are the most interesting, as for example "Daily Talks," which ran from November 1915 through October 1916. Written by Frances Marion for Mary, when both were young and ingenuous, the columns not only provide a wealth of information that rings true, but are a delight to read, even in the Library of Congress microfilms of the *Detroit News,* where I found them.

A seven-part Sunday supplement series on Doug in the *Boston Post* (1921) also contained a ring of truth under the purple prose. And all through their career, the *Motion Picture News* and the *Motion Picture World* carried weekly accounts of what was going on in the film world; complete sets of each are available in the Library of Congress.

Major collections of material examined include the thousands on thousands of clips and photographs stuffed in folders and boxes in the Robinson Locke Collections in New York; the United Artists, Daniel Blum, and Triangle collections in Madison, Wisconsin; the Western History collection in Denver; and, of course, those in the Museum of Modern Art, the Library of Congress, the American Film Institute, and the Academy of Motion Picture Arts and Sciences. Sometimes hours of search produced nothing, as was the case in Duluth, Minnesota; sometimes a gem emerged, as when Sister Elizabeth Skiff, asked about a mysterious "Monsignor Masbooth" who was reported in one account, came up with Doug's baptismal certificate signed by none other than Joseph Projectus Machebeuf, the renowned archbishop of Denver who was immortalized in Willa Cather's *Death Comes to the Archbishop.*

In an area in which so much of questionable veracity has been printed, I realize that some of my statements, conclusions, and interpretations may be controversial. For the benefit of anyone interested in pursuing the subject, I am donating all my material—copies of documents, notes on interviews and films, transcripts, and synopses of books and other printed matter—to the Library of Congress where it will be available for study.

Booton Herndon

Charlottesville, Virginia
July 1977

SOURCES

PERSONAL INTERVIEWS

FAIRBANKS FAMILY

Douglas Fairbanks, Jr.
Letitia Fairbanks Smoot
Mary Margaret Fairbanks Chappelet
Lucille Fairbanks Crump

MOTION PICTURE INDUSTRY

Allan Dwan
Frances Marion
Charles O. Lewis
Richard Talmadge
Miriam Cooper
Hal Mohr
Karl Struss
May McAvoy
Donald Crisp
Roy E. Aitken

Anita Loos
Matty Kemp
Lillian Gish
Blanche Sweet
Johnny Mack Brown
Lucky Humberstone
Eddie Sutherland
William Bakewell
John Mantley
Frank Neill

Dorothy Jordan
Raymond Klune
Bobby Rose
Ray Renahan
Teet Carle
Billie Dove
Harry Brand
Slim Moorten
Raoul Walsh

FILM HISTORIANS

David L. Parker
Paul C. Spehr
George Pratt
James Card

Marshall Deutelbaum
Tino Balio
Douglas Moore
Walter Korte

Anthony Slide
Arthur C. Lennig
David Shepard
William K. Everson

OTHER AUTHORITIES

Seymour Rabinowitz, M.D.   William H. Harbaugh
Paul D. O'Brien   Patrick J. Bird
Lorillard S. Tailer   Donald G. Cooley
Ralph Hancock   Richard S. Crampton, M.D.
Mrs. Harry W. Robinson   Lauretta Bleck Edlund

TAPED INTERVIEWS

Mary Pickford with George Pratt, Eastman House
Mary Pickford with Arthur B. Friedman, Oral History Department, Columbia
  University

BIBLIOGRAPHY

Books

Aitken, Roy E. *The Birth of a Nation Story.* Middleburg, Va.: Denlinger, 1965.

Anger, Kenneth. *Hollywood Babylon.* New York: Straight Arrow, 1975.

Baxter, John. *Stunt.* New York: Doubleday, 1974.

Balio, Tino. *United Artists.* Madison: University of Wisconsin Press, 1976.

Bitzer, G.W. *Billy Bitzer, His Story.* New York: Farrar Straus and Giroux, 1973.

Bogdanovich, Peter. *Allan Dwan.* New York: Praeger, 1971.

Brown, Karl. *Adventures with D. W. Griffith.* New York: Farrar Straus and Giroux, 1973.

Brownlow, Kevin. *The Parade's Gone By.* New York: Ballantine, 1968.

Case, Frank. *Tales of a Wayward Inn.* New York: Stokes, 1938.

Chaplin, Charles. *My Autobiography.* New York: Simon and Schuster, 1964.

Colman, Juliet Benita. *Ronald Colman.* New York: Morrow, 1975.

Connell, Brian. *Knight Errant.* London: Hodder and Stoughton, 1955.

Cooke, Alastair. *Douglas Fairbanks: The Making of a Screen Character.* New York: Museum of Modern Art, 1940.

Cooper, Miriam. *Dark Lady of the Silents.* New York: Bobbs-Merrill, 1973.

Crawford, Joan. *A Portrait of Joan.* New York: Simon and Schuster, 1968.

Cushman, Robert. *Tribute to Mary Pickford.* Los Angeles: American Film Institute Theatre, 1970.

DeMille, Cecil B. *Autobiography.* Englewood Cliffs, N.J.: Prentice-Hall, 1959.

Drinkwater, John. *The Life and Adventures of Carl Laemmle.* New York: Heinemann, 1931.

Douglas, William O. *Go East, Young Man.* New York: Random House, 1974.

Eels, George. *Hedda and Louella.* New York: Putnam, 1968.

Fairbanks, Douglas, Jr. *The Fairbanks Album.* New York: New York Graphics Society, 1975.

Gish, Lillian. *D. W. Griffith, The Movies and Me.* Englewood Cliffs, N.J.: Prentice-Hall, 1968.

Goldwyn, Sam. *Behind the Screen.* New York: Doran, 1923.

Griffith, Linda Arvidson. *When the Movies Were Young.* New York: Dutton, 1925.

Griffith, Richard. *The Movies.* New York: Bonanza, 1957.

Hall, Ben B. *The Golden Age of the Movie Palace: The Best Remaining Seats.* New York: Crown, 1975.

Hampton, Benjamin P. *History of the American Film History.* New York: Dover, 1970.

Hancock, Ralph, and Fairbanks, Letitia. *The Fourth Musketeer.* New York: Holt, 1953.

Harriman, Margaret Case. *The Vicious Circle.* New York: Rinehart, 1951.

Hart, William S. *My Life East and West.* New York: Houghton Mifflin, 1929.

Henderson, Robert M. *D. W. Griffith, His Life and Work.* New York: Oxford University Press, 1972.

_____. *D. W. Griffith, The Biograph Years.* New York: Farrar, Straus and Giroux, 1970.

Higham, Charles. *Ziegfeld.* Chicago: Regnery, 1972.

Horgan, Paul. *Lamy of Santa Fe.* New York: Farrar, Straus and Giroux, 1975.

Howard, Leslie Ruth. *A Quite Remarkable Father.* New York: Harcourt Brace, 1959.

Janis, Elsie. *So Far So Good.* New York: Dutton, 1932.

Jobes, Gertrude. *Motion Picture Empire.* New York: Archon, 1966.

Knight, Arthur. *The Hollywood Style.* New York: Macmillan, 1968.

Lahue, Kalton C. *Kops and Custard: The Legend of Keystone Films.* Norman, Okla.: University of Oklahoma Press 1968.

_____. *Dreams for Sale.* New York: Barnes, 1971.

_____. *Gentlemen to the Rescue.* New York: Barnes, 1972.

Lasky, Jesse L., Jr. *Whatever Happened to Hollywood?* New York: Funk and Wagnalls, 1975.

Loos, Anita. *A Girl Like I.* New York: Ballantine, 1975.

_____. *Kiss Hollywood Goodbye.* New York: Viking, 1975.

Lord, Walter. *The Good Years.* New York: Harper and Row, 1960.

Macdonald, Dwight. *On Movies.* New York: Berkeley, 1969.

Mast, Gerald. *A Short History of the Movies.* New York: Pegasus, 1971.

_____. *The Comic Mind.* New York: Bobbs-Merrill, 1973.

Manvell, Roger. *Charles Chaplin.* Boston: Little Brown, 1974.

Marion, Frances. *Off With Their Heads.* New York: Macmillan, 1972.

Moore, Colleen. *Silent Star.* New York: Doubleday, 1968.

Münsterberg, Hugo. *Photoplay: A Psychological Study.* New York: Appleton, 1916.

Niven, David. *Bring On the Empty Horses.* New York: Putnam, 1975.

Niver, Kemp. *Mary Pickford, Comedienne.* Los Angeles: Locare, 1969.

Parrish, Robert. *Growing Up in Hollywood.* New York: Harcourt, Brace Jovanovich, 1976.

Pickford, Mary. *Why Not Try God?* New York: Kinsey, 1934.

_____. *Sunshine and Shadow.* New York: Doubleday, 1955.

Pratt, George. *Spellbound in Darkness.* New York: New York Graphics Society, 1973.

Ramsaye, Terry. *A Million and One Nights.* New York: Simon and Schuster, 1926.

Rosen, Marjorie. *Popcorn Venus.* New York: Coward McCann, 1973.

Rosenberg, Bernard. *The Real Tinsel.* New York: Macmillan, 1970.

Rotha, Paul. *The Film Till Now.* London: Jonathan Cape, 1930.

St. John, Adela Rogers. *The Honeycomb.* New York: Doubleday, 1969.

Sarris, Andrew. *The American Cinema.* New York: Dutton, 1969.

_____. *The Primal Screen.* New York: Simon and Schuster, 1973.

Schickel, Richard. *The Stars.* New York: Bonanza, 1962.

_____. *His Picture in the Papers.* New York: Charterhouse, 1973.

Spears, Jack. *Hollywood, The Golden Era.* New York: Barnes, 1971.

Slide, Anthony. *The Griffith Actresses.* New York: Barnes, 1973.

Sullivan, Mark. *Our Times.* New York: Scribner's, 1926.

Tabori, Paul. *Alexander Korda.* London: Oldburne, 1959.

Talmey, Allene. *Doug and Mary, and Others.* New York: Macy-Masius, 1927.

Ulman, Emory Washburn. *Young Lawyer U. N. Truth's First Case.* Brooklyn, N.Y.: Cullinan, 1922.

Wagenknecht, Edward. *The Movies in the Age of Innocence.* Norman: University of Oklahoma Press 1963.

Walker, Alexander. *Sex in the Movies,* Baltimore: Penguin, 1968.

_____. *Stardom.* New York: Stein and Day, 1970.

Walsh, Raoul. *Each Man in His Time.* New York: Farrar, Straus and Giroux, 1974.

Wellman, William. *A Short Time for Insanity.* New York: Hawthorn, 1974.

Windeler, Robert. *Sweetheart.* London: Allen, 1973.

Zukor, Adolph. *The Public Is Never Wrong.* New York: Putnam, 1953.

ARTICLES

By Douglas Fairbanks

"Combining Play With Work." *American,* July 1917.
"The Development of the Screen." *Moving Picture World,* 21 July 1917.
"One Reel of Autobiography." *Collier's,* 18 June 1921.
"How I Keep Running in High." *American,* December 1921.
"Why Big Pictures?" *Ladies Home Journal,* April 1924.
"A Huge Responsibility." *Ladies Home Journal,* May 1924.
"Let Me Say This for the Films." *Ladies Home Journal,* September 1924.

By Mary Pickford

"Daily Talks." *The McClure Newspaper Syndicate,* 1 November 1915–31 October 1916.
"The Portrayal of Child Roles." *Vanity Fair,* December 1917.
"The Greatest Business in the World." *Collier's,* 10 June 1922.
"My Own Story." *Ladies Home Journal,* July-September 1923.
"When I Am Old." *Photoplay,* May 1925.
"Mary Is Looking for Pictures." *Photoplay,* June 1925.
"Mary Pickford Awards." *Photoplay,* October 1925.
"Ambassadors." *Saturday Evening Post,* 23 August 1930.
"What Religion Means To Me." *Forum,* August 1933.
"Why Die?" *Liberty,* 17 August 1935.
"My Whole Life." *McCall's,* March-May 1954.

Other Sources

Bates, Billy. "The Pickford-Fairbanks Wooing." *Photoplay,* June 1920.
Belasco, David. "An Actress from the Movies." *Cosmopolitan,* October 1913.
———."When Mary Pickford Came to Me." *Photoplay,* December, 1915.
Bell, William Campton. "A History of the Denver Theatre During the Post-Pioneer Period (1881–1901)." Ph.D. dissertation, Northwestern University, July 1941.
Bisch, Louis E., M.D. "Why Can't They Stay Married?" *Photoplay,* November 1927.
Boss, B. Duncan. "The Complete List of all the DOUGLAS FAIRBANKS Motion Picture Stories (1915–1934)." Unpublished monograph prepared for Twentieth-Century Fox and presented to Museum of Modern Art.
Card, James. "The Films of Mary Pickford." *Image,* December 1959.
Cheatham, Maude S. "On Location with Mary Pickford." *Motion Picture,* June 1919.

Connolly, Myles E. "Douglas Fairbanks." *Boston Post,* 16 October–27 November 1920.

Creel, George. "A 'Close-Up' of Douglas Fairbanks." *Everybody's,* December 1916.

Donnell, Dorothy. "Mary Pickford Lives for Today." *Motion Picture,* July 1936.

Fairbanks, Douglas, Jr. "Mary Pickford." *Vanity Fair,* June 1930.

Fernsworth, Athene. "How Mary Pickford Stays Young." *Everybody's,* July 1926.

Fletcher, Adele Whitley. "Mary." *Motion Picture,* June 1922.

––––––. "As They Were." *Motion Picture,* November 1920.

Gow, Gordon. "Doug." *Films and Filming,* May 1973.

Harmetz, Aljean. "America's Sweetheart Lives." *New York Times,* 28 March 1971.

Harriman, Margaret Case. "Sweetheart." *New Yorker,* 7 April 1954.

Hicks, David. "Looking Back at Early Denver." *Westerners' Round-Up,* July-August 1974.

Hornblow, Arthur, Jr. "Douglas Fairbanks, Dramatic Dynamo." *Motion Picture Classic,* March 1917.

Howe, Herbert. "Mary Pickford's Favorite Stars." *Photoplay,* June 1924.

Johnson, Julian. "Mary Pickford: Herself and Her Career." *Photoplay,* November 1915 to March 1916.

Johnston, William A. "Box Office Verdict." *Saturday Evening Post,* 10 November 1923.

Kegler, Estelle. "Interview with Owen Moore." *Photoplay,* December 1912.

B.L. "A Dressing Room Chat With Douglas Fairbanks." *Theatre,* 1912.

Larkin, Mark. "Biography of Douglas Fairbanks." *United Artists,* Revised January 1933.

Lindsay, Vachel. "The Great Douglas Fairbanks." *Ladies Home Journal,* August 1926.

––––––. "Queen of My People." *New Republic,* 7 July 1917.

McKelvie, Martha Graves. "Surely, It Can't Be Mary." *Motion Picture Classic,* July 1918.

"Mary Pickford and Her Husband, The Luckiest Man in the World." *Minneapolis Sunday Tribune,* 25 February 1917.

"Mary Pickford: She Tunes In On God, a 24-Hour Station." *News-Week In Religion,* 10 November 1934.

"Mary Pickford's Own Story of Her Married Life With Owen Moore" (court records of her testimony at divorce trial). *Chicago Herald-Examiner,* 9 May 1920.

Mayer, Arthur L. "The Origins of United Artists." *Films In Review,* August 1959.

Mercer, Janet. "The Fairbanks' Social War Is On." *Photoplay*, August 1936.

The Motion Picture News, 1915–30.

The Moving Picture World, 1915–27.

Mullet, Mary B. "Mary Pickford Describes Her Most Thrilling Experience." *American*, May, 1923.

Naylor, Hazel Simpson. "The Fairbanks Scale of Americanism." *Motion Picture Magazine*, February 1919.

"One Mary in a Million." *Movieland*, December 1945.

Paddock, Charley. "If You Think You Can." *Collier's*, 28 November 1931.

"Paramount." *Fortune*, March 1937.

Ranck, Edwin Carty. "Mary Pickford—Whose Real Name Is Gladys Smith." *American*, May 1918.

Sangster, Margaret E. "Mary Pickford's Search for Happiness." *Photoplay*, February 1935.

Schickel, Richard. "The Silents Weren't Just Voiceless Talkies." *The New York Times Magazine*, 28 November 1971.

———. "Doug Fairbanks: Superstar of the Silents." *American Heritage*, December 1971.

St. John, Adela Rogers. "The Married Life of Doug and Mary." *Photoplay*, February 1927.

———. "Why Does the World Love Mary Pickford?" *Photoplay*, December 1921.

Smith, Frederick James. "Mary Had a Little Tear—A Serious Interview With Mary Pickford." *Motion Picture Classic*, September 1917.

———. "The Unspoiled Mary Pickford." *Photoplay*, September 1914.

Taylor, Charles K. "Doug Gets Away With It." *Outlook*, 14 April 1926.

———. "The Most Popular Man In the World." *Outlook*, 24 December 1924.

Wallace, David H. "That Personality of Douglas Fairbanks." *New York*, 13 August 1913.

Whitaker, Alma. "Mrs. Douglas Fairbanks Analyzes Mary Pickford." *Photoplay*, November 1927.

Woollcott, Alexander. "The Strenuous Honeymoon." *Everybody's*, November 1920.

Wright, Edna. "Mary Pickford Plus 'Silent Money Talk'." *Motion Picture Classic*, March 1917.

———. "A Weekend With Mary Pickford." *Photoplay*, March 1915.

Zeidman, Bennie. "Owen Moore." *Picture Play*, May 1916.

———. "Trailing Dynamic Douglas Fairbanks." *Photoplay*, May 1917.

Zyda, Joan. "Mary Pickford Speaks From Another Age." *Los Angeles Times*, 3 March 1974.

COLLECTIONS AND REPOSITORIES

Robinson Locke Collection, Library and Museum of the Performing Arts, New York Public Library at Lincoln Center (contains thousands of clippings and tear sheets, many undated and unidentified)

Library of Congress, Washington, D.C.; Patrick J. Sheehan, Barbara Humphries

Library and Museum of the Performing Arts, Theatre Collection, New York Public Library at Lincoln Center; Paul Myers, Steven Ross

George Eastman House, Rochester, N.Y.

Wisconsin Center for Theatre Research, United Artists Collection, Aitken Collection, Daniel Blum Papers, Madison, Wisconsin; Susan Dalton

Charles K. Feldman Library, American Film Institute, Beverly Hills, Calif.; Ann Schlosser

Margaret Herrick Library, Academy of Motion Pictures Arts and Sciences, Los Angeles, Calif.; Mildred Simpson

Museum of Modern Art, New York City; Eileen Bowser, Charles Silver

Alderman Library, Fiske Kimball Fine Arts Library, University of Virginia, Charlottesville, Va.

Western History Department, Denver Public Library; Eleanor M. Gehres, Kay Wilcox

Oral History Department, Columbia University, New York City; Elizabeth B. Mason

Library, Association of the Bar of the City of New York

Harvard University Library and Archives, Cambridge, Mass.; Harley Holden, Bonnie B. Salt

Archives, Archdiocese of Denver, Colorado; Sister Elizabeth Skiff

Beverly Hills Visitors and Convention Bureau, Beverly Hills, Calif.; Roz Meyers

Library, *Los Angeles Times*, Los Angeles, Calif.; E. Kenneth Hayes

Museum of the City of New York

British Museum

Quigley Photographic Archive, Georgetown University Library, Washington, D.C.; George M. Barringer

Louisiana Collection, New Orleans Public Library; Collin Hamer

Special Collection, Tulane University Library, New Orleans, La.; Constant Griffith

National Park Service, Washington, D.C.; Tom Wilson, Jack Geyer

East High School, Denver, Colorado

Fairbanks House, Dedham, Mass.; Arthur Flood

Duluth Public Library, Duluth, Minn.; Nancy Sells

American Jewish Committee, New York City; Morton Yarmon, Betty Lande
American Society of Cinematographers, Hollywood, Calif.
Colorado School of Mines, Golden, Colorado
Philipsburg Manor
Board of Geographic Names, Washington, D.C.; Donald Johnson

FOR VIEWING FILMS

Library of Congress, Washington, D.C.
Museum of Modern Art, New York City
American Film Institute, Beverly Hills, Calif.
Blackhawk Films, Davenport, Iowa
Audio Brandon Films, Inc., Mount Vernon, N.Y.

Index

Film titles are in italic